GREAT
Historic Houses
OF AMERICA

GREAT
Historic Houses
OF AMERICA

Phyllis Lee Levin

Coward-McCann New York

Produced in association with Country Beautiful Corporation
24198 West Bluemound Road, Waukesha, Wisconsin

COUNTRY BEAUTIFUL: *Publisher and Editorial Director:* Michael P. Dineen; *Executive Editor:* Robert L. Polley; *Senior Editors:* Kenneth L. Schmitz, James H. Robb; *Associate Art Director:* Wilbur A. Howe; *Editorial Assistants:* Carolyn Muchhala, Lawrence Kenney, Janice M. Puta; *Executive Director, Sales and Marketing:* Richard W. Stone; *Production:* Frank Bruce; *Circulation Manager:* Trudy Schnittka; *Administrative Secretary:* Donna Griesemer; *Editorial Secretaries:* Christine Maynard, Darcy Davies.

Country Beautiful Corporation is a wholly owned subsidiary of Flick-Reedy Corporation: *President:* Frank Flick; *Vice President and General Manager:* Michael P. Dineen; *Treasurer and Secretary:* Bok Robertson.

Frontispiece: The west drawing room at Oak Hill, Loudoun County, Virginia (Photo: courtesy Mrs. Thomas N. DeLashmutt)

CONTENTS

NEW ENGLAND

MIDDLE ATLANTIC

SOUTH

MIDWEST

WEST

Augusta, Maine
BLAINE HOUSE

Imposing Mansion of the "Plumed Knight"

All photos: courtesy Maine Department of Economic Development

For her birthday on November 20, 1862, Harriet Standwood Blaine's husband, James Gillespie Blaine, deeded her a "mansion house" and her share, like that of so many wives of political figures, of two lives, one "all variety, wide-awake, gay; the other all Aunt Susan, sewing machine, children." Since then the Blaine House in Augusta, Maine, has been the setting for many notable occasions and dramatic events.

The Blaines had met in Kentucky when he taught mathematics at Western Military Institute in Georgetown and his future bride taught at Mrs. Johnson's School in Millersburg. Blaine, who had been born in Brownsville, Pennsylvania, and graduated from what is now Washington and Jefferson College, was the great-grandson of Colonel Ephraim Blaine, commissary general of the American Revolutionary army. Harriet, whose father was a prosperous wool merchant, was educated at the Cony Academy in Augusta and then studied at Mr. and Mrs. Cowles' School for Girls in Ipswich. They moved to Augusta in 1854 where Blaine edited and in time partially owned the *Kennebec Journal*, an influential paper that brought him recognition and a governor's mission to examine prisons and penitentiaries in search of ways of improving Maine's penal system, an appointment as delegate to the Republican National convention, representation in the state legislature and from then on a career of national and international horizons.

His history for ten years was "really the history of Congress" since Blaine was a member of all its principal committees. Beginning in 1862, he served fourteen years in the House of Representatives, three times as speaker. The fourteenth amendment of the Constitution, giving citizenship

Above: Since 1920, Blaine House has provided fifteen state governors and their families with a vast, precisely furnished house.

Opposite: A gracefully curving staircase ascends to the second floor from the entrance hall. Minerva looks down from her niche.

11

Above: When the *U.S.S. Maine* was decommissioned in 1920, her silver, including this loving cup, was returned to Maine and later given to Blaine House.

Opposite: The reception room walls are covered with beige silk paper, handmade in Japan, and the draperies are Italian damask.

to everyone born in the United States, passed during Reconstruction, was "substantially" Blaine's proposition. He was the first in Congress to oppose the claim that the public debt, pledged in coin, could be paid in greenbacks, a champion of American shipping and the "master-spirit" who presided over the Pan-American Congress. Blaine became a senator but resigned to become Secretary of State in Garfield's cabinet, a position he filled again under Benjamin Harrison.

Blaine lost the Presidential nomination in 1880 and the office itself the next time around mainly because he was deserted by the Independent Republicans, who were called "the Mugwumps." But he was also damaged by his permitting the Reverend Samuel D. Burchard to label the Democratic Party "the party whose antecedents are rum, Romanism, and rebellion," implying that Blaine was against Roman Catholics, which was not true. The continuing shadow cast by the incident of the Mulligan letters was the final cause of the distrust that smogged Blaine's name, despite the fact that he thought he had cleared himself of charges that he had received, while a Congressman, $64,000 from the Union Pacific Railroad Company as payment for "undefined services," which his opponents called graft. His rebuttal at the time was based on letters from the company officers and bankers who were said to have negotiated the draft, claiming they knew of no such transaction. He was exonerated by the House, and though there were the staunch followers who thought of Blaine as an "armed warrior, like a plumed knight" marching down the halls of the American Congress to throw his "shining lance full and fair against the brazen foreheads of the defamers of his country, and the maligners of his honor," the opposition party's limerick haunts his name to this day: "Blaine, Blaine, James G. Blaine, Continental liar from the State of Maine." The Democrats chanted this in their successful Presidential campaign of 1884 that elected Grover Cleveland President of the United States.

The Blaines had been married twelve years when they purchased the mansion built over a three-year period by Captain James Hall of Bath on a lot "nine rods north and south and twelve rods east and west" of the road leading from Augusta to Hallowell. By 1872 they had added a conservatory, combined the sitting and dining room into a large family dining room (now the State Dining Room), enclosed the veranda, added a cupola and brought up five children (the first and sixth died in infancy in Kentucky). The times when the family was together in Augusta were Mrs. Blaine's times of contentment. When she was alone with the company of six servants she could not bear "the orderly array of my life," she wrote her children. "I miss the envelopes in the gravy, the bespattered table linen, the uncertainty of meals, for you know he always starts out on his constitutional when he hears them taking in dinner. I miss," she concluded, "his unvarying attention, and as constant neglect." Mrs. Blaine was as eloquent about her sons as her husband. Her sensitive and honest letters find her bracing herself with a "half-bottle of champagne" as she writes about missing her boys. "They know all I ever knew — and I have forgotten much — they are fresh and untiring as the sun which never sets — they are

loving and want sympathy — old enough to be companions, too young to assert their rights, taking everything as of grace, and of their fulness I am a partaker." The mother who was perfectly content to be "used, absorbed, obliterated if need be" was meticulously interested in all of her children. To her daughter Maud she wrote, "I cannot imagine your not loving to study, and if you will study, you will learn. If you learn, you will be learned."

The Blaines were often away from Augusta for long periods and Mrs. Blaine fretted over the Augusta mansion. "If I could feel happy about the Augusta house and children, I should know how to cultivate patience, that homely but friendly herb, but with a house half put to rights, a half-way cook, and half a family, how can you be enjoying a perfect whole? No one sympathizes with my misgivings. . . ." She admitted that her husband "does not hesitate to call it selfishness."

In 1893, James G. Blaine died of Bright's disease; his wife lived until July 15, 1903. Blaine House passed into Harriet Blaine Beale's possession and was given to her son Walker on his twenty-first birthday. When Walker died in battle in 1919 in France in the St. Mihiel Drive, Mrs. Beale gave the house to the State of Maine, which spent nearly $185,000 that year to restore it. The rambling frame mansion is painted white with green shutters and is surmounted by two large cupolas. Its twenty-eight rooms, nine fireplaces and nine bathrooms have, since 1920, provided fifteen state governors and their families with a vast, precisely furnished house in excellent repair.

The entrance hall is elegant but inviting, with bright yellow wallpaper in a Greek goddess motif and two slate-topped

Above: The family dining room features painted Chinese scenic wallpaper of the kind popular in the mid-eighteenth century.

Opposite: A marble bust of James G. Blaine surveys the Blaine Study. Above the fireplace is a painting depicting Lincoln reading the Emancipation Proclamation to his cabinet.

15

Above: This 1825 gilded French clock of classical motif once belonged to a member of the Harrison Gray Otis family of Boston.

Opposite above: The original Duncan Phyfe chairs in the State Dining Room are among the most valuable pieces in the house.

Opposite below: A massive antique brass woodbox is one of the notable pieces in the light, airy and informal Sun Room.

Empire-style pier tables (one a copy). A gracefully curved staircase ascends to the second floor and, part way up, the Roman goddess Minerva looks down from a niche in the wall. It is one of the few items, outside of Blaine's Study, that dates from his residence in the house.

The reception room, to the left, is more classically formal, lined with Japanese beige silk paper, curtained with Italian damask and lit with twin chandeliers of Czechoslovakian glass hanging from an ornamental plaster ceiling. Two distinctive Corinthian columns stand at the point which originally divided this room into front and back parlors before Blaine combined them into a single room. The imposing gilt-trimmed mantels are made of black marble that Blaine imported from Italy. Above each hangs an ornately carved gilt mirror. The furnishings range from Empire to Sheraton style and Martha Washington and Williamsburg chairs. The 1825 French clock on the marble-topped table once belonged to the renowned Harrison Gray Otis family of Boston.

Across the hall is the State Dining Room, which Blaine also created by combining rooms. The twelve original Duncan Phyfe chairs, among the most valuable pieces in the house, have cream and gold brocade seats which match the curtains and contrast with the light green carpet and green and white striped wallpaper. The Coromandel screen is about 175 years old and is thought to be from Honan Province in China. The large sterling silver soup tureen and two vegetable dishes engraved with a pine cone and pine needle motif and state seal had originally been a gift from the state to the battleship *Maine* in 1895. After the ship was blown up in Havana harbor in 1898 the silver was dredged up unharmed and later sent aboard a new *U.S.S. Maine.* Shortly after the ship was decommissioned in 1920 the silver was returned to Maine and given to Blaine House.

The family dining room, adjoining the State Dining Room, features painted Chinese scenic wallpaper above the dado that was most popular in the mid-eighteenth century. Its dominant delicate blue shade complements the darker blue draperies with ball fringe. Adjoining the reception room is the charming Sun Room which derives its name from the considerable amount of light allowed into the room by the French doors running the length of the room. Once a veranda, it faces the state house.

Blaine's Study holds most of the original furnishings still in the house and his belongings from elsewhere. His books fill one wall and the others are covered with an unusual striped wallpaper, a reproduction of a paper Blaine chose for this room in the 1860's. It was the same pattern he had seen in President Lincoln's study in the White House. Blaine used the handsome mahogany desk and chair while he was a U.S. Senator. On the desk is a small pass dated April 7, 1865, bearing the signature, "A. Lincoln," allowing "the bearer Mr. Blaine to pass from City Point to Richmond and return."

The landscaping of the gardens, originally designed by the Olmsted brothers, is prudently maintained, the new blending with the old, the hemlock, hybrid rhododendron, azaleas complementing the cherished lilacs, beautybush, forsythia and hydrangea. There is also a formal garden within view of the mansion dining room, and a private garden that enjoys the cheerful comments of a small but vigorous waterfall.

Cambridge, Massachusetts
THE LONGFELLOW HOUSE

The Poet's "Italian Villa"

When Henry Wadsworth Longfellow, poet and professor of modern languages at Harvard University, left his room at Mrs. Stearn's, mainly because he could not "endure boarding homes," he moved into "two large and beautiful rooms" in the Craigie house where he hoped to be "entirely my own master, and have my meals by myself and at my own hours." "I form to myself a vision of independence," he wrote to his father. What Longfellow could not possibly have envisioned at that moment was that he had moved into the Craigie house for the remaining forty-five years of his life, to live there with his wife and five children and to write some of his most memorable poems there. One day he would have the house named and preserved in his honor.

Between solitary professorship and marriage there was a lonely gap of six years in which Longfellow, a widower of thirty, enjoyed and despaired of his life in Cambridge, Massachusetts, depending on how he thought he was faring in the pursuit of the hand of the "dark ladie" who held his reason "captive." In the beginning he found his life in Cambridge "very quiet and agreeable." Spring was a marvel to him. "Nothing can well surpass the beauty of Cambridge at this season. Every tree is heavy with blossoms, and the whole air laden with perfume." He thought his residence in the old Craigie house "a paradise" and he considered himself successful as a teacher. His lectures were going "very much to my own satisfaction, feeling no more embarrassment, than if I were eating dinner." Though given to understatement about

Above: Longfellow lived in his handsome Georgian-style house with flair and affluence. *Opposite:* The five Louis XVI armchairs in the parlor are of carved walnut and are upholstered in delicate flowers on a pale background. (Photos: Louis H. Frohman)

The ornate chair near the study fireplace is made from the wood of "the spreading chestnut tree" which Longfellow referred to in "The Village Blacksmith."
(Photos: Louis H. Frohman)

himself, Longfellow must have been at ease with life at that time — or at least with his work — for he admitted, "instead of being a source of anxiety, these lectures are a sort of pleasure to me." He wore a broad-brimmed black hat, a black frock-coat, a bright waistcoat, boots, light-colored trousers with straps, a black cane, and in winter he went "much" into Boston society, into Cambridge society "almost never."

But, as his stay in Cambridge lengthened, Longfellow's moods darkened. He had given up society "entirely" for the apparently unrequited love of the "dark ladie," Frances Appleton, on whose account he said he led a "maimed" life that was "grim as death." The combination of this disappointment and winter threw the would-be suitor into despair. "Things go on in the usual jog-trot, commonplace style, ... the purgatory of snow, mud and rain," ruining what was left of his disposition. He was still happy with the Craigie house, thinking it looked like an "Italian villa," and he observed a routine about his days, breakfasting at seven on tea, toast and waffles, dining at five or six, sometimes in Boston, after which he would walk in the Common, and then back to Cambridge. But he was not reading much and he was wasting time over the *affaire de coeur*. He wanted action, wanted to travel, "am too excited — too tumultuous inwardly — and my health suffers from all this," he wrote a friend.

Mrs. Craigie's death from cancer in 1841 made the house "gloomy" and Longfellow's future there "rather uncertain." There was a reprieve when it was taken for a year by Joseph

E. Worcester, the lexicographer, and then a trip to Europe clouded with a feeling of despondency. "... I have let /The years slip from me and have not fulfilled/ The aspiration of my youth, ..." Longfellow wrote.

Miraculously, in May of 1843, his life took a sunnier course. The dark lady had turned acquiescent and the poet was able to write to a friend, "On striped paper, as on a triumphal banner, I send you this greeting, and joyful tidings, which will make me feel beautiful over the Alleghenies. Lo! I am engaged to Fanny Appleton! The great vision of my life takes shape."

Longfellow married Fanny Appleton in July and was given the Craigie house by his father-in-law that autumn, a much appreciated present. It was for him, "a fine old house, and I have a strong attachment from having lived in it since I first came to Cambridge." It reposed on five acres and the Charles River wound through the meadows in front. Longfellow planted an avenue of linden trees behind the house. "I have also planted some acorns," he wrote, "and as the oak grows for a thousand years, you may imagine a whole line of little Longfellows, like the shadowy monarchs in *Macbeth*, walking under their branches, through countless generations."

What is the Longfellow House today and was once Mrs. Andrew Craigie's house, has a hold on the historical past that dates back to before the American Revolution. It was built in 1759 by Major John Vassall whose grandfather had built the house in Quincy that was bought later by John Adams. Vassall, a single-minded Tory had had to abandon this house (one of seven loyalist homes along what was known as "Tory Row") when the loyalists grew unpopular in 1774. Afraid of mob violence, he fled to Boston and in 1776 headed for England. Vassall was subsequently declared an exile and his estates confiscated by an act of the Continental Congress.

With his departure, the house served as a hospital after the Battle of Bunker Hill, and still later, it housed Colonel John Glover's "amphibious regiment" of Marblehead fishermen, an event that has caused some people to consider Longfellow's house as the "first headquarters of the American navy." It is the events, however, of the time between July 1775 and March 1776, that provide Longfellow House with its most inspired historical moments. George Washington arrived in Cambridge on July 2, 1775, to take command of the continental forces and stayed in the house of the President of Harvard College before making his permanent headquarters in the John Vassall house two weeks later. There was a long winter ahead, and Mrs. Washington, who was asked to join her husband, arrived on December 11. She was escorted by her son, John Parke Custis, and his wife, and by Washington's nephew, George Lewis, the entire party making the journey from Mount Vernon in a chariot drawn by four horses, with postillions dressed in scarlet and white livery. During those difficult times, the only reception the Washingtons gave was a Twelfth Night Party in the parlor, on January 6, 1776, to celebrate their seventeenth wedding anniversary. Longfellow, in later years, affected by Washington's occupancy, wrote not only of his children descending "the broad hall stair," but of the first President: "Up and down these echoing stairs, /Heavy with the weight of cares, /Sounded his majestic tread."

The newel post of the front staircase is extremely deeply carved and the balusters are of three different types.

The mahogany dining table served many distinguished guests
over the years, Charles Dickens among them. The red
lacquer and gold Buddhist altar table was brought home
from the Orient by Longfellow's son. (Photo: Louis H. Frohman)

Longfellow wrote most of his poetry on this standing desk in the study.
(Photo: courtesy Longfellow House)

On March 17, 1776, the British were forced to evacuate Boston and General Washington left Cambridge on April 4, to continue the war on Long Island. Vassall's house was sold to Nathaniel Tracy, a Newburyport shipowner, later to Thomas Russell, a wealthy Boston merchant, and then to Andrew Craigie, the first Apothecary General of the Continental Army and later one of the wealthiest men in the country. It was Craigie who added a large ell at the back, converting the former kitchen into a dining room, also adding porches and other comfortable touches. However, he ended up in bankruptcy with his widow turning to lodgers for her income, among them three presidents of Harvard.

In 1913, the Longfellow's four remaining children formed the Longfellow House Trust to which they deeded the house with a substantial endowment with the provision that descendants might continue to live there. The first floor, which has the most historical rooms, is now open to the public. Mrs. Longfellow had died tragically when her dress caught fire in 1861 and it was said that her husband grew a beard to mask the scars he had sustained in putting out the fire. They had lived in this handsome Georgian-style house with flair and affluence, and among myriad private mementos — paintings (by Stuart and David among others), pictures, drawings, busts, bronzes that were meaningful to them and representative of their interests and friendships. Books were, and are, everywhere, even in the dining room.

Today, sitting atop a double terrace facing south, the imposing two-storied frame house displays an expansive hip roof containing four outstanding elements: a massive yellow chimney at either end, a white balustraded widow's walk, a white-trimmed pediment with delicate fanlight in the center of the front and, flanking the pediment, two rather large dormers. Painted yellow, with neat white trim and a white door sheltered by a small bracketed overhang, the façade has four white, two-story pilasters with Ionic capitals, one at either end and two flanking the entrance.

The hallway runs through to the Blue Entry in back which connects with the ell. It and the front staircase, as well as all the other first-floor rooms, have white-painted wainscoting. The newel post of the front staircase is extremely deeply carved and the balusters are of three different types. The parlor to the left of the hall has served history hospitably on many occasions, welcoming leaders of the Revolution as well as Prince Talleyrand and the Emperor of Brazil. The wallpaper, curtains, rug and upholstery are decoratively patterned in flowers on a gray background; the five Louis XVI armchairs of carved walnut are also upholstered in delicate flowers on a pale background. Red tasseled and knotted valances framed with gilt cornices convey a festive-without-being-fancy spirit to the room. In the corner between the windows is a carved walnut corner cabinet characteristic of the Gothic Revival in America. The mantel and overmantel, the most elaborately carved in the house, are surmounted by a broken pediment supported by fluted Corinthian pilasters. On each side are arched and paneled niches, the one to the right containing an elegant marble bust of Mrs. Longfellow.

Longfellow's study, directly across the hall from the parlor, was Washington's dining room, and is where "grave Alice, laughing Allegra, and Edith with golden hair" would enter through "three doors left unguarded" to find their father resting after work at his standing desk. The portraits on the wall include one of Nathaniel Hawthorne, Longfellow's classmate at Bowdoin, and one of Emerson by Eastman Johnson. The heavy ornate chair at the right of the fireplace is made out of the wood of the "spreading chestnut tree" which Longfellow had referred to in his poem "The Village Blacksmith." It was a gift in 1879 from the schoolchildren of Cambridge.

The study is directly connected with the library behind it. Originally square, like the other rooms in the original section of the house, it was probably used by Major Vassall as the dining room and later as Washington's office. Longfellow used it as a music room. In 1793, when the room had been lengthened by Craigie, two fluted Corinthian columns were added to support a heavy entablature in the middle of the long north wall. The Italian and French bookcases are ornately carved in brown oak, and contain many of Longfellow's beautifully bound books by French, Italian and German authors. One of the finest pieces in the library is a side chair used by Martha Washington when she lived in the house.

Across from the library is the dining room which an anteroom links to the parlor. It was used as the kitchen until 1793 when Craigie placed the kitchen in the new ell. The round mahogany table in the center served many distinguished guests over the years, Charles Dickens among them. Against the walls are the two finest tables in the house — Sheraton folding card tables, with inlaid satinwood panels and borders. One of the house's most interesting tables is the red lacquer and gold Buddhist altar table, brought home by Longfellow's son Charles from a trip to the Orient in the early 1870's.

The garden behind the house was created and cherished by the Longfellows. The influence here is Italian and it is both formal and colorful, the sundial bearing one of Longfellow's favorite mottos borrowed from Dante: *Think that this day will never dawn again.*

The Italian and French bookcases in the library contain
many of Longfellow's foreign books, with gold-tooled,
white vellum and green leather bindings. (Photo: Louis H. Frohman)

Quincy, Massachusetts

ADAMS OLD HOUSE

A Great Family's Colonial Mansion

Above: The Adams Old House is a pleasant, colonial-style house with gabled, mansard roof and gray clapboards. *Opposite:* The second-floor study is dominated by a Louis XVI *secrétaire à abbatant* from France. (All photos: Creative Photographers)

Quincy was an oasis to both Abigail Adams and her husband John. As the first lady of the land marooned in a "castle of a house . . . the President's House," which she found twice as large as a meeting house, she was pressed for funds to maintain it and obliged to keep thirteen fires daily "or sleep in wet and damp places." No wonder she wrote to her sister, "I long for my rose bush, my clover field, and the retirement of Quincy, and the conversation of my dear sister and friends."

Quincy to Abigail meant a pleasant, isolated, colonial-style house eight miles from Boston with a gabled mansard roof, gray clapboard siding and green shutters. John Adams, who had visited this house with Abigail, bought it while he was overseas serving as United States Minister to Great Britain from a descendant of its original builder, Major Leonard Vassall, who had begun its construction in 1731. The purchase of a new home had been inspired by the conviction that the Adams family would no longer be comfortable in the salt box left by Adams's father, Deacon John, in which they lived until their appointment abroad in 1783. The larger house, with two bedrooms on the second floor and three small rooms in the attic, grew, over years of necessary additions, to twenty rooms. It acquired an ell, a study, a mahogany-lined sitting room, and a number of names that did not stick for very long. "Mr. Jefferson lives at Monticello the lofty mountain. I live at Montezillo, a little hill," said Adams. Montezillo was also referred to as a "wren's house," the Old House, Peacefield and Stony Field, but in all her letters to her sister Mary Cranch, Abigail never referred to the house as anything else but the place where it stood, Quincy.

The couple certainly seemed split in their initial impression of their acquisition. John Adams thought of it as "but the farm of a patriot . . . from whence are to be seen some of the most beautiful prospects in the world." He did admit that it was "in so much disorder as to require my whole attention to repair it." Abigail's pronouncement on the original state of Quincy was more succinct. She found the garden "a wilderness and

The outstanding pieces in the Long Room are Abigail Adams's Louis XV *fauteuils,* part of a set bought in France in the 1780's.

the house a mere barracks." But years of work "to make my farm shine" made it possible for Adams to write from Philadelphia to his son John Quincy that "one day spent at home would afford me more inward delight and comfort than a week or winter in this place."

John Adams had graduated from Harvard in 1755, studied and practiced law, served in the Massachusetts House of Representatives; as a member of the Continental Congress he had pleaded eloquently for separation from the colonies, for backing for the Declaration of Independence. He was an effective if blunt diplomat, serving in France as a member of the American Commission in 1778 and as minister plenipotentiary for negotiating a treaty of peace and a treaty of commerce. As Minister to the Court of St. James he made it clear to His Majesty George III that he "avowed no attachment but to my own country." Dedicated, visionary, prudent, he unfortunately did not have a popular touch and was maligned during the Presidency for which he beat out Jefferson the first term and lost to him the second.

Abigail suffered bitterly over Adams's failure to commu-

The Paneled Room takes its name from the fine Santo Domingo mahogany paneling installed by Major Vassall, the original owner.

nicate his true excellence to the people, regretted at times the sacrifices he had made personally to serve his country. "It has been my lot in life to spend a large portion of it in publick life," she wrote her sister, "but I can truly say the pleasantest part of it was spent at the foot of Pen Hill in that humble cottage when my good gentleman was a practitioner at the bar, earnt his money during the week, and at the end of it pour'd it all into my lap to use or what could be spaired to lay by. Nobody then grudged us our living, and 25 years of such practise would have given us a very different property from what we now possess." But Abigail was a visionary as well as a practical housewife and recognized that a more comfortable life "might not have given us the second rank in the United States, nor the satisfaction of reflecting by what means and whose exertions these states have arrived at that degree of liberty, safety and independence which they now enjoy."

Abigail Adams, who was sometimes referred to by her Quincy neighbors as the "Duchess of Braintree," was not only articulate but, it seemed, almost tireless. It always seemed that she "had rather have too much than too little" to do.

The portraits of George and Martha Washington in the dining room were painted in 1790 by Edward Savage, a New York artist.

"Life stagnates without action," she said and she was sure she "could never bear to merely vegetate." Though she was often far away from Quincy, her instructions and plans for her home were imaginatively conceived and meticulously thought out. The construction of the large extension at one end of the house which includes the long room, the east entry and the upstairs study, was directed by mail. "I know the President will be glad when it is done," she wrote her sister in 1798, "but he can never bear to trouble himself about any thing of the kind, and he has no taste for it, and he has too many publick cares to think of his own affairs." And it was her sister, too, that she would ask before visits "to have the house open and aired, the beds shook up. If there was time and a fine day, I should like to have them sun'd. as they have not been slept in for a long time." She would also wish "some coffee burnt and ground, some bread and cake made," "that wine be drawn from the casks in the cellar and that punch be made by the gallon of Jamaica rum and brandy."

When Abigail was finally ensconced at Quincy, visitors remember a "middle-size woman in the dress of the matrons who were in New England." She tended to wear a black bonnet, a short cloak, a quilted petticoat and the high-heeled shoe, "everything the best but nothing different from our wealthy and modest citizens," and was often to be found shelling her beans for a family dinner, "conversing freely." She was regarded by some as a "spoiling mother" whose children were of "disproportioned genius." Her first son John Quincy became the sixth President of the United States while her second son Charles was "popular, gregarious and unstable" and died in 1800 at the age of thirty. Her daughter, who made no secret of an unhappy marriage, died in 1813. Through disappointment, discomfort, illness and tragedy, Abigail Adams was staunch. "I bend to disease, totter under it, but rise again for a while, recover a degree of health and spirits, feel grateful, I hope, for the reprieve. . . ."

John Adams lived on twenty-six years after his term in Presidential office. At Quincy, he read Horace and Livy, put his papers in order, served as president of the American Academy of Arts and Sciences. He bought more land, painted apple trees to discourage the tent caterpillars, and supervised the carting of seaweed to fertilize the fields. "I enjoy life and have as good spirit as I ever had," he wrote in his last years, "but my fabric has become very weak, almost worn out." He was concerned over "this period when disorder, indiscipline, and disobedience of every kind, fashioned into a kind of science, are vindicated as right and inculcated as duties," yet he found many consolations that are meaningful, probably for as long as humanity endures. He felt he would leave the world "better than we found it — superstition, persecution, and bigotry are somewhat abated, governments are a little ameliorated, science and literature are greatly improved and more widely spread. Our country has brilliant and exhilarating prospects before it." This was a far more heartening outlook than that of his great-grandsons Brooks and Henry who predicted that "by its nature and substance, United States democracy was foreordained to degredation and decay."

Charles Francis Adams, John's grandson, had supposed "an ancestral mansion in this country . . . an absurdity. The continuation of families is so uncertain," he said, "and the changes of habitation so much depend on the growth of the neighborhood that it is idle to expect permanency." Despite his pessimism, the Adams home was recognized, not surprisingly, as having permanent historic interest; in 1947 Abigail's cherished Quincy, filled with family heirlooms and paintings, its nearly five acres including the library, garden and stables, was given to the Federal Government by the Adams Memorial Society. Now the public may visit the home of this astonishing family who have served their country and their fellow men as diplomats, writers and ambassadors, apparently with tireless dedication.

The oldest part of the house, built in 1731, consists of the Paneled Room, west entry and dining room on the ground floor, two bedrooms on the second floor and three smaller

The main entry hall and stairway are characterized by an austerity that contrasts with the elegance found in the rooms.

rooms in the attic. The Paneled Room, the dwelling's best parlor, takes its name from the fine Santo Domingo mahogany paneling installed by Vassall, the original owner. It has gone through several alterations. John Adams painted the room white after the death of Abigail, but his grandson removed the paint in 1850 and installed silver hardware on the doors. A small Chippendale gateleg table with claw-and-ball feet has been added, but the most treasured piece is the American Chippendale-style sofa upholstered in red velvet with mahogany trim. When he was ninety years old John Adams sat here to have his portrait painted.

The Waterford candelabra and China Trade porcelain in the dining room were owned by Abigail Adams, while the sideboard belonged to the family of Evelyn Davis who married the Adamses' youngest great-grandson Brooks, the last of the family to occupy the Quincy house. The portraits of George and Martha Washington here were painted in 1790 by Edward Savage, a New York artist.

Above the Paneled Room is the Presidents' Bedroom which contains the canopy bed in which Abigail died. Its damask valance is the original hanging. Many of Abigail's famous letters were written on the neoclassic desk near the window, but perhaps the most charming feature of the room is the fireplace with its facing of Sadler tiles from Liverpool, purchased by John Quincy Adams as a gift for his mother.

The large gabled ell which John Adams added in 1798-1800 contains the east entry, the Long Room and the upstairs study. The outstanding pieces in the Long Room are Abigail's exquisite white-painted Louis XV *fauteuils*, part of a set of twelve bought in France in the 1780's. The double sewing chair and the four-seated ottoman from England belonged to the Charles Francis Adamses, as did the gilded Empire chair which was purchased at a sale of James Monroe's furniture in 1861. Three Adams family golden wedding anniversaries were celebrated in this venerable room.

The second-floor study, used by four generations of the family, is dominated by the Louis XVI *secrétaire à abbatant* which John Adams brought from France. The chair in the corner is where he died July 4, 1826, on the same day as his friend Jefferson. John Quincy Adams's celestial and terrestial globes are on each side of the fireplace whose white marble was cut in Philadelphia about 1880.

In 1869, Charles Francis Adams added thirty feet for servants' quarters to the kitchen ell on the west side and the following year he built a separate building, the stone library, overlooking his grandmother's formal garden. It was here that the scholar-editor worked for many years to put his family's papers in order. These papers, like the Old House itself, are, each in their different ways, eloquent reminders of the contributions of one remarkable family to a nation's history.

The most charming feature of the Presidents' Bedroom is the fireplace with its facing of Sadler tiles from Liverpool bought by John Quincy Adams as a gift for his mother.

Portsmouth, New Hampshire
JOHN PAUL JONES HOUSE

Where the Dashing Captain Waited

Above: Jones never owned the patrician house bearing his name, though he roomed here two different times. (Photos: Hans Wendler, FPG) *Opposite:* Fine Sheraton chest crafted by John Skillins boasts serpentine front with graduated drawers and ball-and-claw feet.

The most romantic and controversial American naval figure, John Paul Jones was born in Scotland, served in Russia, died in France, is reburied at Annapolis and remembered in New Hampshire in the sea town of Portsmouth by having the house where he boarded renamed in his honor. It was at Mrs. Purcell's on Middle and State streets, now called the John Paul Jones House, where he lived in the best front bedchamber during the year 1777 while the sloop of war *Ranger* was being built at Langdon's Island and where he returned on August 31, 1781, while he supervised the construction of the seventy-four-gun ship *America.*

Jones had been born John Paul, but at twenty-six had changed his name to conceal his identity while waiting to be judged for killing one of his sailors in a wage dispute. John was the fourth child born on July 6, 1747, to a "good Scots gardener," and a "smart, clean little woman" housekeeper, both of whom worked for the landowner William Craik of Arbigland. At the age of thirteen he packed a sea chest, left with his parents' blessing and Mr. Craik's handshake, and boarded a fishing vessel as ship's boy, outward bound to Barbados and Virginia and on his way to a memorable and torturous career which in the end found him "depressed and gloomy" when he reflected on the "little good" accomplished by the United States Navy after the high expectations that

Between canopied Sheraton field bed and Queen Anne highboy stands mahogany Windsor writing chair, circa 1740. (Photos: Hans Wendler, FPG)

had been held for it in 1776. "The public has been put to a great expense," he said, "yet the poor seamen have, almost in every instance, been cheated, while the public has reaped neither honor nor profit. . . ." Jones, who has been called a murderer and a hero, served as an American agent in France and later, on the advice of Thomas Jefferson, accepted an offer from Catherine the Great, to serve in the Russian navy for one year, from 1788 to 1789. The Russian epic ended in a scandal, with Jones being accused of attempting to rape a ten-year-old girl. He vehemently denied the charge, saying it was "an imposture invented by the mother of a depraved girl."

He died and was buried in an unmarked grave in France at the age of forty-five, his body retrieved a century later and brought to America where his words are code to naval officers to this day. A captain of the navy, Jones said, "ought to be a man of strong and well connected sense with a tolerable education, a gentleman as well as a seaman both in theory and practice — for, want of learning and rude ungentle manners are by no means the characteristick of an officer."

After his first stay in Portsmouth, he sailed as the *Ranger's* commander in November 1777, to bring news to the French court of the great American victory at Saratoga, and the flag he flew was one that the Helen Seavey Quilting Party members had sewn from their own dresses, marking the first time the Stars and Stripes had ever flown over the ocean. Thus it was the first American flag to be recognized by a foreign nation, acknowledged with a nine-gun salute at Quiberon Bay in France. When Jones returned to Portsmouth on his second trip he was welcomed by colonels and generals, by "young girls and widows" who seemed surprised to find him "in manners far from brutal as the report has spread about him," but on the contrary, "quiet and mild-mannered" in society. "He has much knowledge of naval affairs and speaks, contrary to the custom of Englishmen, tolerably good French" was one observation and Jones spent a merry Christmas in Portsmouth with "plenty of rum punch and plum pudding."

Of medium height and square build, Jones, while in Portsmouth the second time, sent to Boston for "a piece of good linen for shirts, and a piece of cambric for stock," and for a guinea's worth of "good hair powder." Portsmouth was an agreeable place to wait for a ship, even though work on the *America* was proceeding at a frustratingly slow pace due to lack of money. Still, there was horse racing to pass the time and a dancing school whose sixty members met "in a handsome ball" every month. Candles were lit after tea and dancing did not end until two in the morning. The people were "affable" and "even the country people, including the little children," came out to greet strangers. "It is not possible to describe the beauty of the congregation or the elegance of their clothes, made in the fashion of the latest taste in France," one Italian nobleman wrote, after going to meeting on Sunday. The *America* did not make it to sea until eight months after the war was over, so Congress gave her to France to replace a ship they had lost in Boston Bay.

Jones paid $10 a week to Sarah Purcell for board and lodging for himself and his steward, or $510 for one week short of a year's stay in one of Portsmouth's most patrician eighteenth-century houses. It was built by Captain Gregory Purcell, the dashing "master mariner" who married the niece of Governor Benning Wentworth. Despite social position and supposed wealth, Purcell's widow was forced to invite lodgers into the frame house built in 1758 in the seaport town that became a shipbuilding center due to abundant timber close by. In 1793, Mrs. Purcell sold her house to Woodbury Langdon, one of Portsmouth's prominent merchants, for 1,600 pounds and it turned over within the Langdon family and among a number of others until finally coming into the hands of the Portsmouth Historical Society in 1919, with the help of a descendant of the first Woodbury Langdon.

Today Portsmouth is a house-proud city, aware of its irreplaceable architectural treasures and of its heroic early place in American history. There is continuing restoration of a number of distinguished homes such as the Purcell house, renamed in honor of John Paul Jones. Although several of Portsmouth's splendid dwellings are of Georgian and Federal design, the John Paul Jones House, while eluding either category, holds its own nobly as one of the finest examples of the kind of frame house built by many of the town's leading

A fire bucket hangs from carved and paneled hallway arch. Windsor settle is shiny black, in contrast to muted reds of the floor.

citizens during the eighteenth century. Standing two and a half stories with pedimented lintels over the first-floor windows and the two third-floor end dormers, the house has been expanded a number of times over the years, which is also typical of many Portsmouth houses.

The entrance hall, extending almost the length of the house, contains the excellent wainscoting to be found in almost all the principal rooms on the ground floor, as well as the warm red-painted floor found also in the upstairs hall, the parlor and dining room. The hall is dominated by the beautifully carved arch with fluted pilasters and the distinctive staircase with its balusters of three different patterns, said to have been carved by sailors at sea who sold them to builders when reaching port. The newel post is composed of four individual spiral-turned balusters on a single base, and on top is a wooden peace button in the shape of a cross, placed there by the builder of the house after it was completed to indicate that the owner was satisfied and that the builder had been paid. Peace buttons are quite common in homes along the East Coast and in the South.

Warm red floor complements paneling in parlor displaying Babcock piano.
(Photo: courtesy John Paul Jones House)

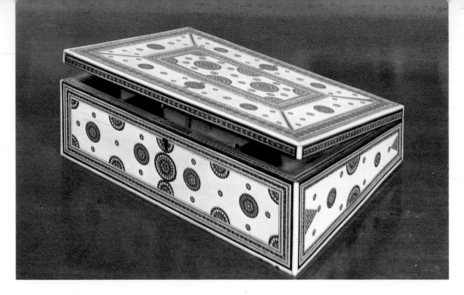

Delicate Indian writing box
shows finely incised geometric patterns
in ivory. (Photo: Hans Wendler, FPG)

Several prominent American cabinetmakers are represented in the house. Langley Boardman of Portsmouth made two of the chairs in the parlor about 1790 and the piano in this room was produced by Babcock of Boston around 1820. However, the three pieces made by John Skillins, of the famous Boston family of woodworkers, are among the most valuable in the house — a small drop-leaf table in the pantry with Queen Anne legs, a round tilt-top table in the dining room, and in the upstairs hall, a fine chest of drawers with serpentine front and ball-and-claw feet which Skillins made for his third wife. Also in the spacious hall are two Windsor comb-back rockers and a fine Empire sewing table.

In addition to the Skillins table, the dining room has an inlaid Hepplewhite secretary, eight Chippendale chairs, an inlaid side-server made by Boston cabinetmaker John Seymour, and a fine collection of glass, including Liverpool pitchers, Waterford glass and a Stiegel flip glass. Over the white wooden mantel of the fireplace, which is faced with original blue and white Delft Biblical tiles, is a small mirror with a mat that was embroidered by Lady Wentworth, the wife of the last Royal Governor of New Hampshire.

The parlor has two windows with built-in seats and Indian shutters which are found on other windows in the house. The furniture here includes an elegant tilt-top table with snake's-head-feet and a fine Hepplewhite card table. Many New England seacoast homes had objects that sailors brought back from the Orient and collections of these can be found in the parlor and the Langdon Room upstairs. Perhaps the finest piece is the ivory writing box from India delicately incised with geometric designs.

The largest bedroom upstairs has a beautifully preserved Sheraton field bed and a Queen Anne highboy. The Windsor writing chair near the window belonged to one of Portsmouth's early postmasters and dates from about 1740.

Across the hall in the room where John Paul Jones stayed is a fine chest of drawers, probably made by Gaines of Portsmouth, and a set of late Sheraton "fancy" chairs with their original gold and black paint. A sedate, twelve-by-fifteen-foot room, bedless at present, it has white curtains and an oriental rug on the gray floor, with blue wallpaper called "Sailor's Farewell." Filling a large part of the space are glass cases that display models of ships built in Portsmouth, a copy of the flag John Paul Jones flew and a letter written by him. Here also is a model of the *Ranger*, the ship that originally caused the dashing and controversial hero to come to Portsmouth where today much of the flavor of a prosperous eighteenth-century seaport has been recaptured.

Coventry, Connecticut
NATHAN HALE HOMESTEAD

Family House of a Hero

Above: The simple, severe Nathan Hale Homestead is classically early American architecture. *Opposite top:* The writing armchair in the Judgment Room reproduces the one owned by Deacon Hale. *Opposite bottom:* The parlor's most charming piece is the Connecticut Queen Anne maple tea table like the one Nathan's mother once had. (All photos: Louis H. Frohman)

The spy in "citizen's brown clothes with a round broad-brimmed hat" had left camp on Harlem Heights one mid-September evening in the year of 1776. Accompanied by a sergeant, Stephen Hempstead, he traveled fifty miles north, to the shore of Norwalk, Connecticut, boarded a small boat and rowed across Long Island Sound to Huntington Bay. There, presenting himself as a schoolmaster and loyalist disgusted with the "rebel" cause and in search of work, he visited the British camps drawing their fortifications and writing his notes in Latin, folding the thin but strategic papers under the inner sole of his shoes, from which he had carefully removed the silver buckles at the start of this precarious adventure. His mission completed, he returned to Huntington Bay and, early for the boat scheduled to return him to Norwalk, he spent the night at the Widow Chichester's tavern. It is thought he was recognized here by a Tory cousin, Samuel Hale, for what he was, Captain Nathan Hale of the Continental Army, serving its commander in chief, George Washington.

On September 7 and again a week later, Washington had called a council of war at the house of the Quaker merchant, Robert Murray, on Murray Hill. The American army on Manhattan Island was in perilous condition after its retreat from Long Island — in desperate need of money, clothing, doctoring. There were only 14,000 men, and they were scattered, to the British army of 25,000. Washington had decided to abandon the city and move on to Harlem Heights, send the sick to New Jersey and their stores to Dobbs Ferry. The enemy's next move was crucial to them. Washington wrote: "As everything, in a manner, depends upon obtaining intelligence of the enemy's motions, I do most earnestly entreat you . . . to exert yourselves to accomplish this most desirable end. . . . I was never more uneasy than on account of my want of knowledge on this score."

At another council of war at Mr. Murray's, the decision was made to send a competent person with military and scientific background, in disguise, into the British camps. Lieutenant Colonel Knowlton asked for a volunteer for this mission. Nathan Hale alone answered. Now, his mission completed, Hale waved to a boat rowing toward him as he stood on shore expecting to embark in moments for his return to Norwalk and to safety. "Surrender or die" was the response to his wave. Word of his presence had reached the British, and he was seized, taken to the British guard ship, *Halifax,* and then to General Howe's headquarters at the mansion of James Beekman. There at Mount Pleasant, at the high bank of the East River at Turtle Bay as it is called today, at Fifty-first Street and First Avenue, he was confined to the greenhouse on the property and condemned to hang the next morning, on September 22, 1776. The precise place of Hale's execution, or his burial, is unknown, but his last words at the age of twenty-one, are indelible: "I only regret that I have but one life to lose for my country."

One of the most moving aspects of Hale's life is that it was such a brief one. He was one of twelve children, born in Coventry, Connecticut. He entered Yale at sixteen and graduated with highest honors. He was almost six feet, "broad chested" and blue-eyed. He taught first at East Haddam and then at the Union Grammar School in New London. "I love my employment," he wrote, ". . . have time for scientific study . . . and my salary is satisfactory."

Hale's schoolmastering ended on April 21, 1774, with news of bloodshed at Lexington and Concord and his voluntary enlistment as a lieutenant in Colonel Charles Webb's regiment. Two years later his father, Deacon Richard Hale, mourned, "A child I sat much by . . . is gone." One month and nine days after Nathan's death, his family moved into a new house which is now an official memorial to the valiant young schoolmaster and, in a larger sense, to the Puritan family that produced him. Shortly after their move, the smaller structure adjacent to it, where Hale had been born, was pulled down.

The clapboard house is classically early American architecture, simple and severe — with an austere beauty nevertheless. Two and a half stories tall, with gable roofs, it has two chimneys over the main section and one over the ell. There are no overhangs or architectural ornamentation, but the clapboards are graduated, narrow above the baseboard, increasing in width above. Part of the ell was built at the same time as the main portion, and the north wall of the old house, Hale's birthplace, was grafted to the south side of the ell. Several years were required to finish the interiors, and the fine paneling and woodwork reflect changes of taste and the work of various craftsmen. The so-called schoolroom, with the simplest paneling, was perhaps done first. Owned and maintained by the Antiquarian & Landmarks Society, Inc., of Connecticut, the dwelling has been turned into one of the most inviting house museums in Connecticut.

A central hall divides the parlor and Judgment Room from the dining room and schoolroom. The latter two rooms are

separated by a second hall that leads to the "coffin" door in the center of the south gable end. The parlor in the northeast corner has well-executed green-painted paneling covering the entire wall around the fireplace and contains probably the most recent furnishings in the house — the Sheraton "fancy" chairs that belonged to Nathan's sister Joanna. The Chippendale-style wing chair in the corner is covered with eighteenth-century bright red damask.

The Judgment Room, where Deacon Hale and some of his sons acted as justices of the peace, provides a realistic glimpse into early governing procedures. The writing armchair reproduces the one owned by Deacon Hale, and the Daniel Burnap tall clock, a Hale possession, was made in nearby Andover. Otherwise the room is appropriately austere, with a plain plank-covered dado. This is repeated in the rustic dining room except that, as in the parlor, the wall around the fireplace is completely paneled. Joanna's china, pewter and copper kettles are here, and over the fireplace is the fowling piece Nathan Hale used as a boy.

The fabrics in the house are unusual. Most of them are original materials, some of which were found in trunks in the attic when the homestead was acquired by Antiquarian and Landmarks Society in 1948. It is in the six upstairs bedrooms where the most unusual fabrics are to be seen, and three of these rooms have Hale beds. In the chamber over the schoolroom the curtains and bed hangings of eighteenth-century rose-red furniture check are original fabrics and contrast with the blue and white resist coverlet on the bed and with the white walls. But the most colorful room is the parlor chamber, or northeast bedroom, which also has the most sophisticated wood trim in the house. This joinery is painted a robin's egg blue while the bed hangings are rose-colored toile.

When Nathan Hale visited his family in January 1776, he probably heard plans for the new house being discussed, and his brother Enoch no doubt kept him informed by letter of its progress. The simplicity of the homestead, which also displays a considerable degree of refinement and craftsmanship for its time and place, reflects the character of the Hale family and of the son and brother who died a hero.

Over the fireplace in the dining room is the fowling piece Hale used as a boy. The slat-back chairs were made in Coventry.

Lebanon, Connecticut
JONATHAN TRUMBULL HOUSE

First Among the Patriots

Jonathan Trumbull told his children "not to live merely, but to live well," that virtue "ought to be the daily object of all government, and especially that of ourselves." This Connecticut Yankee, an impeccable political figure during Revolutionary times, stood five feet seven inches tall, had a Roman nose, dark eyes, a "sallow countenance," a short neck and was considered a "handsome figure and very active," who fervently believed that "the Lord reigneth." He carried a piece of myrrh in the pocket of his embroidered waistcoat "both as a guard for himself against the miasm of the sick room, and for the benefit of invalids." Trumbull was of Scottish and English ancestry, graduated from Harvard where he had studied the classics. Later, when his brother was lost at sea, he "abandoned his early and favorite pursuit," theology, to help his father, a prosperous trader and planter.

At twenty-five, Trumbull married Faith Robinson, a "blooming girl of seventeen" of Dutch ancestry, the great-granddaughter of John Robinson who led the first Pilgrim emigration to the New World. It was an alliance that placed Jonathan among the elect. The couple settled in Lebanon, Connecticut, "on a moderately hilly surface . . . with a chocolate-colored soil . . . well adapted for grass and grains," and at Trumbull's father's death in 1755, Jonathan and his family, which now included six children, moved into the pristine house that his father had built during the years between 1735 and 1740, at the intersection of Town Street and Colchester. He proceeded to prosper as a merchant, trading in the West Indies and England, in Amsterdam and Hamburg, in oil, flaxseed, potash, lumber, fish, whale fins, and skins and furs. He imported in turn what was in demand by the colonists: woolen clothes, silks, scythes, nails, glass, brass firearms, and all sorts of crockery, cutlery, and ironware and pewter. Trumbull pioneered in direct importation from the mother country, and "sloops, schooners, brigantines, and snows," either chartered or owned by himself, frequently furled their sails in New London Harbor, at the wharf in Norwich, or along the banks of the Connecticut River, full of goods and merchandise for the enterprising tradesman of quiet, agricultural Lebanon.

Trumbull's "house and home-estate" was worth over four thousand pounds. He owned valuable furniture, a library, a store adjacent to his dwelling, land at East Haddam, farms "beautifully spotted with rich acres of woodland, an extensive

Above: Austere Trumbull House has a massive chimney linked inside to secret escapes necessitated by British attacks. *Opposite:* Family china with Chinese red key pattern and gray Turnbull medallion is exhibited in dining room. (All photos: J. Linton Houser, FPG)

share in the 'Five Mile Propriety'," as it was called in Lebanon, plus a stock of domestic animals. However, his estate, truly a large one for the day, was destined to sink, in large part, from his grasp, reverses that were rendered inevitable partly by the times and partly by the patriotic generosity of its owner during the convulsive Revolutionary struggle.

But Trumbull as a merchant is only a "shadow of the whole man." With his entrance into public life and especially with his relationship to Washington, we have a fuller-dimensioned portrait. He studied law and was elected to the assembly in 1773 where he was speaker for three years. He was county judge of Windham County for seventeen years, chief justice of the colony, and in 1769, he became governor, one of the first in the colonies to be elected by the people. He remained governor until voluntary retirement in 1784.

As soon as he heard of the Battle of Lexington, in April 1775, the Revolution's opening skirmish, he dispatched troops to embattled Massachusetts, and he was to be the only colonial governor to side with the colonies in the war. Beginning soon after Lexington, Trumbull and his sons and son-in-law began furnishing arms, tents, food and clothing to the Continental Army. Much of this was loaded on to ox sleds from the front room of his store, which was adjacent to his house.

The desperate need for these supplies was revealed in the letters Trumbull received, anguished letters that told of prisoners who "fared very hard," who had not clothing enough to "cover their nakedness," causing many of them from mere necessity to enlist in the service of the enemy. "Can't we by some means or other send them in some tow shirts & trowsers, which will make them comfortable in the warm weather?" pleaded Thaddeus Burr. And from Jedidiah Huntington: "We have invalids without number, owing to the constant fatigue of the army marching by night & day, thinly clothed, many without shoes or stockings, indifferently provided for, no vegetables." The cry went out for blankets (only 130 had been received from the continent), for breeches, for shoes and stockings. A great number had "no breeches or scarcely a substitute; linen overalls worn almost out are little better than nothing."

In the back room of Trumbull's store hundreds of meetings of Connecticut's Council of Safety were held between sessions

Queen Anne splat-back chair doubled as Trumbull's church pew. Governor's heart-shaped trademark is carved on Chippendale daybed.

Kitchen display includes pewter plates, spinning wheel and chairs combining fiddle-shaped splat-back with cane seat.

of the General Assembly, giving it the name War Office. Frequent conferences occurred in Trumbull's home between John Adams, Thomas Jefferson, John Jay, Lafayette and Washington, and many times Washington would say, "Let us consult Brother Jonathan." In August 1776, when Washington informed Trumbull of the need for more troops, he dispatched nine regiments of 350 men each, in addition to the five Connecticut regiments already provided, and they arrived in New York in time to halt the British advance. It is not surprising that Washington later stated that "but for Jonathan Trumbull, the war could not have been carried to a successful conclusion," and said he was "among the first patriots."

Jonathan Trumbull lost his son Joseph, the first Commissary General of the United States, in 1778, and in 1880, his son John was imprisoned in London on charges of treason committed in America, the same year as the death of his wife. Trumbull's exchange of letters with Washington is a fascinating study, and of his contemplated retirement he wrote, on April 20, 1784, "A month more, I trust, will bring me to the haven of retirement; in the tranquility of which I hope to have leisure to . . . cultivate those seeds of private friendship, which have been planted during the tumults of war. . . ."

Trumbull received many honors but none more fitting for a man with his constructive interest in education (he had founded a school in Lebanon), than the honorary degrees from Yale and from Edinburgh, Scotland. He had made crystal clear to his sons' teacher, Thomas Marsh, that he did not mean "to send them to college to spend their time and my estate in a careless, idle, and foolish manner, but in the hopes they may thereby become better qualified for service and usefulness to themselves and others." His son, Jonathan, Jr., was paymaster general and private secretary to General Washington and eventually Governor of Connecticut. His daughter Mary married William Williams, the son of a signer of the Declaration of Independence. His son John, the artist, was perhaps the most remarkable Trumbull of all. John's special contribution during the War of Independence was to sketch plans of the British works, and he was appointed second aide-de-camp to General Washington. He studied with Benjamin West in London, and it was in his studio that he painted his *Battle of Bunker Hill* and *Death of Montgomery*, both now hung in the Yale School of Fine Arts. His other works include portraits of Washington, Clinton, Hamilton, Jay, John Adams.

The Trumbull House, which was a considerable mansion for its time and place, now belongs to the Connecticut Daughters of the American Revolution. After it passed from the family, it was moved by yoke of oxen to its present pleasant location atop a grassy knoll studded with tall, full trees that shade the house and wide sloping front lawn. Standing two and a half stories, the austere white-painted frame dwelling is surmounted by a steep gable roof with a massive square chimney rising from the center. Of the nine twelve-over-twelve-light

Parlor holds Trumbull's candle stand and Queen Anne tea table. A Winthrop desk with bookcase stands near chair with original rush seat.

windows in front, the four ground-floor ones, as well as the double doorway, display simple pediments. Along the top of the doorway, below the pediment, six panes form a transom light that brightens the hall. Gifts and loans have helped to furnish the inside with many period pieces, some of them original Trumbull possessions. These include the Queen Anne splat-back chair in the Governor's dayroom that he carried to church to use in his pew. Beside it is the small Chippendale daybed in which it is thought he died. The same heart shapes are cut into its headboard that are found in the shutters of the house, a symbol Trumbull used as something of a personal trademark.

The valuable Trumbull pieces in the unpretentious parlor are the 1750 Chippendale-style chair with original rush seat at the Winthrop desk with glass-enclosed bookcase, the American Queen Anne tray-top tea table, tilt-top birdcage table and the graceful candle stand. Displayed in the dining room are the remains of a set of china with a band in Greek key pattern in Chinese red and a medallion in gray of a bull with its head turned to one side. Turnbull was the original name of the family, whose forbear, Ruel Turnbull, was credited with saving King Bruce of Scotland when he was attacked by a bull and rewarded by a coat of arms bearing the mark of the bull.

The Long Room, or keeping room, is one of the house's most inviting rooms, with its plain blue-painted woodwork and its collection of rare pewter. It is thought that here is where Washington held his many war conferences. But the lingering and fearful presence of war is felt most strongly in the Governor's workroom upstairs. Here is the mahogany writing desk with double kneeholes at which he worked so long and hard, making supplies available to Washington's army and doing much of the solitary labor necessary in governing during wartime. The room's only window is a shuttered opening twenty-seven inches square, placed high enough above the person seated at the desk to prevent stray bullets from hitting him. Just to the left of the window is a "sentry box" where a man stood guard day and night.

Hartford, Connecticut

MARK TWAIN HOUSE

"Part Steamboat, Part Medieval Stronghold"

To passersby pausing at 351 Farmington Avenue in Hartford, Connecticut, in 1874, the new three-storied residence of Samuel L. Clemens, more renowned as Mark Twain, and his wife Olivia, was "one of the oddest buildings in the State ever designed for a dwelling, if not in the whole country." The stately mansion was a classic American success story, "a reminder that it was possible to be born in a two-room clapboard house in Florida, Missouri, a village of one hundred inhabitants, and to become world-famous, marry a rich and beautiful woman, and live a life of domestic bliss in a house that was the marvel of Hartford."

Clemens came to Hartford first when he was thirty-three years old, to talk to Elisha Bliss about publishing *The Innocents Abroad.* A year after his marriage to Olivia Langdon of Elmira, New York, the couple decided to settle among friends such as Isabella Beecher Hooker, half-sister of Harriet Beecher Stowe in Nook Farm Colony, a section of Hartford favored by artists and writers. Edward Tuckerman Potter of New York, who had designed the Church of the Heavenly Rest, was hired to draw the plans for the house which took more than a year to complete for a most impatient and changeable client. The result was "part steamboat, part medieval stronghold, and part cuckoo clock," nineteen rooms and five baths inside a brick house patterned in black and

Above: Mark Twain House combines steamboat-style balconies with painted brick patterns on the exterior.

Opposite: Langdon family silver epergne and smoke screen of onyx tiles share prominence in dining room. (Photo: courtesy Mark Twain Memorial)

scarlet, festooned with balconies, turrets and porches, and trimmed with fern-bearing flower boxes every angle of the way. The interior, decorated in 1881 mainly by Louis Comfort Tiffany, lived up to the promise of the exterior. One could safely say Tiffany caught the spirit of the architect and spared nothing — not a stenciled wall, not a stained-glass window, not a glass tile. The brass smoke shield above one fireplace contained forty-two onyx Tiffany glass tiles in all. The furniture was heavy, "opulently inlaid and carved with cherubs, gargoyles, sphinxes and griffins," the carved furniture came from Venice as well as Olivia's home in Elmira, New York. Clemens gloried in his possession and when he returned to his home after a trip abroad he confessed to "a furious desire to have us all in this house again and right away, and never go outside the grounds anymore forever — certainly never again to Europe." Clemens found "ugly, tasteless, repulsive" all the domestic interiors he had seen in Europe by comparison "with the perfect taste of this ground floor, with its delicious dream of harmonious color, & its all-prevading spirit of peace & serenity & deep contentment; ..." he thought his "the loveliest home that ever was."

Clemens also managed to do some of his most memorable work there. But not with the "writing convenience" he had been "wailing" about for private correspondence. The writing box frustrated him, so did the "delicate glass vase" on top of it, and in the end he wanted "no more women's conveniences, for I will none of them." The same was true for his professional writing. The large divan in the corner of the study he found "much more comfortable to lie there and smoke than to stay at my desk. And then these windows — I was constantly getting up to look at the view; and when one of our beautiful heavy snow-falls came in winter, I couldn't do anything at all except gaze at it." As a result, he moved upstairs to the billiard room where his desk was carefully placed so he could see "nothing but the wall in front of him and a couple of shelves of books."

It was in the billiard room of his Hartford house in the winter and Quarry Farm, Elmira, in the summer that Clemens wrote *The Adventures of Huckleberry Finn, The Adventures of Tom Sawyer, The Prince and the Pauper, A Connecticut Yankee at King Arthur's Court.* He was described by his friend William Dean Howells, "at the crest of the prosperity which enabled him to humor every whim or extravagance." He and his wife were "whole-souled hosts, with inextinguishable money, and a palace of a house." In "amplitude, luxury and freely expressed affection, the house on Farmington Avenue was the opposite of Clemens's cramped birthplace and of his childhood in what he remembered as a loveless household." Clemens and his wife, and his daughters Susan, Clara and Jean lived with pleasure and gusto and the spirit of the servants was equal to that of the master. Their butler George "had come one day to wash windows and remained for eighteen years." Clara said the only time he looked after anyone's needs was when there was company; otherwise when there was only family at the table "he preferred listening to the conversation, to passing them food."

The staff of seven servants in the Clemens household included a coachman named Patrick McAleer who persuaded Clara that if she curried the calf every morning and put a

saddle and bridle on him he would turn into a horse. And Kate Leary, the maid, found her own biographer in later years. Kate Leary served breakfast to the family at about half-past seven, but the Clemenses never came until about 11 o'clock. Mrs. Clemens rang for Kate who brushed her hair, helped her to dress. After breakfast, Mr. Clemens went to his billiard room to write, leaving "strict orders not to have anybody disturb him — oh, for nothing." He would reappear about half-past five and dine at six. Mrs. Clemens "always put on a lovely dress for dinner, even when we was alone," and they had music during dinner, cranked from a music box in the hall.

Above: Harriet Beecher Stowe occasionally played this drawing room piano.
Cast of Mercury is original.
(All photos: J. Linton Houser, FPG)

In the billard room, Twain
engaged in both writing and
recreation. Table was Twain's,
a gift from his financier.

Below: Library holds Susy's rocker and
high-relief oak mantel from Scotland.
Wall and ceiling stencils are by Tiffany.

The grown-ups were not the only ones to enjoy life at 351 Farmington Avenue. The children loved to perform in plays, loved to dress in their mother's clothes, inviting neighbors to participate in the festivities. They also played charades in the drawing room and for the story of Hero and Leander, Clemens, as the impassioned lover who had to swim across the Hellespont, wore a bathing suit, a straw hat tied under his chin and a hot-water bottle slung across his chest. The Prince and the Pauper was played in the library in front of the conservatory, and to Kate Leary, "it looked just like a real palace." The children thought themselves a "very happy family" and Susy said their father was the "loveliest man I ever saw or ever hope to see — and oh, so absent-minded." She and her sister loved his "perfectly delightful stories" and used to sit and listen on each arm of the chair as he told them.

Samuel Clemens reached the age of fifty "in what seemed the fullness of success from every viewpoint." As a writer "he sat upon the highest mountaintop." As the principal partner in the ambitious New York publishing house, Charles L. Webster and Company, he had become "already the most conspicuous" publisher in the country. The typesetting machine patent he regarded as the chief invention of the age and invested $300,000 toward its perfection. Unhappily, the "beautiful miracle remained permanent but not profitable" — simpler and cheaper machines were invented, and Ulysses S. Grant's memoirs, for which he had paid $350,000, did not sell. The Clemenses' fortunes were changing, if not vanishing.

In 1891 the family decided to go to Europe to economize and four years later, after a lecture tour with his wife and Clara, Samuel decided to settle in London where Kate Leary was to bring both Susy and Jean. Susy, within the week of receiving her father's cable asking them to sail at once, fell ill and died shortly in the family home in Hartford of spinal meningitis. At Susy's death, all birthdays that had been "milestones on the march of happiness," became only "gravestones" and "the spirit of the dead" hallowed the house for Clemens. Mrs. Clemens would never enter it again; her husband did once more "when it was tenantless and forlorn" and found it a "holy place and beautiful."

Samuel Clemens died in 1910 at the age of seventy-four. He thought his daughter Susy had died at the "fortunate time of life . . . at twenty-four, such a girl has seen the best of life — life as a happy dream. After that age the risks begin; responsibility comes, and with it the cares, the sorrows, and the inevitable tragedy."

On April 19, 1902, the house was put up for sale, advertised in the *Hartford Courant* as a "most beautiful and valuable residence" . . . a "rare opportunity." In 1903 Richard M. Bissell moved in with his family and in 1917 the house was leased to the Kingswood School. The Mark Twain Library and Memorial Commission bought the property in 1929, renting out portions to the public library, and at last in 1956 the house was to be restored by the commission to the condition it was in when it "spoke out its eloquent welcome" to the prosperous and successful author known as Mark Twain.

The process of restoring and refurnishing is not quite complete, but the Mark Twain House stands today as a

Hall and stairway continue steamboat décor and Tiffany stencil, here in a design of gold on olive-green background.

remarkable memorial to the man and the gilded age in which he lived. The rooms have been furnished appropriately for the period and the family's taste. Particular care has been given to the restoration of the interior décor.

Like some of the exterior porches and other architectural details, the folding doors in the front hall and the staircase are reminiscent of the style which has been called "Mississippi steamboat." The stenciled walls in the hall were reproduced in 1967 from the original Tiffany design. A year later the elegant silver-on-peach stenciled wall design by Tiffany in the drawing room was restored. This room includes a pier glass, a crystal and gilt chandelier, two side chairs and a plaster cast of Mercury by Karl Gerhardt, a protégé of Mark Twain — all original pieces. The bust of Mrs. Clemens was done in Elmira before her marriage. Occasionally in the morning, while the Clemenses lived here, the elderly Harriet Beecher Stowe would wander into this room unannounced to play the piano.

The fireplace in the dining room has the smoke shield with the onyx tiles. The silver epergne on the table belonged to Mrs. Clemens's family and was used at her wedding.

The library served as the family living room, and it was here the charades and family dramatics were enacted. The rocker belonged to Susy. The high-relief and elaborately carved oak mantel, brought from Scotland by the Clemenses in 1874, was removed from the house when it was sold in 1903, but was returned in 1958. At the south end of the library is the wide, arched opening into the glass-enclosed conservatory, the first area in the house to be restored. The compact, semicircular design was suggested by the Clemenses' neighbor, Mrs. Stowe, who influenced the design of several Nook Farm conservatories. The period plants here are arranged around a pebble walk encircling a small central fountain.

Clemens's own bedroom, known as the Mark Twain Bedroom, contains the elaborately carved mahogany Italian baroque bed the Clemenses bought in Venice in 1878. Clemens called it "the most comfortable bedstead that ever was, with space enough in it for a family. . . ." He was particularly fond of the carved angels atop its heavy spiraled columns. The dresser, rocker and small desk are also original.

The Mahogany Room, or guest room, was called "a royal chamber" by William Dean Howells, author, editor of *Atlantic* and one of Clemens's close friends. Original pieces in the first-floor room are the marble-topped commode, the dresser with large mirror and the substantial bed with half-tester, paneled headboard and footboard, and the inlaid, diamond-shaped English tiles on the sideboards. The dominant color of the walls and carpet is rich green. Sir Henry Irving, Bret Harte and George Washington Cable are among those who slept in this room and made use of the large porch off of it called the *Ombra*, the Italian word for "shade." But the room also recalls tragedy, for it was here that Susy was carried when she was struck down with the disease that killed her.

Altogether, the Mark Twain House is an extraordinary and expressive dwelling. Clemens thought it had "a heart, and a soul, and eyes to see with, and approvals and solicitudes, and deep sympathies," — that it was for his family "of us, and we were in its confidence, and live in its grace and in the peace of its benediction."

56

Twain's Venetian baroque bed is mahogany, carved with heavy
columns and angels — "the most comfortable bedstead that ever was."

Katonah, New York

JOHN JAY HOMESTEAD

Rambling Farmhouse of the First Chief Justice

Top: Modest and comfortable, the John Jay Homestead was expanded into a gracious shelter. (All photos: Pendor Natural Color)
Above left: Hanging in the front parlor is a compelling portrait of Jay in the robes of Chief Justice.

John Jay occupied exactly two rooms as United States Secretary of Foreign Affairs and a study made by a Congressional committee in 1788 reveals that records and papers could be reached without "delay or difficulty. ... Upon the whole ... neatness, method and perspicuity" were evident throughout the department. It would not take another Congressional committee to apply the same description to the Jay Homestead that John Jay built in Bedford, New York, on a site bought by his maternal grandfather, Jacobus Van Cortlandt, and inherited at the death of his father, Peter Jay, a wealthy New York merchant of Huguenot descent. Jay chose an idyllic spot for his home: on top of the highest hill in the area, overlooking a wide meadow below, surrounded by woods. Two-story, modest, comfortable, painted gray-green with sienna shutters, the farmhouse has been expanded over the years into a gracious shelter for generations that have included another judge, as well as a Minister to Austria.

Jay, who was born on December 12, 1745, was one of ten children brought up in Rye, New York. His parents, he thought, were "actuated by sincere and fervent piety," and had "warm hearts and cheerful tempers" and a "remarkable degree of equanimity." In turn, the father admired Johnny's "grave disposition," and recorded that his son learned "exceedingly well," had a "disposition for books" and was generally so promising that he wrote a friend, "I cannot forbear taking the freedom of hinting to you that my Johnny gives me a very pleasing prospect." Johnny was sent to a grammar school kept by the Reverend Mr. Stoope, the Swiss-born pastor of the French church at New Rochelle where there was "little food and much scolding," and French to be learned both from contacts in the village as well as in the parsonage. At King's College, now Columbia University, Johnny was subjected to ridicule because he had trouble articulating clearly, particularly when he pronounced the letter "L" and he read so fast that he was impossible to understand. To remedy his difficulties he bought a book by Sheridan, probably his *Lectures on Elocution*, and read aloud to himself behind closed doors, halting carefully after every word until he acquired complete control over his voice. He also kept paper by his bedside for jotting down valuable ideas "even in the dark." After college there was law school and later a commission of colonel of the militia, the beginning of his service to his country for the next illustrious twenty-seven years of his life.

Jay was aristocratic, conservative and a strong nationalist. Paradoxically, he was also visionary and liberal. He was a member of the first Continental Congress and eventually its president. He wrote the "Address to the People of Great Britain," a forerunner of the Declaration of Independence (he happened to be in New York on business and so missed signing it), that led the colonists of New York to breaking with the mother country "at the risk of our lives and fortunes." He drafted the constitution of New York State which was adopted, "with some regrettable omissions," while he called on his dying mother. "I should also have been for a clause against the continuance of domestic slavery and for the support and encouragement of literature," he said. Jay thought "they who know the value of liberty, and are blessed with the enjoyment of it, ought not to subject others to slavery." He was an emissary to Spain, Secretary of State for Foreign Affairs after the Revolution, first Chief Justice under the new Constitution and New York's governor from 1795 to 1801 when he retired to Bedford where he lived until 1829.

Jay had felt "the impulse of duty strongly" during his years of public service. His conception of his responsibilities and lofty commitment, which, in theory anyway, is espoused by the high court even today, is articulated in a note to his brother: "My official situation with respect to foreign ministers, renders it improper for me to place myself under personal obligations to any of them. . . ." Jay could also be extremely skeptical and practical at times. To Washington he wrote, "We have, probably, had too good an opinion of human nature in forming our confederation."

For John Jay, as for most men in public service, there was the dilemma "between personal considerations and public ones." When there was talk of sending him to England in 1794, "if possible to avert a war," he wrote his wife Sarah, that no appointment "ever operated more unpleasantly upon me." Jay thought, however, if he helped to prevent "the effusion of blood and other evils and miseries incident to war," that he and his wife would have "reason to rejoice." His wife's reply is moving, as much for what is implied as what is written. "Your superiority in fortitude, as well as every other virtue," she wrote her husband, "I am aware of, yet I know too well your tenderness for your family to doubt the pangs of separation. Your own conflicts are sufficient; they need not be augmented by the addition of mine."

Jay left Albany at the end of his second term in office to go to Bedford with his daughter to complete the enlarged, still unfinished farmhouse that had been occupied by his farm manager. Jay reported to his wife, who was too feeble to withstand the wear of the work entailed in Bedford, that the "noise and hurry of carpenters, masons, and labourers in and about the house are inconveniences to be submitted to, but not to be chosen by convalescents or invalids. When our buildings are finished, and things put in order, there will be an end of many disagreeable embarrassments. I hope . . . we shall all be together again." And they were, for the year before her death, a time about which Mrs. Jay said, "I have never enjoyed so much comfort as I do here."

The dining table is an original Jay piece, circa 1770, and the American Chippendale chairs are thought to have belonged to him also.

Bedford was forty-six miles from New York and three miles from the post road where mail and the newspapers, "which furnish a history of the times," were delivered once a week. "Attention to little improvements, occasional visits, the history which my recollections furnish, and frequent conversations with the 'mighty' dead . . . who, in a certain sense live in their works," made Jay feel that retirement had lived up to his expectations and that, had "Mrs. Jay continued with me, I should deem this the most agreeable part of my life."

Major alterations and additions on the Jay farmhouse, which had originally been built from 200,000 bricks ordered to be done at the building site and completed in 1787, did not begin until 1800. Of the five rooms that comprised the original farmhouse, three of them — the front parlor and dining room in front and the Victorian parlor in the rear — are off a central hall, while the library adjoins the Victorian parlor and the Red Kitchen is off a small hallway in the rear of the house.

Richly embellished by time and many sophisticated purchases, today the house is a fascinating gallery of portraits of America's innovators, including DeWitt Clinton, inventor and Governor of New York, painted by Ezra Ames, and Timothy

The chairs and settee in the library were crafted between 1860 and 1880 especially to complement the authentic Gobelin tapestry upholstery depicting fables of La Fontaine.

Dwight, President of Yale College, by John Trumbull. These are in the central hall along with Jay's Federal bookcase, made about 1810 of five superimposed sections with massive brass bail handles at the sides.

To the left, the front parlor, whose floor boards were uncovered during restoration, is a dignified facsimile of Jay's period. The cornice is molded and the green and white wallpaper with leafy motif is a reproduction of early samples found during restoration. The beige-painted mantel with pilasters and dentil molding is based on period styles and the fireplace is faced with brownish-red and white Delft tiles. The Duncan Phyfe game table was Jay's own, as was the hand-carved ivory chess set, and the celestial globe, which Jay brought back from England in 1794, was charted by Nevil Madklyn. Hanging over the piano is a compelling portrait of Jay in the robes of Chief Justice, a copy made by John Wesley Jarvis for Jay from the original by Gilbert Stuart that now hangs in the National Gallery.

Across the hall is the dining room that has been used as such over the decades without interruption. The table, an original Jay piece, circa 1770, may be expanded by adding drop-leaf tables, and the American Chippendale chairs, also believed to have belonged to Jay, are upholstered in horse-hair. The initials "J.J." are on each piece of Jay's Chinese Export Lowestoft set, circa 1800. The mantel is identical with the one in the front parlor except it lacks the dentil molding and the fireplace is faced with handsome blue and white Delft Biblical tiles.

The Victorian parlor behind the front parlor is significant chiefly because of its marble mantels and French doors which John Jay II added and the parquet floor which was moved here from the front parlor during restoration. However, the library represents another especially successful transformation from the office Jay originally added in 1800 along with a small bedroom adjoining. Both the books and the furniture are valuable and unexpected — the books dating back to Jay's college texts in Latin and Greek, the chairs and settee crafted between 1860 and 1880 especially to complement the authentic Gobelin tapestry upholstery depicting fables of La Fontaine on the seats and *Les Amusements Champêtres* on the backs. The red damask, gold-trimmed draperies contrast nicely with the cream-colored walls and glass-enclosed bookcases. The Meissen rose-patterned tea service belonged to Mrs. John Jay II, and throughout the house there are other family treasures: The American Chippendale cupboard, a Jay heirloom, and the grandfather's clock, owned by John Jay's brother Peter, are in the upstairs hall. In the William Jay Bedroom the canopy bed, made about 1830, is a family piece and the bedspread on it was worked by several ladies in the family.

John Jay's house was lived in by his family until it was bought by Westchester County and presented to New York State as an historic site in 1958 and restored and opened to the public in 1964 as a tribute to an esteemed American. Jay had his own ideas on this subject: "The esteem of the estimable is certainly of great value, but the transient praise of the multitude, like feathers blown on and off by the passing breeze, can weigh but little."

A massive fireplace in the kitchen is a feature of many colonial dwellings. The rustic furniture was very functional.

Johnstown, New York

JOHNSON HALL

Last Baronial Hall in America

The young Irishman from County Meath was called Sir William Johnson by His Majesty George II, "Chief Big Business" by the Iroquois and "one of the most baffling characters in American history" by his biographer. Johnson, who has been portrayed "on the one hand, a patron of the arts, encouraging religion," on the other hand "a voluptuary, a libertine and a land grabber," wore the uniform of a British provincial officer, yet painted his face for Indian ceremonial occasions and indulged in war dances. It is no wonder that Johnson has been described variously as an "imperialist, the Napoleon of the Wilderness," and as a "strong and fearless man, a natural leader, a builder of empire, a student of human nature and a tower of strength of his King and country." He has been compared to Cecil Rhodes, "whose efforts brought England an empire in India and Africa, as well as great honors

and personal possessions, for their services to their country."
William Johnson, "European and Mohawk, colonist and Baronet," was also, concludes one historian, "the Dr. Jekyll and Mr.
Hyde of the pre-Revolutionary times."

Even a brief look at Johnson's life indicates that he deserved
his flamboyant reputation. Born in Smithtown, County Meath,
Ireland, in 1715, he was brought to America to act as an agent
for his Uncle Peter Warren who had purchased, with others,
fifteen thousand acres of land south of the Mohawk. According
to legend, another reason for his emigration was the need to
wean a "wayward youth" away from his attachment to an
Irish colleen in the port town of Drogheda, an act that was said
to color Johnson's adult conduct toward women forever.

Some time after he arrived in America, Johnson was made a
liaison officer between the province of New York and "certain
Indian nations." Also, he began an extensive fur trade in 1738
and started acquiring land. After learning the Mohawk language and customs, he was formally adopted into the tribe
and given the title *Wa-ra-i-ya-ge*, "he who does much business." His bonds with the Indians were reinforced by his
alliance with an Indian woman after the death of Catherine
Weisenberg, a Palatine German girl who died after bearing his
three oldest children, including his son and main heir, Sir
John. With Mary Brant, his Indian housekeeper, who was
sometimes referred to as the "Brown Lady Johnson," he
fathered eight more.

In 1755 Johnson was named sole agent and superintendent
of the Six Nations and all other Indians inhabiting British
territory north of the Carolinas and the Ohio River. Active in
campaigns against Ticonderoga and Fort Niagara, and in the
capture of Montreal, he helped to maintain Iroquois loyalty in
the French and Indian War. The Treaty of Fort Stanwix in
1768, negotiated by Sir William and other royal governors
with 3,400 of the Six Nations and their dependent tribes, was
thought to be "the most important treaty ever executed on the
North American continent" because it established the first
definite western boundary for the province of New York. It is
the opinion of some that, for his negotiations with the Indians,

Above: The wide boards on Johnson
Hall's facade were cut to resemble blocks of
stone. (Photo: Glen S. Cook) *Opposite:* This
early painting shows Indians of the Six
Nations gathered for council at Johnson
Hall. (Photo: Courtesy Knox Gelatine, Inc.)

The focal object in the Blue Parlour is a portrait of Sir William Johnson by Matthew Pratt. (All remaining photos: Glen S. Cook)

Sir William's role as an "outstanding Indian diplomat of the colonies can hardly be over-estimated. . . ."

Also for his negotiations with the Indians, William Johnson was rewarded with a vast tract of land — at least sixty thousand acres and perhaps more — extending between East and West Canada creeks, on the north side of the Mohawk River. Earlier, in 1751, Johnson, then a Colonel, had bought some fifty thousand acres on the western allotment of the Kingsborough Patent, and it was on this land that he built his fourth and last house, Johnson Hall.

It stands on a slight elevation some four miles back from the Mohawk. The master builder, Samuel Fuller of Schenectady, produced a noble Georgian-style mansion made of wood from Johnson's own forests and mill, boards that were extra wide and cut to resemble blocks of stone, and hardware made on the site, resulting in a structure fifty-five feet wide and thirty-eight feet deep and two stories high, with a hip roof and two chimneys. It was "executed with the charm which flows out of ample time, sound workmanship and unexcelled material."

The atmosphere surrounding Johnson Hall was of another ilk: part Indian, part German, many-faceted and quite startling to visitors who stopped for a day or a week.

"Here this singular man lived like a little sovereign; kept an excellent table for strangers, and officers, whom the course of their duty now frequently led into these wilds, and by confiding entirely on the Indians, and treating them with unvaried truth and justice, without ever yielding ... what he had once refused, he taught them to repose entire confidence in him; he in his turn became attached to them, wore in winter almost entirely their dress and ornaments, and contracted a kind of alliance with them. ..."

Another insight into Johnson Hall's inhabitants indicates, "On its white side, Johnson Hall was an Irish establishment, and one can always get up a dance and a frolic in such society." Tucked among the Negroes, half-breeds and Indians, were Doctor Daly, Lawyer Lafferty, Schoolmaster Wall, Financial Adviser Robert Adems and Secretary Guy Johnson, all Irish, and a son-in-law and butler who were German. Johnson seemed to preside over a brilliant and unpredictable pageant, taking an interest in everything about him, ordering a French horn, a "common hunting horn" and a "good loud trumpet" from his London bankers, importing hounds and grapevines, and advising his son-in-law, "If you can get a bargain of any good piece of household plate, and fashionable, I would have you buy it to the amount of one hundred pounds, but not unless it is good and cheap."

Johnson died in 1774 and his son Sir John went to Canada, raised and commanded a regiment there, remaining loyal to the Crown throughout the war. As confiscated property, under the Acts of Attainder, Johnson Hall was sold to James Caldwell of Albany in 1779 for $30,000 in public securities or the equivalent of perhaps $5,000 in cash. Over the years, it passed through several hands until, in 1906, the State of New York purchased it. As a National Historic Landmark today, Johnson Hall appears gem-like in its neat symmetrical compactness. Painted white with dark green shutters on its twenty-two windows, the mansion displays a pedimented door that is flanked by windows the same height as the others, but only two lights wide. An identical pair of narrow windows is found flanking the odd window above the door that is framed by two fluted pilasters. Each floor contains extremely wide, spacious central halls and four large rooms, all areas fully furnished with pieces that have in common an austere simplicity, a number of them original Johnson possessions. An attic and a cellar complete the mansion.

The two front rooms on the first floor are the Blue Parlour to the left and the White Parlour to the right, named by the Johnsons after the color of the painted woodwork in each room. Both rooms were used as dining rooms at times, so it is appropriate that the Blue Parlour presently is furnished as a dining room. The color of the paneled wainscoting and wooden molding in this particular room, as well as the entire fireplace wall, duplicates as nearly as possible the delicate light blue

Sir William's Study and Bedroom holds his desk and an immense ledger he used to record the accounts of various of his tenants.

Tables abound in the White Parlour: A fine Queen Anne drop-leaf and a Chippendale-style card table are against the wall.

the Johnsons used originally. Hanging over the mantel is the room's focal object, a famous portrait of Sir William done from life in 1772 by Matthew Pratt. An important piece is the simple Queen Anne oval table and six early Chippendale chairs with delicate pierced slats and foliage sprays lightly carved on the back rails and around a shield-shaped opening. A fine double gateleg table completes the furnishings.

Across the hall the White Parlour holds several notable pieces, among them a Chippendale armchair with plain legs that belonged to Sir William and an excellent Chippendale wing, or fireside, chair with ball-and-claw feet and richly carved legs. Tables abound: A fine Queen Anne drop-leaf and a superb Chippendale-style card table with extremely graceful lines rest against the wall, while another fine double gateleg stands in the middle of the room. Beside each chair is a plain tray-top table with turned shafts. Here, too, a portrait hangs above the wooden mantel, this one of Sir John Johnson, Sir William's son, done in 1771 by John Mare.

The two back rooms on the first floor, the Children's Bedroom and Sir William's Study and Bedroom, are accessible through doors located at the extreme rear of the hall. In Sir William's Study behind the White Parlour, two bookcases with cabinets are built into the wall on either side of the fireplace. The wooden mantel and overmantel, as well as the bookcases, are painted a soft blue. Open on Sir William's desk is an immense ledger used for recording the accounts of various of the Baronet's tenants, reminding us that this was a place of business. The desk chair is a handsome Chippendale, and opposite the desk is Sir William's austere low-post bed and a Chippendale side chair.

A broad stairway with one landing leads up from the right side of the hall to the spacious subdued second-floor hall with its contrasting gray woodwork and large, pale red oriental rug. The four bedrooms off the hall are gay, brightly colored rooms, particularly the one over the Blue Parlour. Its cream-colored paneled wainscoting complements nicely the gold bedspread, white canopy and beige wallpaper with its gold pattern. Bright blue curtains and valance frame the two windows, while blues and reds and golds dominate in the oriental rug.

In the opposite corner of the second floor is Mary Brant's bedroom with its plain pencil-post tester bed and mahogany chest. Here, too, the colors are imposing: a rust chair rail and molding accent the Indian-red curtains with white peacocks and vines. A bright bedspread has the same dark shade of Indian blue seen in the rug.

After visiting Sir William at his third home, Fort Johnson, the Swedish naturalist Peter Kalm wrote back, "A new sorrow did darken my heart, when I remembered that you, Dear Sir, yet did live . . . as a child of Israel in the middle of the Sons of Enakim where the most . . . look upon you with a more sowr eye and darker face, than a bull can do; I wonder, Sir, that you don't grow ten times sick in a day in such place." Johnson entertained the same variegated company at the more gracious Johnson Hall, but hopefully Kalm might have found things here more agreeable.

Above: A rust-colored chair rail and molding in Mary Brant's bedroom accent the Indian-red curtains with white peacocks and vines. *Below:* The mansion's four bedrooms are all off the spacious second-floor hall.

Tarrytown, New York
SUNNYSIDE

European Romanticism on the Hudson

Above: Sunnyside's Dutch stepped gables at either end give it a romantic, even eerie appearance. (All photos: Country Beautiful)

He might write that the world was in the "form of an orange," but for Washington Irving in the year 1810, it was clearly oyster-shaped and his for the asking. He was the best-selling and highest paid author of the year; his book, *A History of New York . . . by Dietrich Knickerbocker*, earned a record $2,000. And although Emerson and Whitman sniffed that it was only "shallow burlesque," Charles Dickens wrote, during a visit to New York some years later, "I do not go to bed two nights out of seven without taking Washington Irving under my arm." Dickens was not alone in his hospitable feelings toward Irving. The Americans, British, French, Germans and Swedish as well took him to their hearts and recognized him as America's authentic literary figure and it seems that no honor was too great for him. He could have been the Mayor of New York or Secretary of the Navy and he had the nomination for a seat in Congress. He did serve as the Secretary of the United States Legation in London, accepted an honorary degree of Doctor of Laws from Oxford and served as U.S. Minister to Spain, while completing the biography of Oliver Goldsmith during those years between 1842 and 1845.

Washington Irving was the eleventh child born to Scottish-English parents. His father was a prosperous hardware merchant but as a young man he chose to study law, principally it seems because it was free from "the risks and harassing cares of commerce." He took the grand tour of Europe for two years, sketching and writing and, in 1807, he began his varied and celebrated writing career. In his own words, he "attempted no lofty theme, nor sought to look wise and learned." He addressed himself to the "feelings and fancy of the reader more than to his judgment." Irving, a "mild little

During the first ten years of his occupancy, Irving used the study virtually as a one-room apartment, doing most of his writing here.

man," said to be terrified of making speeches in public, was dauntless between the covers of his literary work. He was frivolous with the colonial Dutch, tireless as a biographer — his five-volume *Life of George Washington* helped to perpetuate a hero — enamored of adventures at sea and Christopher Columbus in particular, and intrigued by the Indians, especially the noble leader, "Philip of Pokanoket," of whom he writes in *The Sketch Book of Geoffrey Crayon, Gent.*

As a result of a collaboration with his brother and a friend at the start of his career, Irving had produced the Salmagundi papers. Salmagundi was a dish of meat "chopped up with pickled herring, onion, oil, vinegar, pepper and whatever else inspired the cook." The literary version was a conglomeration of political satires, drama criticism, essays and sketches of New York life.

The freedom with which he assembled these pamphlets is not so different from the eclectic manner in which he rebuilt his beloved house, Sunnyside, which he bought in 1835. Irving owned twenty-four acres on the banks of the Hudson River twenty-five miles north of Manhattan and thought the surrounding area "one of the most agreeable neighborhoods I ever resided in." He was delighted with his neighbors, "generally in opulent or at least easy circumstances," and thought them "well-bred and well-informed." He admired the "delightful little parties," the "elegant little groups of females." He was almost embarrassingly eloquent about the picnics, those "picturesque assemblages, on some wild woodland joint jutting into the Tappan Sea, with gay groups on the grass under the trees; carriages glistening through the woods; a yacht with flapping sails and fluttering streamers anchored about a half

The 1805 sofa in the parlor is attributed to New York cabinetmakers Slover and Taylor. Portrait of Irving is by John Wesley Jarvis.

mile from shore, and rowboats plying to and from it, filled with lady passengers."

Irving's house, originally a farmhouse built in the late seventeenth century and lived in at one point by a branch of the Van Tassel family, was remodeled in what is described as a "highly personal style," part Regency, part Victorian, part defying definition. Its Dutch stepped gables at either end of the house, surmounted with ancient weathervanes that came from old buildings in New York, gave the house a romantic, almost legendary, even eerie appearance. Irving's development of this house, in which he was assisted by his friend, the painter George Harvey, who lived in Hastings, is indicative of his maturing interest in European romanticism.

Irving complained about "tardy masons," waiting for them to finish the outside work of the cottage "all in vain." He devised a recess to hide the slope of the roof and then he decided to paper it with a striped design "so as to resemble the curtain of a tent." Irving, who had an artist's eye and had been encouraged to take up painting as his career, was intrigued by the attic room where "the very irregularity became a source of ornament." He even designed cast-iron benches that would have "backs inclined a little and . . . smooth at the top so as to admit of a lounging position and to be leaned upon."

Sunnyside might have been the very spot Washington Irving was describing in *The Legend of Sleepy Hollow*: "a retreat whither I might steal from the world and its distractions," but it is rather doubtful that it was a retreat in any realistic sense. Friends and admirers came from far and near to pay homage, family visited for months and in ten years Sunnyside acquired a three-story tower with a slanting room, sometimes called the Pagoda, whose four rooms housed servants and sometimes overflow guests. Sunnyside was inherited by Irving's nieces, Catherine and Sarah, after his death in 1859. It was in 1945, when it was sold to Mr. John D. Rockefeller, Jr., that plans for its restoration were made and finally completed in 1961.

On the west side of the central hall is the dining room which contains mahogany Sheraton dining chairs with Gothic Revival backs that belonged to Irving. Most of the glass, ceramics and silver here were purchased by Irving during his many years of residence in Europe. Silver spoons on the table are stamped "H Cheavens" and are engraved with the Irving family crest. The portraits are of a diplomat and writer, John Pendleton Kennedy, and his wife, both frequent guests at Sunnyside.

Across the hall is the study, which was, for Irving, the heart of the house. During the first ten years of his occupancy at Sunnyside, he used this room virtually as a one-room apartment. He moved to an upstairs bedroom only after additions to the house were made in 1847. It was here that Irving did most of his writing and where he received most of his visitors. At one end is a romantically conceived draped alcove containing a divan with loose pillows against a wall of books. The partners' desk, labeled in silver, was given to him by his publisher G.P. Putnam. Everything is in its original place, according to several drawings of the room done when Irving lived here, and the books are in almost pristine condition.

The center of family life was the parlor which has a beautiful view of the river. The square rosewood piano was often played by Irving's nieces, Catherine and Sarah, who frequently accompanied him as he played his flute. In front of the fireplace are two Martha Washington chairs and a classical sofa, circa 1805, by the New York cabinetmakers Slover and Taylor. The oil of Irving is by John Wesley Jarvis, and at the far end of the parlor is a small picture gallery displaying original drawings done by various artists of Irving's day for his books.

Upstairs is a unique arrangement of interior architecture, a combination of sloping barrel ceilings and interesting arches devised by Irving to make a harmonious whole. Here as everywhere his highly personal tastes dominate, although the influence of Andrew Jackson Downing — a friend of Irving's who tried to codify in written form the conventional tastes of early nineteenth-century America — can also be seen.

The second-floor bedrooms contain furnishings from painted cottage styles to American Empire beds and a rare bed of cast iron, probably made at one of the foundries along the Hudson. Irving's bedroom in the southeast corner is directly over his famous study. The Sheraton tester bed, as well as the paisley dressing gown and walking stick, are thought to have been his. It was in this room that he died in 1859.

Now that the house has been restored to the way it was during the 1850's, it is once more Irving's "snuggery," a truly "little old-fashioned stone mansion, all made up of gable ends, and as full of angles and corners as an old cocktail hat."

Irving owned the mahogany Sheraton dining chairs with Gothic Revival backs as well as most of the glass, ceramics and silver.

Cove Neck, Long Island, New York
SAGAMORE HILL

A Rough Rider's Victorian Retreat

Above: Theodore Roosevelt wrote many of his letters at his desk in the Sagamore Hill library. (All photos: Sondak, FPG)

When he was leaving the White House, Theodore Roosevelt wrote to his son Kermit: "I have had a great run for my money, and I should have liked to stay in as President if I had felt it was right for me to do so; but there are many compensations about going; . . ." that he and his wife were "looking forward to a life of interest and happiness. . . ."

Roosevelt's adult life had begun at Sagamore Hill; the ten years he lived on after serving as twenty-sixth President of the United States ended there in "that nook of old-time America" where his children and their cousins enjoyed "just the proper mixture of freedom and control." But probably none of the children loved Sagamore Hill more than its owner and builder, Roosevelt himself. He enjoyed the cherry trees, the peach and apple trees, regretted the demise of the May flowers and bloodroot, anticipated the anemones and bellwort and the violets, could identify every bird he ever saw and enjoyed having "the warblers troop through the woods." Roosevelt wrote at Sagamore Hill, governed there (it was his summer White House), a statesman, naturalist, soldier, orator and historian about whom it was said "a man who could do so much could not do everything perfectly, though few have ever done so many things so well."

Among other things Roosevelt accomplished was to design a house that anticipated and fulfilled a way of life for a remarkable man and his large and honorable family.

Roosevelt's father's family was Dutch, his mother's Huguenot and Scotch-Irish. He graduated from Harvard in 1880 and

married Alice Lee of Chestnut Hill, Boston. He had spent summers near Cove Neck, the Long Island peninsula on which Sagamore Hill now stands, and two months after his marriage he paid $10,000 in cash and assumed a twenty-year mortgage for $20,000 for 155 acres from Thomas Youngs. Roosevelt completed Columbia Law School and was in his third term in the New York Assembly when he hired the architectural firm of Lamb and Rich of 486 Broadway, incorporating his own ideas with their plans for his new house. To a friend he wrote: "I did not know enough to be sure what I wished in the outside matters, but I had perfectly definite views what I wished in inside matters, what I desired to live in and with; I arranged all this so as to get what I desired insofar as my money permitted; and then Rich put on the outside cover with but little help from me." Roosevelt wished for a big piazza where he could sit in rocking chairs "to look at the sunset," a library with a "shallow bay window looking south," a parlor at the western end of the lower floor and big fireplaces for logs. "I had to live inside," he said, "and not outside the house and while I should have liked to 'express myself' in both — as I had to choose, I chose the former."

The house is a large, friendly, though formal one, designed for an affluent man to live with his family, to visit with his friends, to write and work in and to hold treasures. Two weeks before Roosevelt was to sign a contract to begin work on the house his wife Alice died after giving birth to her brilliant, now famous namesake, Alice Roosevelt Longworth. Roosevelt's

The angular, twenty-three-room mansion stands on a site exposed to the strong winds of Long Island Sound.

75

A pastel portrait of Mrs. Roosevelt
by Philip Laszlo is displayed in her drawing
room. A treasured Aubusson rug covers the floor.

mother died within twelve hours of her daughter-in-law and the house that was to have been called Leeholm was eventually named "Sagamore Hill," after Sagamore Mohannis, who, as Chief of his tribe, had signed away his original rights to the land on which Roosevelt built. The property was deserted by its owner and his home built in his absence while he spent two years after his tragedies on a ranch in western Dakota. It was completed in 1885 and the next year, he brought to this house his new bride and an old friend, Edith Carow, with whom he proceeded to build a successful life and a remarkable family of five more children.

Sagamore Hill is a twenty-three-room Victorian mansion, the first floor is brick, the second and third floors are clapboarded. Standing on a site exposed to the strong winds of Long Island Sound, the house is solidly built, with foundations twenty inches thick. Roosevelt's beloved and spacious piazza looks out from the south and west sides of the house over Oyster Bay Harbor. The ornamental clapboarding and porte-cochere are features typical of the 1880's.

On the first floor are a large center hall, the dining room, Mrs. Roosevelt's drawing room, the library that served as Roosevelt's study, the kitchen and the Trophy Room, or North Room, which was added in 1904-1905 when Roosevelt felt the need to expand in order to accommodate the many visitors to the summer White House. It was designed by an old friend, C. Grant La Farge, son of the famous painter John La Farge, and it is a momentous room, thirty feet wide and forty feet long, both impressive and personal, ornamented with columns of Philippine mahogany and stuffed with treasures.

On the north wall between a pair of tall windows is a large portrait of Roosevelt surmounted by a carved and gilded American eagle crafted by Gutzon Borglum. Above is a Presidential flag personally designed by Roosevelt. On the huge mahogany mantel are bronze sculptures, *Bronco Buster* by Frederic Remington, and *Kit Carson* by Frederick Mac-Monnies. This unique room, with its enormous oriental rug from a Sultan of Turkey, elephant tusks from Abyssinia, exotic furs and countless books, was hugely appreciated by its owner. "You cannot imagine how delighted I am with the new room," he wrote La Farge. "Really, I like it better than any room in the White House, which, as you know, is my standard of splendor!"

Though the Trophy Room is obviously the most spectacular part of the house, the rest is always interesting and a little unexpected because it so vividly reflects the breadth of interests of the entire Roosevelt family. The dining room, like the drawing room and library, was restored with the help of photographs taken in 1903. The Italian furniture, bought by the Roosevelts in Florence, provided an intriguing setting for the embroidered silk screen at the door that was a present from the dowager Empress of Japan. The Roosevelt silver and china is also here.

Mrs. Roosevelt's drawing room, in contrast to her husband's great room, is comfortable but graceful, in the original shades of blue, in contrasting textures of damask and lace, arranged around a soft and treasured Aubusson rug. The original pressed-tin ceiling has been carefully reproduced, and prominently displayed is a pastel portrait of Mrs. Roosevelt by Philip Laszlo.

Roosevelt spent most of his waking hours at Sagamore Hill in the library, or study, where he wrote many of his letters (150,000 are known to exist), thousands of articles and thirty books. Important official messages came over the nickel-plated telephone on his desk as he sat in his swivel chair. The walls are papered with a floral border. An oddity is the rhinoceros-foot inkstand.

On the second floor, Mr. and Mrs. Roosevelt's bedroom contains the set of lightwood, elaborately carved furniture purchased by the President's father at the Philadelphia Centennial in 1876. The walls of the bathroom, with its mahogany-railed bathtub, are painted their original Pompeian red, and Alice Roosevelt's bedroom has all of her childhood furnishings. The third floor has four restored rooms, including the fine collection of weapons in the Gun Room.

Roosevelt had written to his son Ted: "I always believe in going hard at everything, whether it is Latin or mathematics, boxing or football, but at the same time I want to keep the sense of proportion." This he managed throughout his life. The historian who wrote the *Naval History of the War of 1812* was also the ornithologist who recorded one day in March of 1879 that the *Parus atricapillus* not only "places its nest in deserted woodpecker holes, etc., but frequently excavates a burrow for itself . . . and is very fond of using the fur of the pine mouse as lining." Again, the Rough Rider of the Spanish-American War was also the winner of the Nobel Prize for peace as a result of a conference with the envoys of the warring Japan and Russia that ended in the Treaty of Portsmouth. The President of the Police Board of New York City also enjoyed hunting buffalo in the Badlands of North Dakota. The politician who thought that the young were with him and that it "is only the timid, elderly gentlemen that I have to fear," was also the poet and naturalist who wrote, "No one, but he who has partaken thereof, can understand the keen delight of hunting in lonely lands." As President, Roosevelt alternated messages to Congress with those to his children, writing to tell them, on his various trips, of treasures to divide "when I get back," reporting on "a little live lizard" named Bill which he explained was "called a honored frog, very cunning, who lives in a small box." He also took the time to report on a badger

Roosevelt's children and their cousins enjoyed "just the proper mixture of freedom and control" at Sagamore Hill: They swam, skated in winter and served tea to their teddy bears.

named Josiah who was "very well and eats milk and potatoes." In seeking to keep a sense of proportion Roosevelt's balance seemed almost flawless.

Theodore Roosevelt's four sons fought in World War I. Theodore was gassed, Archie crippled and Quentin killed. And still he was able to write: "With all my heart I believe in the joy of living; but those who achieve it do not seek it as an end in itself." Roosevelt died in his sleep one year later, on January 6, 1919, at the age of sixty. His wife lived on at Sagamore Hill enduring the death of Theodore Roosevelt, Jr., who was killed in Normandy in 1944, four years before her own death in 1948, at the age of eighty-seven.

In 1950 the house and eighty-three acres of land were purchased by the Roosevelt Memorial Association and donated to the Federal Government by authority of Congress on July 12, 1962. The official dedication ceremonies occurred a year later. The house is completely restored as authentically as possible, with the help of relatives' memory and actual documents, to its peak Victorian comfort. The third-floor maids' quarters, having served in past years as a museum for guns and documents, has been returned to its original appearance and its contents removed to the small museum installed in the home of Theodore Roosevelt, Jr., called Old Orchard.

In the momentous North Room, Roosevelt's portrait is surmounted by a carved eagle crafted by Gutzon Borglum.

Morristown, New Jersey
FORD MANSION

Landmark of the Revolution

Above: The Ford Mansion has been described as a "wooden Palladian mansion of the Dutch-English transition." *Opposite:* The room used by General and Mrs. Washington has the original secretary-desk where he wrote his dispatches. (Photos: J. Linton Houser, FPG)

"They have it much in their power to lead us a very disagreeable dance," said George Washington about the British in the year 1777. He was worried about defending four crucial areas: the Hudson highlands, Lake Champlain, the Delaware between Philadelphia and the sea, and the Jersey plains, and he could not decide whether the British would "either try to cut the United States in half at the Hudson River or try to take Philadelphia." He had come to one conclusion: The situation was grave. "I think we are now in one of the most critical periods which America ever saw. . . . It is our business to prepare for the worst."

It was just three days after the battle of Princeton, on January 6, that the general and his staff stopped off in Morristown, thirty-five miles from New York, to "accommodate and refresh." The town, settled in 1710 and named for Governor Lewis Morris, was described as "a very clever little village situated in a most beautiful valley at the foot of five mountains." The village was protected by an outer rampart, a chain of hills surrounding the New York-Philadelphia roads, and Washington realized then that Morristown was an ideal post for blocking the British soldiers' passage to Philadelphia. Two years later, in December of 1779, he returned to set up winter quarters in an ample, gracious white house, four miles from the heart of the town, at the invitation of its mistress, Mrs. Jacob Ford, Jr.

Jacob Ford, Jr., one of the pioneers in the iron business, was "no doubt the leading man in Morristown," and when the house was completed in 1774, it was considered the town's finest residence. Ford supplied the community and surrounding region from his different forges and, as one of the two members representing Morris County at the House of Assembly, he had been responsible for an eleven-point resolution, the fifth one of which stated: "That unanimity and firmness in the colonies are the most effectual means to relieve our suffering brethren at Boston, to avert the dangers justly to be apprehended from that alarming act commonly styled the Boston Port Bill, and to secure the invaded rights and privileges of America." He had died here of pneumonia, contracted in service, just three years after building what became Washington's headquarters and to which Washington brought a brilliant entourage of "polite, sociable gentlemen." They included Alexander Hamilton, a "quick, proud, bony-faced young man, with cold blue eyes and smiling mouth," and generals Quaker Nathanael Greene, German Baron Friedrich von Steuben, Polish Thaddeus Kosciusko, and Virginia's "Light Horse Harry" Lee.

In January 1880, Washington wrote: "I have been at my present quarters since the 1st day of December, and have not a kitchen to cook a dinner in — nor is there a place at this moment in which a servant can lodge with the smallest degree of comfort. Eighteen belonging to my family and all Mrs. Ford's are crowded together in her kitchen, and scarce one of them able to speak for the colds they have." Soon a log kitchen and a log cabin office were added to the premises, as was the presence of Mrs. Washington. No person "suffers more by an absence from home than myself," the general admitted, and the erratic mail delivery he found "rather mortifying, as it deprives me of the consolation of hearing from home on domestic matters. . . ."

But even during that crucial winter, with 250 guards posted about the premises, there was a day-to-day pattern of life affording a certain amount of pleasure. The fifers and drummers practiced regularly because Washington found "nothing . . . more agreeable and ornamental than good music," and he wished them to continue "on these accounts and for his own ease and satisfaction." A visitor to Washington's headquarters that winter found that Washington's "tall, noble stature and just proportions, his fine, cheerful, open countenance, simple and modest deportment, are all calculated to interest every beholder in his favor, and to command veneration and

Washington conferred frequently with his staff officers in his office and possibly used one of the two Windsor chairs there now. (Photo: courtesy National Park Service)

Near the doorway of the bedroom used by the Washingtons is the general's camphor-wood camp chest. (Photo: Houser, FPG)

respect. He is feared even when silent, and beloved even while we are unconscious of the motive." The visitor noted that the table was "elegantly furnished and provisions ample, though not abounding in superfluities," that the "civilities of the table were performed by Colonel Hamilton and the other members of the family, the general and lady being seated at the side of the table," and though Washington smiled placidly, a loud laugh "seldom if ever escapes him." The general was "polite and attentive" to everyone, as was Mrs. Washington, who, according to the visitor, combined "in an uncommon degree, great dignity of manner with the most pleasing affability, but possess no striking mark of beauty."

Upon the death of Colonel Ford's grandson, Henry A. Ford, in 1873, Ford Mansion was purchased for $25,000 by four New Jersey citizens who organized the Washington Association of New Jersey to preserve the structure. For nearly sixty years after the house was opened to the public this group collected many of the outstanding furnishings,

The Queen Anne dining table and four matching chairs in Mrs. Ford's living and dining room are Ford family pieces. (Photo: J. Linton Houser, FPG)

manuscripts and art objects now in the house. In 1933 the association gave Ford Mansion to the Federal Government as part of the Morristown National Historical Park and six years later the restoration to the 1779-1780 period was completed.

The Ford Mansion has been rather formidably described as a "wooden Palladian mansion of the Dutch-English transition," built in the style of Inigo Jones who has sometimes been called the "English Palladio." The two-and-a-half-story main section is surmounted by a dentil cornice and hipped roof, flanked by two large square chimneys. But the chief feature of the exterior is the elaborately decorated Palladian doorway with a more restrained second-story Palladian window directly over it. The main section has a central hall flanked by two rooms on each side, and the two-story east wing contains the kitchen and buttery and servants' rooms above.

To the left, the large room used by General and Mrs. Washington as both a living and dining room contains the original secretary-desk where he wrote his dispatches. Surmounted by a scrolled pediment or bonnet top with rosettes and urn finial, it has round-topped panels and claw-and-ball feet. Also in this room with white walls and beige woodwork are Washington's drop-leaf table and a fine Queen Anne chair upholstered in blue. Unusual is the iron fireback in the fireplace, cast in 1758 at Oxford Furnace, New Jersey.

Across the hall is the combination living and dining room where Mrs. Ford lived with her family during the time the mansion was used as Washington's headquarters. The Queen Anne dining table and four matching chairs are Ford family pieces that were in the house at the time. Inside the built-in cupboards the original paint made of brick dust and buttermilk is preserved, and in front of the cupboard nearest the doorway is a tea table with a cup and saucer that were owned by Martha Custis before she married Washington.

In the rear of the house to the left of the hall is a simple, unadorned room that served as Washington's office. Here, where he conferred frequently with his staff officers and commanders, are two Windsor chairs that were in the mansion during Washington's occupancy, one with a writing arm.

The upper hall, which was sometimes used for small social gatherings, has an inviting Palladian window, and is hung with a delicately styled brass chandelier made in London. The delightful harpsichord was also made in London in 1715 by Jacob Kirckman. There are three bed chambers off the hall and the outstanding one, in the southwest corner, was occupied by the Washingtons. The excellently carved Chippendale dressing table in the corner, perhaps the dwelling's finest piece, was in the house during the winter of 1779-1780, and the camphor-wood chest near the doorway was the general's.

The most important visitor to stay in the comfortable southeast guest room was Lafayette, in May 1780. The outstanding pieces are the graceful pencil-post bed and the handsome curly-maple highboy that was in the house during Washington's stay. The cowhide trunk under the window belonged to the Revolutionary War surgeon of Morristown, Dr. Jebez Campfield. The Aides' Room next to the guest room, where some of Washington's aides-de-camp slept, contains an iron camp broiler and folding field bed, a rare relic from Revolutionary times.

As Washington noted, it was the kitchen in the east wing, a large room and the warmest one in the house, that served as a gathering place during the coldest days that historic winter. It is now completely furnished with colonial utensils and cooking tools and the banister-back armchair is a Ford family piece that was here at the time. The spring of 1780 brought warmer weather and welcome news. Lafayette informed Washington that a French army was on the way to help the Americans and the commander in chief left Morristown shortly with rekindled hope in the future.

The most important visitor to stay in the comfortable guest room was Lafayette, in May 1780. (Photo: J. Linton Houser, FPG)

Elizabeth, New Jersey
BOXWOOD HALL

Home of Washington's Reluctant Commissary

Like the ancestors of John Jay, the first Chief Justice of the United States Supreme Court, those of Elias Boudinot were Huguenots escaping from the province of La Rochelle after the revocation of the Edict of Nantes in 1685. Instilled with the idea that freedom was a prize worth seeking and sacrificing for, it had not, however, been simple for Boudinot to turn his back on England, where his grandfather had sought refuge and his father married his mother. And in the beginning, he admitted, "Nothing was farther from our ideas, than a state of independence on the country from which we drew all our ideal principles of happiness & enjoyment." In 1775, Boudinot was chosen a member of the Provincial Congress of New Jersey and when a "proposition was made by a few weak & violent men for raising a regiment of troops," it was opposed by "all the men of note & understanding as a measure wholly against our duty of allegiance to Great Britain and rejected as contrary to every sentiment or desire of our constituents. . . ."

By 1777, Boudinot had given up the luxury of sentiment. George Washington had written him asking that he accept a commission as "Commissary-General of Prisoners in the Army of America." When Boudinot "politely declined the task," Washington "very kindly objected to the conduct of gentlemen of the country refusing to join him in his arduous struggle." Washington had reassured Boudinot that "he had nothing in view but the salvation of his country, but it was impossible for him to accomplish it alone," that "if men of character and influence would not come forward and join him in his exertions, all would be lost. . . ." Boudinot, "Affected by this address, . . . consented to accept the commission. . . ."

Above: Built between 1750 and 1763, Boxwood Hall today is faced with red-painted cedar shingles. (All photos: J. Linton Houser, FPG)

From this assignment, Boudinot, a lawyer who had studied with his brother-in-law Richard Stockton, a signer of the Declaration of Independence, went on to serve his state and his country unceasingly. He was a member and eventually President of the Continental Congress, a secretary of foreign affairs briefly, a member of the national House of Representatives, a director of the United States mint, a founder and first President of the American Bible Society and a trustee and benefactor of the College of New Jersey, now known as Princeton University. For all the breadth of his public career, his dedication seems to have been more a matter of conscience and discipline than private inclination. To his wife Hannah he had written during their courtship days, "It will be most for your advancement, as well as happiness, to take the world as you find it, and endeavor to convert even the prejudices of fashion and common life into such proper channels, as to make them subservient to your advancement in usefulness. . . ."

Boudinot found it difficult to be separated from his home and his wife and daughter Susan, his "one ewe lamb." From Valley Forge he wrote, "I miss my bed as the weather is bitter to lay on blankets. . . ." He was concerned about his wife, who was in Trenton, not being able to reach Philadelphia with "two horses in one day," and he fretted about his daughter's dilatory correspondence: "I am sorry you are not more fond of letter writing as you would find great improvement from it & after a little while it would become easy & familiar. . . ."

Elias Boudinot, the early patriot and American statesman earned still another, though lesser distinction: that of being one of the first commuters and suburbanites. He and his wife bought their home in Elizabeth Town, called Boxwood Hall, ten years after their marriage in 1762, and he then proceeded to commute to nearby Newark to his law offices until he

Below: The alcoves flanking the fireplace in the Dayton Room are framed by intricate plasterwork with grains-of-wheat motif.

Above the sideboard is the mansion's most treasured piece, a Federal mercury-glass mirror with two two-branch sconces.

accepted his commission as colonel with George Washington.

Built between 1750 and 1763 for Mayor Samuel Woodruff, Boxwood Hall is a plain, symmetrical, two-story house rising behind green shrubbery across the front and faced with dark red-painted cedar shingles. The cedar-shingled gable roof is pitched rather steeply and has a wide chimney at each end. Eight of the nine windows in the facade have red shutters and the odd window in the center, over the white door, is crowned with a fanlight and flanked by columns of narrow windows.

The house has surprisingly elaborate interiors, hardly hinted at by the chaste exterior. On the right of a twelve-foot-wide central hall extending to the rear of the house is a broad handsome staircase with original beige-painted hand-turned balusters and newel post with acorn motif and striking dark mahogany banister. The width of the hall enables it to accommodate graciously the two landings.

To the left of the entrance is the Boudinot Room, a parlor containing, as do all the other furnished rooms in the house, eighteenth-century American pieces that closely resemble the original furniture. Among these are two fine tables — a mahogany birdcage tilt-top, circa 1780, and a late-eighteenth-century mahogany Hepplewhite card table. The delicate brown of an elegant grandfather's clock made by Elizabeth Town clockmaker John Brokaw, circa 1790, harmonizes perfectly with the typical early American light and dark beige wallpaper with its circles of rose-colored flowers above the original off-white wainscoting. The rarest attraction here, however, is the mantel which is faced with marble from a now-extinct quarry in King of Prussia, Pennsylvania.

Across the hall is a colorful parlor called the Dayton Room, twin of the Boudinot Room except for two bright-red arched alcoves flanking the fireplace. Framing these spaces is intricate plasterwork with a grains-of-wheat motif. Over the fireplace is a portrait of General Jonathan Dayton who bought Boxwood Hall from Boudinot between 1795 and 1800. The eggshell-colored silk and cotton moiré curtains ably complement the dark beige wallpaper with its mid-eighteenth-century English and French design depicting flowers, doves and shepherdesses. The mantel here is a prized possession: a carved Adam design executed in France, circa 1801, with cherubs across the top and a bellflower design on the pilasters. A Queen Anne oak tea table dating from 1760 and a clock with Chippendale case are valuable additions.

Behind the Boudinot Room, the dining room is given an air of colonial formality by its gray-blue woodwork and fireplace faced with blue Delft tiles illustrating Biblical scenes. Above the Hepplewhite-style sideboard is the mansion's most treasured piece, a large Federal mercury-glass mirror in gilt frame with an eagle and horns-of-plenty, circled with twenty-six acorns and hung with two two-branch sconces. Also here are three large English pewter chargers, one of them dated 1718. Complementing the blues of the woodwork and tiles is the dark blue wallpaper with stripes and urns of fruit and flowers. The remaining room on the first floor is a museum room with display cases showing muskets and swords and such early household utensils as candle molds, scales and pottery.

Of the four rooms upstairs, only one is presently furnished as a bedroom. It contains an attractive canopied bed whose posts have fluted columns ending in flame finials. The gay, multicolored wallpaper is a copy of crewelwork and has an off-white background that blends with the cream-colored wainscoting. Other items include a Franklin stove, circa 1800, and an eighteenth-century hooded cradle.

After General Dayton's ownership, Boxwood Hall had several owners, was operated as a boardinghouse and then was deeded to the Home for Aged Women of Elizabeth. In the late 1930's, it was finally relieved of other tenants and further transformations by the Boxwood Hall Memorial Association and deeded to the State of New Jersey and restored through a WPA project to its original luster.

Boxwood Hall's finest moment came on April 23, 1789. Congress had appointed Boudinot chairman of a committee charged that day with conducting George Washington safely from Philadelphia to New York for the ceremony inaugurating him first President of the newborn nation. Because there could be no safer place to stop for a rest than his own home, Boudinot took the general there for lunch before boarding the ferry to New York where he reported to his wife that "our worthy President was greatly affected with these tokens of a profound respect." Boudinot, a modest and responsible figure on the Revolutionary scene, is suitably commemorated by the respectful restoration of Boxwood Hall.

The gay wallpaper in the bedroom is a copy of crewelwork and has an off-white background that blends with the cream-colored woodwork.

Princeton, New Jersey
MORVEN

"An Outpost of Sensibility"

The first of the Stocktons to make a public impact on America was Richard Stockton, the elder, who migrated from England and settled in Flushing, Long Island, near a stream called Stony Brook. This Stockton signed a petition for the release of one William Wickenden who had been fined and imprisoned in 1656 by Peter Stuyvesant, the Governor of New Amsterdam, for preaching without a license. His grandson and namesake used his signature even more impressively: He wrote it on the Declaration of Independence of 1776.

The Stocktons were numerous, intelligent and enormously wealthy landowners as well as creative and dedicated citizens. The most "lasting accomplishment" of Richard the elder's son John's life was the part he played in bringing the infant College of New Jersey to Princeton. Opened at Elizabeth Town and moved to New Ark with the Reverend Aaron Burr as its second president, its seventy students and President Burr went to Princeton in 1754 because John Stockton and two other benefactors signed a bond for a thousand pounds that made it possible. One of the most unusual students to attend Princeton subsequently was John's great-grandson Robert Field Stockton, a naval officer who developed the first propeller-driven warship in the world for the United States Navy, pioneered the construction of the Delaware and Raritan canal, commanded the United States forces that captured the Mexican stronghold, Los Angeles, in the battle over California, and served in the United States Senate.

Dedicated and as full of achievements as the Stocktons were, the most appealing member of the family was a Stockton by marriage, a young woman named Annis Boudinot who married Richard, the signer, in 1755. The Stockton-Boudinot alliance was further reinforced by Annis's brother Elias marrying Hannah Stockton, her sister-in-law. Annis was handsome, intelligent, enterprising and contagiously romantic. Her

Above: Lovely, sedate Morven is today the home of New Jersey governors. *Opposite:* Two Sheraton settees in the Gold Room are among the mansion's finest pieces. The portrait of John Potter was painted by Thomas Sully.(Photos: J. Linton Houser, FPG)

The crystal chandelier in the entrance hall was a gift of Mrs. Walter E. Edge. A mahogany tall-case clock on the stair landing was made in England in 1780. (Photos: Houser, FPG)

father had been apprenticed to a goldsmith in New York before moving to Philadelphia where he was a neighbor of Benjamin Franklin's, earning his income by selling silver and other merchandise, and serving as postmaster. Annis, with her plain background, fretted in a poem about her marriage to the son of New Jersey's richest landowner: "I found me all thine own in spite of those/Whose cold unfeeling minds would bid us part."

The first section of the house that was to become Morven had been built by Richard Stockton the elder in 1701 on land bought from William Penn in the wilderness of West New Jersey. After Annis's marriage, one of her first acts as mistress of the 5,500-acre "dwelling plantation" was to observe a pleasant custom of that era by planting "bride trees," twin poplars at the entrance of the Stockton Place. Annis not only wrote poetry but also read enough to inspire pen names for herself and her husband: They wrote to each other as Emelia and Lucius. Her reading inspired another variation, a change of name for the Stockton Place. She read James Macpherson's successful forgery, *Poems of Ossian,* supposed translations of heroic lays of the Gaelic bard Ossian narrating the exploits of his father Fingal. Fingal's home was called Morven and shortly after she finished her reading, Annis gave her home the same name. Annis, who adopted white myrtle as her special flower and had herself painted holding a spray of it, furnished her house with such flare, developed the gardens with so much imagination that Morven was considered, because of its mistress's taste and ingenuity, "an outpost of sensibility."

It was the "consequences" of the trip to England Richard Stockton made alone that were to "affect Morven in one way and another for generations to come." In England Stockton visited the garden of the poet Alexander Pope in Twickenham. He took with him a gentleman "who draws well to lay down the exact plan of the whole," so that he could duplicate Pope's garden at home. For his garden he collected Roman brick from the top of Dover Castle, a piece of wood from the five hundred-year-old effigy of the Archbishop Peckham at Canterbury, a fragment of the King's coronation chair, and "the best cement for sticking shells in a large way." Stockton also sent home "a little box of flower seeds . . . with the hope that these will please you for the present," and assurance that he was making "a charming collection of bulbous roots" to send when the danger of freezing was over. On Stockton's return, Morven, with its new treasures and wealth of fresh plantings of cedars, cypresses, royal walnut and Spanish chestnut trees, its mulberries, boxwood and willows, became so luxurious that all their visitors acknowledged that the Stocktons and their six children lived in a "state of splendor."

As the plots thickened, and the colonies were inclined toward separation rather than accommodation, Stockton's thoughts turned from gardening to government. He was made a member of the Supreme Royal Legislative, Judiciary, and Executive Council of the province, and in 1774, judge of the provincial supreme court. On December 12, 1774, he drew up and sent to Lord Dartmouth, Secretary of the Colonies, "An expedience for the settlement of the American disputes," which was in fact a plan for American self-government, independent of Parliament but still owing allegiance to the English Crown. If something of the kind was not done, he warned the noble lord, the result would be "an obstinate, awful, and tremendous war." Four years later while the campus bell tolled, Princeton students burned the college steward's entire supply of tea, together with an effigy of Governor Hutchinson hung with a tea canister around his neck. By 1776 Richard Stockton and his son-in-law Dr. Benjamin Rush signed the Declaration; Princeton was ravaged by fire and sword, Morven pillaged and its east wing left roofless, and by 1781 Stockton was dead and his fortune depleted.

The house, which burned again in 1821, remained in the possession of the Stockton family until 1945 when it was purchased by Governor Walter E. Edge with the intention of giving it to the State of New Jersey, which he did in 1954. The following year the legislature authorized rehabilitation work to restore it to the best possible condition. Today, it is the residence of New Jersey governors and it is regarded, even without lavish moldings or architectural embellishments, as "expressive of a landed, wealthy, educated, refined society."

Constructed of yellow-painted brick trimmed in white, Mor-

The drawing room, or morning room, holds a superb Chippendale-style highboy once owned by Richard Stockton and used at Morven.

93

This lacquered Regency settee was a gift of Citizen Genet, French Minister to the U.S. from 1793 to 1794. (Photos: courtesy N.J. Dept. of Conservation and Economic Developt.)

ven today is a lovely sprawling old house that is sedate and far from elaborate, even in its present, handsomely restored state. The two-and-a-half-story central portion has a low-pitched gable roof with end chimneys and a modest single-story porch with four front pillars. Each of the two-story wings flanking it has smaller, similar porches. Although there is no certainty as to how much present-day Morven resembles the eighteenth-century dwelling, it is believed the dining and reception rooms in the central portion and the drawing room and library in the east wing have not changed very much. The west wing contains service rooms and a foyer used as an entrance to the governor's private rooms on the second floor. Morven's entire first floor has ten rooms and the second floor contains seven bedrooms and a sitting room.

The decorations and furnishings follow, as closely as possible, those of an eighteenth-century country home. Some of the pieces are authentic antiques and others are copies. The west foyer is connected to the central section, where the state rooms are, by a fully paneled passage containing an original Stockton piece — a Regency settee and matching chairs that are lacquered black with gold trim and have cane backs and arms. They were a gift from Citizen Genet, French Minister to the U.S. from 1793 to 1794, after an enjoyable visit to Morven. (President Washington later demanded Genet's recall after he tried to raise troops against Spanish Florida and commission privateers against British commerce.)

In the entrance hall of the central section, a crystal chandelier and handsome gold-leaf mirror are accompanied by a portrait of Commodore Robert Field Stockton and beyond, on the stair landing, is a mahogany tall-case clock made in England about 1780 by George Guelst.

In the dining room, to the left of the hall, the choice pieces are the three-section Regency dining table and the graceful

A three-section Regency table and a graceful Adam-style sideboard with brass rail at the back dominate the dining room.

Adam-style sideboard with serpentine breakfront, carved rosettes and a charming brass rail at the back. To the right, the reception room, or Gold Room, has some of the finest things at Morven — an English Chippendale breakfront, circa 1800, an eighteenth-century gaming table with a trough for chips and two Sheraton settees. The yellow wallpaper is a copy of eighteenth-century flock paper that could have hung here and that gives the room its name. The portrait of John Potter over the fireplace was painted by Thomas Sully about 1841. Partially adjacent to the Gold Room is the inviting drawing room, or morning room, reached through a broad stair hall, perpendicular to the entrance hall, which leads to the east wing. It contains a superb Chippendale-style highboy once owned by Richard Stockton and a straight-back chair that belonged to Elias Boudinot.

Annis Boudinot Stockton lived on at Morven after her husband's death, entertaining her children or visiting with them. Still vigorous in her middle fifties, "She was familiarly called 'the Dutchess,'" said George Washington Parke Custis, because of her "elegance and dignity of manner." She continued to write poetry, favoring her friend George Washington with a number of her verses, including: "Forget not her on Morven's humble glade,/Who feels for you a friendship most refin'd."

Washington, D.C.
THE WHITE HOUSE

Where America's History Resides

"This house is built for ages to come," Abigail Smith Adams prophesied. And rebuilt, she might have added. The minister's daughter, the second President's Puritan wife, was talking about the Executive Mansion that has been painted white since it was burnt down to its Virginia freestone walls when the British captured the fifteen-year-old capital in 1814. Almost from the moment James Hoban, a young Irish architect, won $500 and a gold medal worth $46 for designing the White House, this residence of United States Presidents has been in a state of change. The "honest and wise men" Abigail's husband John hoped would rule under the White House roof have been men of fine and eccentric taste and the times of their power have been tragic and serene. Colonnades and porticoes have been added, foundations rebuilt, fences and greenhouses have come and gone and so have the Tiffany glass pieces that Chester A. Arthur cherished and the sheep that grazed the lawn during World War I when Woodrow Wilson was in office.

For the design of the Executive Mansion, Hoban drew on the Palladian-style architecture that was the rage in mid-eighteenth-century Europe; Château de Rastignac in France and Leinster House in Dublin are its counterparts. Hoban was the first of a number of architects who have contributed to the design of the White House as it stands now in the late

96

Above: The mahogany secretary in the Green Room is attributed to Baltimore cabinetmaker Joseph Burgess. *Opposite:* The table in the State Dining Room is ornamented by superb bronze doré pieces ordered by Monroe.

twentieth century. When Thomas Jefferson was in office (he had entered and lost the original design competition under another name), he asked Benjamin Henry Latrobe, an American architect of English birth, to modify Hoban's plans for the projected South Portico and to provide a North Portico as a sheltered carriageway, though it was Hoban who supervised the restoration after the British fires gutted the mansion.

Two Presidents, Harrison and McKinley, itched for expansion, both favoring the addition of Bulfinch-style cupolas, but the approaching centennial and the architect Glenn Brown revived interest in restoring and expanding along the original lines. It was Theodore Roosevelt who called in the architectural firm McKim, Mead & White to make the additions which now included an office building, and it was in 1927, during the Coolidge administration, that the roof was raised enough to make the old attic into a full third floor. It was Harry Truman who became concerned about the vibrations of the White House floors and had its structural condition investigated. The findings were that the new third story had been laid on old and weakened interior walls that were settling and had cracked. Consequently, during 1948-1952, the entire interior of the building was removed. The old paneling and other details were numbered and stored, a new basement and foundation built and a new steel framework erected within the original exterior walls.

All the rooms in the White House are the result of successive periods of redecoration and renovation. The principal public

A bronze doré fruit basket, also purchased by Monroe, originally had candle branches. It is one of the mansion's greatest treasures.

rooms on the first floor are the huge East Room — extending all the way from the entrance, or north, front of the house to the garden, or south, front — and across the south front, the Green Room, Blue Room, Red Room, and State Dining Room on the west side. Today's Green Room was originally Hoban's "common dining room" and later became a parlor. Little evidence exists to indicate how it was furnished during the early nineteenth century but a small piece of cornice decoration, salvaged in the 1948 renovation, points toward a classic mode. The first room refurnished by the Fine Arts Committee for the White House, it is now a Federal-style parlor as Jefferson might have known it. The green silk damask walls give it its current name and provide a suitable setting for the admirably designed and constructed Federal furniture, classical chandelier, paintings and a superb marble mantelpiece ordered after the fire of 1814.

The Blue Room, an oval drawing room, gleams with its blue and gold silk walls and matching upholstered Bellangé chairs, cut-glass chandelier with matching wall sconces, French gilt bronze pier table and two large looking glasses, and a parquet floor. The blue color originated with the Van Buren administration but many of the furnishings were purchased by James Monroe after he entered the White House in 1817. Although the great mansion had been completely rebuilt since its burning three years before, it remained sparsely furnished. Monroe ordered new furniture, upholstered in pinkish-red silk, from Paris and it became the most lavishly furnished room on the first floor, intended to impress upon the nation and the world the republic's renewed strength after the humiliating occupation of the capital by the British.

Like its sister parlor, the Green Room, the Red Room has a simple, classic décor, but its Empire furnishings of the 1810-1830 period make it stylistically the latest of the three parlors, as one moves from the Green Room (1800-1810) to the Blue Room (1817) to here. Its name comes from the sumptuous cerise silk with gold borders on the walls and the same material with gold design is used to upholster the furnishings, such as the restrained mahogany sofa that belonged to Dolley Madison. During the 1902 renovation the State Dining Room was enlarged and its two matching Italian marble mantels removed to the Red and Green rooms as it was completely repaneled with carved natural oak in the classical style. The comfortable "back stools" in the Queen Anne style and high-backed caned chairs in the William and Mary style accommodate a maximum of 140 guests for dinner.

In the course of White House history, frustrated, happy and busy first ladies have lived within its walls. Eleanor Roosevelt thought "a man in high public office is neither husband nor father nor friend in the commonly accepted sense of the words." Lady Bird Johnson found the White House a challenge, especially since she had always hoped to be "in the heart of things." Abigail Adams thought the country around the White House "romantic but a wilderness," and an establishment that "cannot be born by the present sallery: No body can form an idea of it but those who come into it," she wrote her sister. As the British encroached on the capital in the summer of 1814 and the White House was to be evacuated,

Right: Admirably proportioned and filled with natural light, the President's Oval Office looks out on the Rose Garden.

Below: The Treaty Room on the second floor, formerly the Cabinet Room, displays a gigantic chandelier ordered by President Grant in 1873.

Dolley Madison insisted on waiting "until the large picture of General Washington is secured." Mrs. Madison ordered the Stuart portrait unscrewed from the wall, the frame broken and "the precious portrait placed in the hands of two gentlemen of New York for safe keeping." One of the happiest first ladies was Mrs. Ulysses S. Grant. "My life at the White House was like a bright and beautiful dream and we were immeasurably happy. ... Life at the White House was a garden spot of orchids, and I wish it might have continued forever, except that it would have deterred others from enjoying the same privilege."

Several latter-day first ladies shared Mrs. Madison's determination to preserve White House furniture and treasures, as well as to add to them. It was Mrs. Benjamin Harrison who initiated the custom of having each administration design its own china and it was Grace Coolidge who was influential in having Congress pass a resolution allowing the acceptance of appropriate antiques for White House furnishings. The fastidious beauty of today's White House is mainly due to the brief but appreciative presence of President John F. Kennedy's wife Jacqueline. Mrs. Kennedy formed the Fine Arts Committee for the White House in February 1961, and attracted the help of official and amateur experts in the fields of art and furniture as well as splendid and generous donations that helped to refurbish almost every corner of the White House. The following September of 1961, the 87th Congress passed legislation providing that "Articles of furniture . . . when declared by the President to be of historic or artistic interest, together with similar articles . . . acquired in the future, shall thereafter be considered to be inalienable and the property of the White House." President Lyndon B. Johnson subsequently issued an executive order establishing the Committee for the Preservation of the White House, providing a permanent curator.

Mrs. Kennedy's love of French furniture and food was not unique with the second youngest first lady ever to live in the White House. Presidential admirers of French cabinetmaking included Washington, Adams, Jefferson, Madison and Monroe. John Adams had even brought to the White House from the President's House in Philadelphia a Louis XV drawing room suite he had originally purchased in France. There seemed to be among the early leaders of the United States a general acceptance of France as the fountain of taste and a natural empathy between the young republic and the French empire. While Napoleon was copying the ancient Romans, we were busy copying Palladio's own copies, or at least his somewhat free-hand versions of the ancient buildings. Many of the prize pieces in the White House today were made by Charles Honoré Lannuier who learned his craft in France, came to New York in 1803, and produced over a period of sixteen years remarkable examples of Louis XVI design, acting as a catalyst in bringing the Empire style to America. But the most rewarding aspect of the present splendor of the White House is the intelligent and sensitive manner in which all periods of furniture, portraits, china and silver have been lovingly preserved. Abigail Adams understood history and the significance of the executive mansion. So did Jacqueline Kennedy, who wrote, "Many First Families loved this house — and . . . each and every one left something of themselves behind in it."

Above: The spacious East Room is used as a reception room on state occasions and displays a mahogany piano at the north end.

Opposite: The Blue Room is the main reception room and is hung with blue and gold silk. A cut-glass chandelier and matching sconces on the walls light this exquisite oval room.

Washington, D.C.
DECATUR HOUSE

On Historic Lafayette Square

Above: Stephen Decatur hired Benjamin Latrobe, a noted American architect, to design his house. (Photo: courtesy National Trust for Historic Preservation) *Opposite:* The vestibule combines "Roman ornamental taste and colonial reserve." (All remaining photos: City News Bureau, Inc.)

Observing Stephen Decatur, the "hero of the Caribbean" at the age of twenty-five, a fellow naval officer was "struck with a peculiarity of manner and appearance, calculated to rivet the eye and engross the attention. I had often pictured to myself the form and look of a hero, such as my favorite Homer had delineated; here I saw it embodied." From the time when as a midshipman he helped capture the French vessel *Amour de la Patrie* by ramming a twenty-pound shot through her off the coast of Martinique (and retrieved and captured its captain), until he died a commander by a duelist's shot in Washington, D.C., Stephen Decatur's exploits on behalf of the United States Navy equal, if not surpass, any legends a poet or playwright might devise for the ages.

When Stephen was eight he accompanied his father, who had commanded privateers such as the *Comet* and the *Retaliation* before joining the shipbuilding and trading firm of Gurney and Smith, on an European sojourn. Whether it was sheer delight in the sea or the fact that his siege of whooping cough dissolved, or the combination, Stephen's future was settled in his mind. After attending the Protestant Episcopal Academy in Philadelphia and one year at the University of Pennsylvania, his scholarly preparation for life was abandoned. He joined his father's firm and waited impatiently for an opportunity to go to sea.

The state of the American Navy at that time was, to put it politely, depleted. In 1792 Congress voted to spend $40,000 to purchase peace and to give $25,000 annual tribute to the pirates of the Barbary States, and two years later a bill was passed to provide four ships "to carry forty-four guns and two ships to carry thirty-six guns each." The future of a larger shipbuilding program was insured by George Washington. According to his "best information," he said, "it would seem as if our trade to the Mediterranean, without a protecting force, will always be insecure. . . . These considerations invite the United States to look to the means, and set about the gradual creation of a navy." As a result, the first war vessels in the permanent navy were under way: the *Constitution*, the *Constellation* and the *United States*, on which Stephen Decatur would serve gallantly fifteen years later. It was built, by coincidence, by the firm of Gurney and Smith.

On April 30, 1798, Stephen Decatur received an appointment as a midshipman in the navy and a brave career was at last in motion. Decatur served in the brief naval war with the French, commanded the *Enterprise* and, in 1804, on a little captured craft Decatur named the *Intrepid*, he led an expedition into the harbor of Tripoli to burn the U.S. frigate *Philadelphia* which had fallen into Tripolitan hands. When the *Intrepid* was about a hundred yards from the *Philadelphia*, the *Intrepid's* men scrambled aboard her, setting her on fire and dashing back aboard their own ship, escaping through fire with only one of their men wounded. Decatur's future was sealed. He was recognized as an officer of "too much value to be neglected," his feat termed by Admiral Lord Nelson "the most bold and daring act of the age." At twenty-five he was commissioned the navy's youngest captain.

During the next ten years, as Decatur rose from captain to commander, he commanded the *United States* in the War of 1812 and served in the Mediterranean. In reward for his victories over the corsairs of Algiers, Tunisia and Tripoli in the course of 187 days, he was congratulated and told he had accomplished "more in a few months than all Europe had been able to effect in ages, and have given a lesson not only to Christendom but to the Barbary States that will not soon be forgotten." In December 1815, when a vacancy occurred in the Board of Navy Commissions who superintended, out of Washington, D.C., the building of ships, purchase of naval supplies, promotions and assignments, Decatur was appointed to fill it.

Working in Washington meant finding a home there for himself and his wife, Susan, who was reported to have "made advances" to Commodore Decatur when he was engaged to another lady; their marriage was regarded by some "as a blot on his escutcheon. . . ." Decatur's solution to his housing problem was to build his own. He bought a lot on the corner of President's Square, now Lafayette Square, the corner of H Street and Jackson Place, and hired the esteemed Benjamin H. Latrobe, a noted American architect, to draw up the plans for his intended house. Latrobe, whom Jefferson had appointed Surveyor of Public Building of the United States, produced, as might have been anticipated, a wonderfully balanced, disciplined though luxurious design. It was, some thought, the equal of its model standing in Norfolk, England, and it was eminently suitable for entertaining the Decaturs' important visitors from near and far.

The earliest dated drawings for the Decatur house are from January 1818, when the "curled maple seasoned" and "bird's-eye maple," the plans and "250 Cash of Thomas Town Lime," were ordered. Latrobe was so thoroughly involved in this project that he wrote he had seen "Commodore Decatur often and have been very busily engaged for him."

The Decaturs moved into their new red brick, three-story house in January 1819. The result of the arduous planning and care was a structure with ample space for a childless family and a quite perfect interior. Tragically, the Decaturs, who were considered part of President James Madison's

The gateleg dining table is surrounded by mustard-colored, late Sheraton "fancy" chairs, circa 1810, with cane bottoms.

"inner circle," enjoyed the house they had so painstakingly planned for only fourteen brief months. Commodore James Barron had been suspended from the navy. Decatur barred his readmission, writing the unhappy officer that "your conduct as an officer since the affair of the *Chesapeake*, has been such as ought to forever bar your readmission into the service. . . ." Complicated by outside influences and prejudices, the argument crescendoed and a few months later, on March 22, 1820, Decatur accepted Barron's challenge to a duel. The two men met near the old stage road between Washington and Baltimore at what was called "Valley of Chance," the site of more than fifty duels. Moments after the duel began both men lay wounded, Decatur mortally, and the nation a short while later had lost, in John Quincy Adams's words, "one of its heroes — one who has illustrated its history and given grace and dignity to its character in the eyes of the world."

Decatur's estate amounted to about $100,000 but the depression and decline of property values left his widow depleted and she moved to Georgetown. Writing to President Andrew Jackson in 1833 about some silver and French china, Susan Decatur said she would be "very much oblig'd if you wou'd take the whole for three hundred and fifty. . . ." Finally she was granted a modest pension.

Following Decatur's death, his home had a succession of distinguished tenants, including three secretaries of state — Henry Clay, Martin Van Buren and Edward Livingston — and

The bed in the Commodore's Bed Chamber has French toile hangings that date from about 1816. Decatur was born in this bed.

President Polk's vice president, George M. Dallas. In 1871 the house was purchased by Mary Edwards Beale, wife of General Edward F. Beale, a hero of the Mexican War in California. He was appointed Minister to Austria-Hungary in 1876 by President Grant, a frequent visitor to the Decatur House. In 1956 the house was bequeathed to the National Trust for Historic Preservation by the widow of Edward's son, Mrs. Truxton Beale, who had lived there for more than fifty years. Today part of the restored house functions as offices for the National Trust headquarters staff, but the first and second floors are a museum reflecting Mrs. Beale's as well as the naval hero's era.

The original Decatur house was said to represent what one might expect in an "eclectic, transient, Washington house of the early nineteenth century," and this is evident in the house today. The ground-floor rooms are furnished and decorated in the style of the Decatur period. The floor above, which in Decatur's day was the principal one, is given over to the Beale period of the house. The splendid vestibule, said to combine "Roman ornamental taste with colonial reserve," has a wood-framed and plastered ceiling with a low segmental dome in the center. These facets and the restrained moldings of the walls and ceiling provide a pleasing variety of surfaces. The south door of the vestibule opens to the Commodore's Study which, like the dining room adjacent to it, has a pine mantel painted off-white, original with the house, although both of them were moved to their present locations from the third floor. The décor here is informal and the most valuable pieces are a mahogany Philadelphia false-front desk and a china cabinet made in Baltimore in the early nineteenth century.

In the adjacent dining room to the west, with a herringbone-pattern parquet floor from the Beale period, the gateleg dining table is surrounded by mustard-colored, late Sheraton "fancy" chairs, circa 1810, with cane bottoms. But the choice Decatur piece in the room, and perhaps in the entire house, is his gilt-trimmed *secrétaire à abbatant* in late Louis XVI style.

The north vestibule door opens to the outstanding room in

the house, the Commodore's Bed Chamber, although there was no door here in Decatur's time and the room was accessible only from the hall in front of the service stairs toward the rear of the house. The unadorned four-poster with high posts and French toile hangings, circa 1816, is the bed in which Decatur was born. Also in this room is a lacquered ladies' work table Decatur brought back from Japan for his fiancée, and another Decatur family piece, a Chippendale-style tilt-top table, circa 1770-1780, with scrolled square top and snake feet. The restrained and dignified characteristics of the furnishings are matched by the subdued, but appealing colors — pale blue walls with an orange pattern, off-white woodwork and white draperies, and light maroon bed hangings trimmed in gold.

The spacious drawing room in the southeast corner on the second floor and the smaller drawing room entered through the sliding doors to the north contain the most valuable Beale pieces — Philadelphia Chippendale claw-and-ball-foot armchair with carved knees and carved shell on the chair rail and crest, a pair of Chippendale side chairs, with pierced splats, shell crests and slip seats and an English Hepplewhite serpentine-front sideboard with inlay. The parquet flooring in the drawing rooms are of rare California woods installed by the Beales and, in the north drawing room, the State Seal of California was inlaid with twenty-two of these woods.

The square that came to be called Lafayette was one of the largest squares to be laid out by L'Enfant when he designed the new federal capital, and over the years it was the site for the fine homes of a host of important people. Decatur House, the only original dwelling on the famous square to survive to this day, was, for much of that time, a center for cultural, social, political and military activities in the capital, but this fine structure is remembered today primarily because it was the residence for a few short months of the forceful naval hero who proclaimed the indelible toast: "Our Country! In her intercourse with foreign nations may she always be in the right; but our country, right or wrong."

The parquet flooring in the two second-floor drawing rooms is made of rare California woods installed by the Beales.

Germantown, Philadelphia, Pennsylvania
DESHLER-MORRIS HOUSE

The Germantown White House

Above: During November 1793, and again in the summer of 1794, President Washington lived in Market Square's Deshler-Morris House. *Opposite:* Blue and white Delft tiles around the tea room fireplace depict goats and other animals. (All photos: J. Linton Houser, FPG)

George Washington's restless itinerary, which took him from Williamsburg to Boston and innumerable places in between, includes Market Square in Germantown. There in 1793 in a delightful house built by David Deshler out of the profits on a medicated ointment he had concocted, President Washington lived, because Philadelphia, the nearby capital, was suffering an epidemic of yellow fever that put a "strange and melancholy . . . mask on the once carefree face of a thriving city." Washington traveled from Mount Vernon to Germantown in November and at the suggestion of Attorney General Edmund Randolph, whom he had asked to find him quarters, he moved into what is now called the Deshler-Morris House which at that time was in the possession of an intermediary owner, Colonel Isaacs Franks, a former aide-de-camp to Washington.

Four cabinet meetings held there, between November 18 and November 28, 1793, concerned the war between Great Britain and the colonists' ally France. Washington told his cabinet members, Secretary of State Thomas Jefferson, Secretary of the Treasury Alexander Hamilton, Attorney General Edmund Randolph and Secretary of War General Henry Knox, that he preferred to remain neutral in "affairs, both new and delicate. . . ." The problem was to explain proclamation of neutrality before Congress in such a way as not to seem to infringe upon Congress's Constitutional powers. The address Washington read to Congress on December 3, written at Franks' house, reflects his own final judgment: "It rests with the wisdom of Congress to correct, improve or enforce this plan of procedure."

Besides his private secretary and two servants, Washington had the temporary help of Charles Byerly who cooked for him

Two of the bedrooms have fireplaces faced with rare mulberry-colored Delft tiles, one of the house's prime attractions.

and David Meredith who did the baking. On November 28, Washington "pd. Wm. Bockius per ascot in full for dinners liquors etc. furnished at Germantown . . . $50.46." Washington's rent for the month came to $75.56 after four months of negotiations over a larger bill of $131.56. This one had included Franks' traveling expenses to and from Bethlehem where he was waiting out the yellow fever epidemic, the price of a chair broken during the President's occupancy, the cost of cleaning the house after the President had left it, and the loss of a shilling flatiron, a large fork, four plates, three ducks, four chickens, a bushel of potatoes and a hundred bushels of hay.

Washington's second stay at Franks' house was less strenuous than the first. During the summer of 1794, he and his family moved to Germantown to escape the heat of the Presidential mansion in Philadelphia, just a few miles away. On July 29 the President established his wife and two adopted children in Germantown until the weather broke, and they left on September 20. The reason they had gone to Germantown rather than to Washington's favorite retreat, Mount Vernon, was simply a matter of proximity and wifely objections to being alone. Washington was an extremely busy man whose "public avocations" would not "admit of more than a *flying* trip to Mount Vernon for a few days this summer. This not suiting Mrs. Washington, . . ." Germantown was chosen as a substitute summer house. During this visit Washington was able to relax, as his private letters reveal. He took time to write to his granddaughter that she should not "look for perfect felicity before you consent to wed," and that ". . . love is too dainty a thing to live upon alone."

This momentary Germantown White House was built on two adjoining strips of land on Main Street, two acres with a one-hundred-foot frontage in all, which was bought by David Deshler in 1752. An immigrant from the German state of Baden, whose father served the reigning prince as aide-de-camp during the War of the Spanish Succession, Deshler was sixty years old, solidly entrenched as a respectable merchant on High Street and a member of a committee of enforcement after the signing of the Non-Importation Agreement in 1765. Construction on the house started around 1772 and it was pronounced "finished in the most elegant manner" with grounds that were "in complete order," with a stable and carriage house, a pump in the rear, a large enclosed garden and a "great variety of the best grafted fruit trees."

Washington's occupation was not the Deshler house's first flirtation with history. Just a few years after its builder had moved in, Germantown had been occupied by the British. In 1777, Lieutenant General William Howe established his headquarters in the house from October 2 to 18, as he followed the Continental Army that had withdrawn to the northwest of Philadelphia after Howe had captured the city. After two weeks of harassment by the Americans, Howe ordered his weary army back into lines established around Philadelphia.

In 1804, Isaac Franks sold the house to two brothers, Elliston and John Perot, who, in turn, thirty years later, sold it to the former's son-in-law, a shipping merchant named Samuel B. Morris whose descendant Marriot C. Morris willed it to the United States Government. In the process of its being restored as part of the Independence Hall National Historical Park project, the Deshler-Morris house has acquired many coats of paint and some remarkable examples of eighteenth-century native furniture.

The white-stuccoed house is a graceful one. Its two neat stories are surmounted by a gable roof with a chimney at either end and two dormers with sashes delicately rounded at the top. The nine windows in the façade each display shutters and twenty-four panes of glass imported from Germany, while the recessed doorway is framed by a handsome molded pediment and rounded pilasters. Three soapstone steps lead up to the massive paneled door.

Inside, there is wainscoting throughout the first floor called Tidewater paneling, which is uncommon in Northern homes of the period. To the left of the broad entrance hall is the elegantly restrained parlor, where Washington is believed to have held his cabinet meetings. The walls are white — as they are throughout the house — the fine woodwork is French gray and the fireplace, like the one in the dining room, is faced with gray-veined Pennsylvania marble. Above it hangs a painting of the Washington family relaxing, as they were so often able to do during their stay here. The chief treasure of this room is the crisply detailed secretary-desk of New England origin with ogee scrolled panels and bonnet top. Behind the parlor is the cozy little tea room with a pleasing view of the garden out one window and a delightful fireplace beside, patterned with blue and white Delft tiles.

Across the hall from the parlor is the dining room where Washington probably gave the dinners for his cabinet after their first and last meetings in the house. The woodwork, including the completely paneled wall on the fireplace side of the room, is painted a subdued blue-spruce green. The superb furnishings include Hepplewhite chairs and a beautiful Philadelphia Hepplewhite cabinet holding Chinese Export porcelain — all possessions of the Morris family.

Above the landing of the staircase leading from the back of the hall to the second floor is a small window known as Martha Washington's window because Mrs. Washington, so the story goes, often rested here and chatted through the open window with her next door neighbor. Washington's Bedroom has an eighteenth-century Sheraton canopy bed and the fireplace is faced with blue and mulberry-colored Delft tiles.

The Deshler-Morris House is the oldest existing dwelling that was used by a President as an official residence. So it is fitting that it has been restored as part of the Independence Hall historical project and refurnished, if not precisely as it was in Washington's time, at least as handsomely as it was then and in a manner appropriate to the period.

Above the staircase's first landing is a small window where it is said Martha Washington chatted with her next-door neighbor.

Pottstown, Pennsylvania
POTTSGROVE

Landmark on the Schuylkill

The place was Pennsylvania not Virginia, the crop was iron not tobacco, the house was rough stone instead of brick and there wasn't a colonnade in sight. Still, the background and ambition was precisely that of the Southern colonists of pre-Revolutionary days, for John Potts hoped and succeeded in molding a prosperous and an independent life for his family and townspeople. He built a forge plantation — of the mansion it was said there were "few like it, not many superior" — and as an early real estate developer and urban planner, he created a village which was originally called, as his plantation was, Pottsgrove. He was Justice of the Peace for the entire Philadelphia County and he fathered a family that aided the American cause in the Revolution. And he founded in 1820, in the village whose name was changed to Pottstown, the first commercially important iron furnace in America.

John Potts's father Thomas, born in Wales and settled in Germantown, was brought up as a Quaker and married one. As a widower he moved with three children into the Manatawny wilderness and through hard work and what must have been shrewd manipulation managed to acquire enough capital as an ironmaster to buy ownership of two-thirds of Colebrookdale Furnace, a successful iron producer, and one-third of Pine Forge, which converted Colebrookdale pig iron into bar iron. Through his mother-in-law, John Potts and his wife Ruth became owners of the Warwick Furnace, which by the 1750's was able to supply pig iron to Pine Forge, Pool Forge, Valley Forge, as well as to eight others, part of which he either owned or leased.

Pottsgrove was his latest acquisition. On September 8, 1752, John Potts "Esquire, Ironmaster," paid three pounds an acre (it had been three *shillings* thirty-five years before) for one thousand acres along the Schuylkill River and the Manatawny Creek and proceeded to build a splendid forge plantation with a mansion on the "scale of a castle, the forthrightness of a farmhouse." The walls are two feet thick and have the special "tailored" look imparted by fieldstone and sandstone that is square-cut and, in the front wall, laid in range courses (rows of stone with continuous horizontal joints). The

Above: Pottsgrove's walls are two feet thick and have the special "tailored" look of fieldstone that is square-cut. *Opposite:* The superb fabrics in the drawing room and throughout the mansion were specially designed and woven by Franco Scalamandré. (All photos: J. Linton Houser, FPG)

floors, panels and pilasters are of seasoned pine, the first story 11-1/2 feet high, the second 10 feet high. It is a dwelling of "a character so elegant and substantial" that it surprises observers to this day who know that builders of real training were scarce in mid-eighteenth-century Pottsgrove.

But John Potts did not concentrate solely on his own house. He laid out the village of Pottsgrove in rectangles, bisecting the land with traditionally named King and Queen and Hanover streets. Street-front property could be paid for in "Spanish pieces of eight, or value thereof" and the lessees had to promise to build "one dwelling-house at least twenty feet square of brick or stone," within two years. The village included an inn, a grain mill and a saw mill. When "our Mr. Potts," as Mrs. Benjamin Franklin called him, died on June 6, 1768, he was the most successful ironmaster in the American colonies. His landed estate consisted of nearly four thousand acres in different parts of Pennsylvania and Virginia and was said to be "more highly improved than any other in the thirteen colonies." He had lived "with great dignity at his stately house" and was survived by his thirteen sons and daughters, as well as his wife, who continued to work on in the various forges, or to work for the colonies' causes. Samuel Potts made cannons for Washington's army at Warwick, Thomas served the Continental Armies as a colonel. Jonathan, a surgeon, was Director of the Military Hospitals of the Northern Department. Only John, Jr., sided with England during the Revolution. He was practicing law in Philadelphia when it was occupied by the British. Pessimistic over the future of the colonists, he made his way to Nova Scotia, where he was later joined by his wife and children, and petitioned for land there when his Pennsylvania property was confiscated.

Pottsgrove's most dramatic historical role was brief and desperate. For just about a week, when Washington was trying to block the British from reaching Reading and its enormous army supplies, the general and his army of approximately 11,000 men camped on the outskirts of Pottsgrove. Washington's official reports from that area tell of an army "so fatigued that it is impossible I should move them today." His officers were "wet breast high" and yet had marched through the night suffering from "bear hunger and thirst at the same time." That was around September 18, 1777. A few days later, Washington wrote to Alexander Hamilton: "The distressed situation of the army, for want of blankets and many necessary articles of clothing, . . . inevitably must bring destruction to it, unless a speedy remedy is applied." Camp Pottsgrove was a prelude to a bitter winter at Valley Forge, but it was also a time of a crash rehabilitation program. Hospitals were set up at the Swamp Lutheran and Reformed churches and the Friends' Meeting. The community pitched in to bake bread, deliver supplies of coffee, potatoes, beans, freshly slaughtered livestock and clothing in order to help during these crucial days. By Friday, September 26, Washington sent out word that "We are now in motion." Heartened by the only good news to be heard in months, the victory of Saratoga, Washington led his freshly patched troops on to Valley Forge leaving behind his indelible impact: He had operated out of John Potts's mansion, making it a permanent historical as

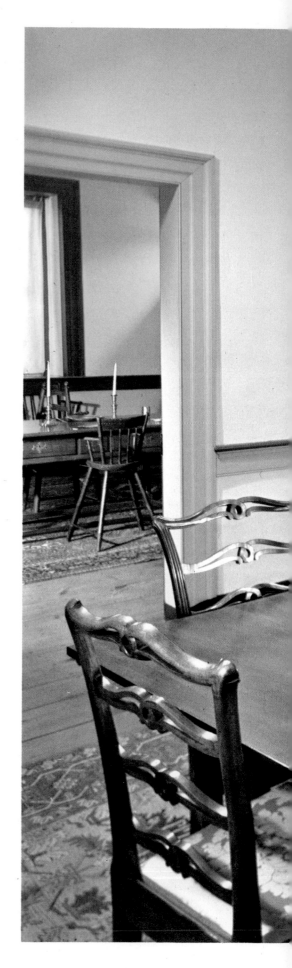

The three-section Chippendale dining table and eight matching chairs are
among the most treasured pieces acquired by the Pottstown Historical Society.

Potts's thirteen children had their meals on the early Pennsylvania German tavern table in the delightful children's dining room.

well as architectural landmark.

Pottsgrove was purchased in 1936 by descendants of John Potts and its restoration was supervised by G. Edwin Brumbaugh who did distinguished research for the restoration of many colonial buildings in Pennsylvania. Over the years, the Pottstown Historical Society has faithfully collected prize examples of the Philadelphia-made furniture that existed in Pottsgrove from 1750 to 1800, when John Potts and his family lived there. The house was opened to the public in 1952.

The main section of the house contains the basic central hall with two rooms off either side of it, a pattern duplicated on the second floor. A one-room, one-story addition extends from the right side, while a larger, two-story ell containing the kitchen is in the rear. It is from the rear that the mansion's rambling appearance can best be seen.

Among the most treasured pieces acquired by the Pottstown Historical Society is the three-section Chippendale table which dominates the front dining room. Made in Philadelphia in 1760, it has impressive proportions, seating twelve when complete. The eight matching chairs are not only a fine complement to the table, but are also rarely found in that number. A four-candle girandole looking glass above the fireplace was crafted in America and dates from 1799.

The superb fabrics in the dining room, and indeed through-out Pottsgrove, were a gift of the famous textile designer, Franco Scalamandré, and were designed and woven by him especially to complement the warm, simple colors of the house's painted woodwork. The yellow damask curtains here are a sunny contrast to the white walls and the unusual shade of mauve gray found in the woodwork. In the library across and down the hall, the tan and brown pattern on a beige background in the curtains and the pale yellow in the Pennsylvania wing chair harmonize subtly with the subdued gray-green woodwork. Also in the library is a walnut birdcage chess table and two Windsor chairs.

Passing through the dining room toward the rear of the house, the visitor enters the unique, delightful children's dining room where Potts's thirteen children had their meals. The tavern table and stenciled dower chest here are necessarily sturdy early Pennsylvania German pieces, and a large smooth burl bowl on the table endures after two hundred years of use.

The second floor of Pottsgrove, which contains four principal bedrooms, is reached by a handsome staircase facing the entrance hall. In the front on the second floor is the master bedroom. Its mahogany four-poster dates from 1790 and has elaborately carved swags on its high posts. Also of interest is the Pennsylvania walnut chest-on-chest with reeded corners and, along the bottom, a delicate "lamb's-tongue" molding with its deep symmetrical profile ending in a tapered edge.

Across the hall is the Martha Washington Room, believed to be the room used by Mrs. Washington during her frequent visits to Pottstown during the merciless winter of 1777. The canopied four-poster is from Charleston, South Carolina, and is the only Southern piece in the house. The superbly woven fabric here, too, is a gift of Scalamandré, "to show my appreciation to the country that has been so generous to a young immigrant," just as the country had been generous two centuries earlier to the ambitious young immigrant Thomas Potts and to his son John.

The four-poster in the Martha Washington Room is from Charleston, South Carolina, and is the mansion's only Southern piece.

Colonial Williamsburg, Virginia
GOVERNOR'S PALACE

Grand Mansion of Seven British Governors

Thomas Jefferson took a measured view of one of the most influential pieces of American architecture, as well as of its setting: the Governor's Palace in Williamsburg, the second capital of the young colony, Virginia. He pronounced the Governor's Palace "not handsome without; but it is spacious and commodious within, is prettily situated, and with the grounds annexed to it, is capable of being made an elegant seat." He thought the college and hospital were "rude, misshapen piles, which, but that they have roofs, would be taken for brick-kilns." And as a whole he despaired that "a workman could scarcely be found here capable of drawing an order." "The genius of architecture," he concluded, "seems to have shed its maledictions over this land." However, his seems to be a minority opinion. Others thought the "Palace and the Williamsburg building the best in all English America . . . exceeded by few of their kind in England."

Williamsburg was the educational, social and governing center of the Virginia colony from 1699 to 1780. It had literally emerged from the ashes of Jamestown, its first capital. Jamestown had never fulfilled expectations as a colonial capital. The colonists would not cooperate in making it the single port of entry, clinging instead to the individuality of plantation life and to the use of private wharves for shipping tobacco or receiving supplies. The accidental burning of the statehouse at Jamestown in October 1698, opened the door for establishment of a more centrally located capital, having better drainage and a more pleasant climate away from the mosquito-infested marshland. "An Act directing the building the Capitol and the City of Williamsburg" nearly eight miles northeast of Jamestown, a "more salubrious situation," be-

Above: The Governor's Palace, home of the English colonial governors, was the colony's social center and also its official residence. *Opposite:* The magnificent supper room has Queen Anne furniture and a Waterford cut chandelier. (All photos: courtesy Colonial Williamsburg)

came law on June 7, 1699. With the removal of the capital, Jamestown wasted away to an "abundance of brick rubbish."

Williamsburg was meticulously laid out from its creation from civic building to private house to boxwood hedge, to gardens "tidy as a child's clean pinafore." The town proper was built on 220 acres, the ground selected by a jury of twelve men from the counties of York, New Kent and James City. The College of William and Mary, reportedly designed by Christopher Wren, was where the House of Burgesses met until 1705 when the capitol was completed. It was on May 1, 1706, that several members of the Council requested Governor Edward Nott "to cause a draught of such a house as by him shall be thought most convenient to be laid before the House of Burgesses." Governor Nott, in turn, asked them "to give such directions . . . as you think proper." Negotiations for a Williamsburg house had begun six years before when the British colonial administrator, Francis Nicholson, had written to the Council of Trade and Plantations: "I am in hopes that . . . there may be money enough in a year or two to build a house for His Majesty's Governor, as also the capitol. . . ." Following Governor Nott's answer, a committee was appointed and a suitable act was passed late in June 1706.

The approach to providing housing for the governor was

An impressive feature of the upper middle room is the gilt hand-tooled Spanish leather wall covering brought from a London house.

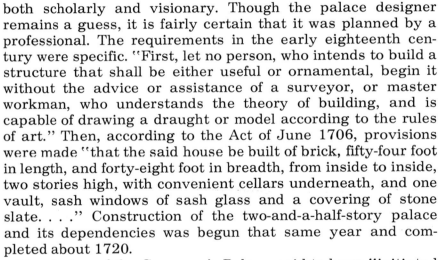

The royal coat of arms above the mantel in the main entrance hall
is oak, but the remainder of the woodwork here is carved black walnut.

both scholarly and visionary. Though the palace designer remains a guess, it is fairly certain that it was planned by a professional. The requirements in the early eighteenth century were specific. "First, let no person, who intends to build a structure that shall be either useful or ornamental, begin it without the advice or assistance of a surveyor, or master workman, who understands the theory of building, and is capable of drawing a draught or model according to the rules of art." Then, according to the Act of June 1706, provisions were made "that the said house be built of brick, fifty-four foot in length, and forty-eight foot in breadth, from inside to inside, two stories high, with convenient cellars underneath, and one vault, sash windows of sash glass and a covering of stone slate. . . ." Construction of the two-and-a-half-story palace and its dependencies was begun that same year and completed about 1720.

The design of the Governor's Palace, said to have "initiated a period of mansion building unequaled in the history of England's colonies," was thought to have originated in England, and was likened to Ashburnham House. The reason it is called a palace is because Spotswood spent so much of the colony's money on its construction. The palace was altered in 1751 and repaired in 1770. During the Revolution it was used as a hospital and accidentally burned in 1781. In 1930 the demolition of a high school on the site laid bare its foundations. Then followed the reconstruction of 1931-1933, carried out faithfully and ingeniously with the financial backing of John D. Rockefeller, Jr., and made possible by the discovery of the Bodleian Plate, a remarkably precise copper engraving found in the archives of the Bodleian Library at Oxford, England, thought to have been intended as an illustration for a work of William Byrd II of Westover.

Shielded from the street by a shoulder-high brick wall, the

123

palace is an admirably graceful building with its dormers, roof balustrade and two-story cupola surmounted by a tall weathervane. Enhanced by spacious gardens, it is a monument to the governors who represented the British Crown — from the English lion and Scottish unicorn stone carvings atop the tall piers of the painted and gilded wrought-iron entrance gate of the handsome forecourt, to the coat of arms of George II and many royal portraits inside the palace. The blend of warmth and grandeur is beguiling. The palace speaks at once of family life and state entertainment, of cozy evenings and official gatherings, for it was the colony's social center as well as its official residence.

The happy combination of solemnity and graciousness found in the palace is especially successful in the six-sided hall inside the entrance door. The woodwork, including the paneling, is a particularly rich, carved black walnut, although the royal coat of arms over the mantel is oak. The floor is laid with black marble squares on white marble background. Ionic pilasters flanking the doorways and arches rest on an elaborately molded dado and support a full entablature. On each side of the hall is a moderately small square room. To the left is the little dining room, with muted gray-blue paneling, where the governor and his family and frequently a few close friends would take their meals. The mantel is of Fleur-de-Pêcher marble worked with a white marble, fluted keystone and is based on fragments of the original, as is the mantel across the hall in the parlor, or reception room. Here the cream color of the paneling is based on documentary evidence dating to 1727. The white marble mantel has a carved central block showing flora and fauna, but most delightful are the panels of inlaid pink-veined marble in the frieze and pilasters. Looking down from above the mantel on the card table set for a game of loo is a portrait of Evelyn Byrd of Westover, whose father was worried when she was unmarried at twenty-one.

A very small room, sometimes called a "closet," but with its own fireplace, separates the parlor from the State Dining Room in the northeast corner of the palace's original section, its largest paneled room. The chimney breast is framed by full-height Corinthian pilasters whose formality is matched by the glittering silver-gilded objects in the room. On the two-part Chippendale-style table are four silver candelabra made by Thomas Pitts of London about 1760 and an exquisite silver epergne, also by Pitts, in a delicate rococo chinoiserie style. The epergne is unusual for its double-pagoda canopy hung with bells. Along the side is a marble-topped gilt table, made in England about 1750, and over it is a gilt looking glass, also English, circa 1760.

Directly across the stair hall from the door to the State Dining Room is the broad staircase. The newel finials are baskets of fruit, a common motif of the early eighteenth century. At the fifth step the stairs pass through a handsome arch. The coved ceiling is decorated with an oval panel enclosing George I's cypher and covering the nail holes on the edge of the treads are inlaid, carved boxwood representations of the four suits of playing cards — spades, hearts, diamonds

Opposite: The little dining room, where the governor and his family and friends took their meals, has a mantel of Fleur-de-Pêcher marble.

Measuring twenty-six by forty-seven feet, the ballroom with its
lofty coved ceiling was one of the great rooms in colonial America.

and clubs. The upper middle room on the entrance side was an
upstairs sitting room. Its most impressive feature is the gilt
hand-tooled Spanish leather covering of the walls, listed in a
governor's inventory of this room. The looking glasses are
English, circa 1740, as is the bookcase with broken-pediment
containing appropriate editions of all the books listed in
Governor Botetourt's 1770 inventory. On the center table, the
tortoise-shell jewel casket, inlaid with mother-of-pearl, was a
gift from Queen Elizabeth II to Colonial Williamsburg during
her visit in 1957. Off this room is the Governor's Bedchamber
with its Chippendale-style tall post bed hung with green and
gold lampas from the late seventeenth or early eighteenth
century. On the same side of the house is the Governor's
Study. Its mahogany tall case clock from Scotland was owned
by Lord Dunmore, the last of Virginia's royal governors, and
the early eighteenth-century oak wing chair is upholstered in
its original brightly colored silk and wool needlework. The two
other principal rooms on the second floor also contain significant pieces: the Great Bedchamber with a mahogany chest
of drawers made in Philadelphia and the small bedchamber
a bombé mahogany chest.

The single-story, ballroom-supper-room wing, extending directly behind the original, central portion of the palace, was added about 1751. The ballroom is reached through the door at the rear of the first-floor stair hall. Measuring twenty-six by forty-seven feet, it must have been one of the great rooms in colonial America. From a letter of Governor Botetourt's estate, it is known the portraits of George III and Queen Charlotte hung here. Two portraits of them by the Scottish painter Allan Ramsay now flank the south doorway. Portraits of Charles II and his queen, Catherine of Braganza, grace the north doorway. The walls are painted light blue and the lofty coved ceiling resembles the drawing room of the later Miles Brewton House in Charleston, South Carolina.

Behind the ballroom is the magnificent supper room. While the rest of the palace is flawless in its examples of eighteenth-century furniture, this room is the most brilliant in conception, and the most original *and* trend-making. Eighteenth-century tastes were influenced by the explorations of Marco Polo and Vasco da Gama and found expression in an enthusiasm for porcelains, silks, lacquers and chintz brought by ship from China and India to Europe and to America. Oriental motifs influenced the design of furniture and ceramics, as well as fabrics of the period, adding a dimension of luxury and fantasy that made for more exultant décor than was visible before this time. The Queen Anne furniture, Waterford cut chandelier, the Chinese-influenced molding and the concave pediments over the doorways, reminiscent of pagodas, add up to a harmonious composition. The floral motif of the hand-painted, eighteenth-century Chinese wallpaper from a house in England emphasizes the nearness of this room to the lovely garden lying directly outside its door.

At its height, Williamsburg's streets were filled with gentlemen in velvets and ruffles, students in academic dress, clergymen in black and judges in scarlet. Williamsburg, named in honor of King William III, resembling "a good country town in England," was alive with balls and banquets, horse races, lawn fetes, theatrical performances, cultural groups such as the Society for the Advancement of Useful Knowledge. Governor Gooch was especially pleased with his parties and pronounced his guests "perfectly well-bred, not an ill dancer in my Gov'mt." The last of the seven governors to live here was Lord Dunmore, who in desperation, on an April night in 1775, ordered the removal of the colony's powder from the magazine on market square. Patrick Henry protested this move and asked for the return of the powder.

"It was at Williamsburg that the demand for liberty was crystallized," and when the resolution to declare the united colonies free and independent states was passed by the members of the Continental Congress, it was said the town "went fairly wild in its patriotic enthusiasm and demonstration," that bells rang and guns crackled. The future capital, Richmond, was considered "more safe and central than any other town situated on navigable water," and Williamsburg's heyday was done.

Charles City County, Virginia
SHIRLEY

The Carter Family's James River Plantation

In plantation society, no young couple maintained a more finely chiseled niche than Elizabeth Hill and John Carter. The marriage of "King" Carter's son to Colonel Edward Hill II's daughter *and* Sir Edward Williams' granddaughter (on her Welsh mother's side) in 1723, united for generations to come two of Virginia's most wealthy and renowned families. The marriage of the daughter of a "gentleman of estate and standing," the heiress of Shirley, to the son of the owner of "the most considerable estate of any man in the country," brought Hill property into the capable hands of the Carter family where it prospers into the ninth generation. Between John and Elizabeth and their descendants they could claim ties with three Virginia governors, including Alexander Spotswood; three signers of the Declaration of Independence; a bishop; two Presidents of the United States; and dozens of lesser luminaries. Their granddaughter Anne, whose son was General Robert E. Lee, grew up at Shirley and in times of stress, when her husband "Light Horse Harry" was in financial difficulties, turned to her ancestral home for respite from her tragic predicament.

As of the year 1616 the twenty-five people who had settled on Shirley Hundred in 1613, were commanded by Capten Maddeson, and were "imployed onely in planting and curing tobacco — with the profitt thereof to clothe themselves and all those who labor about the general business." By 1660 Colonel Edward Hill had patented 416 acres in Shirley and he grew influential as well as prosperous — though he faltered along the way. A member of the House of Burgesses and His Majesty's Council, his force of colonists and friendly Indians were routed in battle with hostile Indians and the "mighty Tottapottomoy," who commanded his Indian allies, was killed causing the assembly to disfranchise and fine Colonel Hill. A similar fate befell his son Colonel Edward Hill II, an elegant gentleman inclined to crimson velvet and lace who followed Governor Berkely during Bacon's Rebellion and was disfranchised by Bacon's Assembly. Defending himself before the governor and King's commissioners he pleaded that he was an "unlearned & unskilled Virginian borne and bred who have not the dress and learning of schools, nor have I the skill to cloath vice like vertue. . . ." He is thought to have built a house on the land sometime before 1700 but by 1740 there is a record of plans by Elizabeth and John Carter for the present mansion and bordering outbuildings — though whether they or their son completed it seems to be a permanent mystery. There is the enduring, but somewhat unlikely theory that the Governor's Palace at Williamsburg was the inspiration.

Whatever its origins, this impressive mansion close by the

Above: The pineapple finial atop Shirley symbolizes hospitality. (Photo: courtesy Va. State Chamber of Commerce) *Opposite:* Charles Carter entertained Washington and Jefferson in the parlor, with its outstanding chimney piece. (Photo: Haycox Photoramic)

Above: The Duncan Phyfe-style dining table is original with the house and the silver tray is rare Britannia standard. (Photos: Haycox Photoramic)

James River is extraordinary even in comparison with other Virginia plantation houses. It was completed by 1769 or 1770, although the date of the present two-story porches on the two fronts is 1831. Approaching the house from the drive on the east, the visitor passes through the forecourt with its four symmetrical dependencies. Beyond, partially hidden by the great ancient trees, is the mansion standing three stories high above the basement, its unusually steep roof containing four dormers along each side and five on each front and topped, quite appropriately, with a large pineapple finial symbolizing hospitality. The mood of the house, both inside and outside, and the history of its owners — especially John and Elizabeth Carter — is one of warmth and hospitality. Shirley's record of friendships, entertainments and agricultural enterprise is a record in microcosm of the manners and mores of the affluent South.

Edward Hill lived with the young Carters for nine years, from 1723 until his death in 1732. Tormented by severe headaches and gout, Hill snored disturbingly and though he was thought to be "a man of no great ambition," he was said to be a man of "honour and good nature, . . ." a man of "good sense and good principles notwithstanding what has been said of him." His daughter Elizabeth was described by their close neighbor William Byrd II of Westover as a "good humour'd little Fairy," and John Carter seems to have been a thoroughly distinguished young man of excellent education. He went to school at Mile End in London and entered Trinity as a Fellow Commoner on January 12, 1714; he attended Middle Temple and was called to the bar in 1720. His father was exceedingly proud of him and wrote "Tis no small satisfaction to me to have a pennyworth for my penny." He urged his son to study, believing "it will prove a cordial at your heart all the days of your life." Young Carter acted as his father's business agent, as solicitor for Virginia affairs in London and, when he was appointed Secretary for Virginia Affairs, he sought an allowance to cover the cost of firewood to heat the records office, for he was deeply concerned that the dampness of the walls would make the preservation of the records impossible.

Shirley seems to have been one of three Carter residences. John's sister was living at Berkeley, married to Benjamin Harrison; another married Mann Page, whose house, Rosewell, was perhaps the grandest of all Southern plantations. John noted that his affairs made it necessary for him "to pass a good part of the year at this part of my estate, and as it is very inconvenient to remove pewter, table linnen and other furniture from Shirley and bak again, by which they are much injured and lost, I have thought it the best way to have a supply at each place."

With the help of slaves and indentured servants, John

Beside the rice-carved tester bed in the downstairs bedroom is the crib used by Robert E. Lee as an infant.

The most striking feature of the square hall and first-floor rooms is their great expanse of paneling. (Photo: courtesy Hill Carter, Jr.)

Carter worked 640 acres of his land. His basic market crop was tobacco, Stout Oronoko, "fit for the Irish market." He grew various grades of tobacco, but also bought up his neighbors' crop to sell in England. He raised wheat and corn, and imported wine from Mr. Rider & Co. of "Madera." A claret drinker by choice, he ordered "madera" to break himself of the habit. "Pray order them particularly to let my wines be white," he wrote, "for I do not like the tinctured or deep colored."

Shirley, with its floating staircase of walnut, its dining room in which hung the Charles W. Peale full portrait of Washington (now in Williamsburg), is filled with many family treasures. Though it was never occupied or burned when surrounded by Yankee forces during the Civil War, the plantation suffered the ups and downs of fortune and was not always in a state of perfection. President Tyler's wife wrote after a visit in May 1854 that she thought Shirley a "fine old place," but that she would arrange it "so differently" if it were hers. She would have wished the parlor in "better taste and in conformity with modern fashion. Old and fine portraits all round the rooms for four generations back and *coats of arms* is over two doors of the hall as in old English style. It seems like perfect affectation, or dislike to spend money . . . that everything should remain so *old fashioned* . . . and yet," she concluded, "it cannot be on account of the *expense* that no change is made where it can be avoided, as we know how liberal the Carters are in other respects."

Shirley's individuality is evident just as soon as one enters from the east side. Instead of the usual center hall running the length of the house, this distinctive mansion has a square hall with a false fireplace and the superb staircase which rises three stories without visible support. But perhaps the most striking general feature of the interior is the great expanse of paneling. All of the rooms on the first floor and the hall up to the soffit of the second-floor stair are completely paneled. Painted a quiet beige, the paneling is basically the same in each of the rooms but some variety is provided by the varying designs of the door frames, cornices and moldings.

Three rooms — the downstairs bedroom, parlor or drawing room, and dining room — open on to the hall. In this bedroom, beside the rice-carved tester bed, is the crib used by Robert E. Lee as an infant. He spent several years in his mother's home and received part of his schooling there. It is the parlor, however, that is richest both in history and decorative associations. Here Charles Carter entertained George Washington and Thomas Jefferson and later visits were made by President Tyler and Theodore Roosevelt. The windows here are in deep reveals and are protected by inside paneled shutters, as they are in other rooms on this floor. The chimney piece in this room, with its rich entablature, rivals the staircase as Shirley's outstanding single item. The backband of the mantel's facing is carved with egg-and-dart ornament mitered with acanthus leaves and the frieze is enhanced with oak leaves banded with ribbons.

This handsome room was the scene of the wedding of Robert E. Lee's mother, Anne Hill Carter, to "Light Horse Harry" Lee. The fine doorway to the north, leading to the dining room, has a modillioned cornice and scrolled pediment, broken in the center for a pineapple finial. The traditional story is that Anne and Harry Lee first met in the dining room while she was desperately trying to hold on to a slipping punch bowl and was gallantly rescued by the man who would become her husband. It is not difficult today to imagine this and many equally charming domestic and social scenes taking place here during the more than two centuries of the mansion's existence. The Duncan Phyfe-style dining table is original with the house, but the most cherished item in this room is the silver tray, a gift to John Carter from his father. It is unique in the United States because it is made of Britannia standard which was estalished by a decree of William and Mary requiring that silver objects be 954/1000ths pure. This silver is rare because the decree was in effect only twenty-two years, from 1697 to 1719.

Each generation seemed to cherish Shirley but there was uncertainty at one point when Robert R. Carter, Hill Carter's son, seemed to prefer the life of a sailor to that of a country squire. Only after a "brisk correspondence," reported by Robert Carter's wife, did he return, "much against his will." He studied, she said, "one profession and made a good living at that and didn't know about farming under these conditions, but it was ordained to be so and we lived a blissfully happy life together. ..." Eventually Robert Carter managed a prosperous plantation, with wheat fields, corn lands, well-kept stock, and gardens and was said to be "a Virginia gentleman of the noblest stamp."

Robert Carter willed Shirley to his wife and two daughters stating that the "last surviver shall have power to vest the entire remaining estate in fee simple and absolute property in an heir that she may select from among the descendants of my father Hill Carter bearing the name of Carter." This Carter is Charles Hill, great-grandson of Hill Carter, master of Shirley during the Civil War, who was a great-grandson of the original Carter residents of Shirley, John and Elizabeth Carter. The tobacco is gone but the Carters remain ... raising corn, barley, oats, tending the gardens and exploring the history of Shirley, that started nine generations and almost four centuries ago.

Charles City County, Virginia
WESTOVER

Home of Virginia's "Most Ornamental Gentleman"

Above: The Old Westover Mansion, an oil painting by Edward L. Henry in the collection of The Corcoran Gallery of Art.
Opposite: Westover's elaborate main doorway is framed by pilasters of the Composite order supporting a broken ogee pediment with pineapple finial. (Photo: John T. Hill)

If there had been no "Black Swann" of Westover to glide across Virginia's pre-Revolutionary landscape, the colony would have to write out of its pages one of the most literate and elegant characters in its entire history and one of the refreshing diary-keepers of any time. William Byrd II was the son of a wealthy father who had been born into a humble goldsmith's family in London. Wanting to compensate for his own erratic education (his grammar was considered eccentric, his misspelling notorious), he intended a superb one for his son. In 1681, at the age of seven, William II sailed for England, to spend the next eight years of his life at Felsted Grammar School in Essex, to read law later at Middle Temple in London, as well as to spend some time in office work both in Holland and in London.

Virginia's "most polished and ornamental gentleman" was also one of England's most fashionable. Though considered a social climber by many, he was an accomplished classics student, an admirer of the restoration dramatists Wycherley and Congreve, a member of the Royal Academy and an ardent and buoyant suitor. Blue-eyed, tall, slender, he was as philosophical as he was successful about his conquests. "The miscarriage of an honerable amour," he wrote in *The Secret Diary of William Byrd of Westover, 1709-1712,* never "disturb'd him so much, but that he wou'd sleep and look much better in his dispair than he did in the hottest of his expectation." Byrd thrived on his life in London and though, at his father's death in 1705, he was called home to Virginia at

Above: The plaster ceiling in the entry hall follows the French rococo style and is a superb example of its period. (Photos: John T. Hill)

Opposite: The eighteenth-century Austrian chairs in the dining room are covered with elegant red cut-velvet.

the age of thirty-one, all his life he maintained a consuming interest in London and admitted that he tore open mail from that city "as eagerly as a greedy heir tears open a rich father's will."

Westover and its original 1,200 acres west of Ducking Stool Point, "two miles above where the great ships ride," was bought by the shrewd, acquisitive, elder Byrd in 1688 for three hundred English pounds and ten thousand pounds of tobacco, and as Receiver General of Virginia he amassed six thousand acres more. William I had dealt ruthlessly with the Indians, lovingly with his own land, and had a sharp eye for a bargain. For his house, built around 1689, he wanted "a looking glass for a chamber to be handsome and neat but cheap." The summer house in his garden, which was considered the finest in the country, was "set round with Indian Honey-Suckle which all the Summer is continually full of sweet flowers in which the birds delight exceedingly."

William II was home from England only a year when he married Lucy Parke, whose nephew Daniel Parke Custis was Martha Washington's first husband, and with whom he shared his life at Westover and in London in the next ten years. Lucy, whom he described as full of "variety enough to satisfy the inconsistency of any man," was a poor plantation manager with a decidedly unreliable disposition. "My wife was out of humor for nothing," Byrd would record in his diaries, in one version or another, time after time. "However I endeavored to please her again, having consideration for a woman's weakness." Despite Lucy, he seemed to enjoy his life at Westover where he lived like one of the patriarchs ". . . in a kind of independence on everyone but providence." His doors were "open to everybody" and he was proud that they would "rest securely in our beds with all doors and windows open, and yet find everything exactly in place the next morning."

Byrd, who owned 130 volumes on medicine always seemed to be prescribing a "vomit" or a "purge" to a member of his family or his plantation. Somewhat of a health fadist, he ran across the snow-covered lawn to plunge into the icy James River twice a week and almost daily he records in his diary of having "danced his dance" which is interpreted by historians as doing his exercise. On an average day Byrd read Greek in Lucian and in Thucydides, or Latin in Terence, settled accounts, scolded the lazy, drank wine that gave him "gripes" and ate pigeons and bacon or apricots that "made his belly ache." He also read Milton, as well as law, played whist and billiards, romped with his wife, and for the most, enjoyed "good health, good thoughts and good humor, thank God almighty."

William Byrd, the "quintessence of Virginia Aristocracy," played a leading role off the plantation as well as on it. He served in the House of Burgesses, the powerful Council of State, as Commander in Chief of the Militia of Charles City County and was Receiver General of the royal revenues, selling this office for five hundred pounds when he went off to London. He represented Virginia as its official agent in London, failed to be governor of either Maryland or Virginia, but offered one thousand pounds for the appointment as lieutenant governor of the latter state, and directed the party

that surveyed the Virginia-North Carolina boundary. He bought and shipped tobacco to English markets and sold supplies to his neighbors, pursued the trade with India that his father had developed, maintained an interest in slave trade and his desire for land was almost his downfall, as well as his saviour. By refusing to allow his wife to sell her land to pay for the debts of her father's estate, he outsmarted himself, since the debts exceeded the value of the land she inherited.

Though he did not find the coal or iron deposits or the gold mines he hoped for on his property, he did lay the foundation for two cities, those of Richmond and Petersburg, on lands in his possession. At the falls of the James and Appomattox rivers, Byrd aspired to places "naturally intended for marts." "There," he said, "we did not build castles only, but also cities in the air." Byrd also dreamed of developing part of the land bordering North Carolina for immigrant habitation. For a real estate promotion booklet printed in German and published by the Helvetian Society, his name was translated so that as proprietor of the new Eden he was known as Wilhelm Vogel.

William Byrd's first wife died in 1716 and eight years later he married an Englishwoman, Maria Taylor, whose disapproving mother he called Medusa, again settling at Westover after a lengthy hiatus. Just when Westover was built in its present style is a matter of speculation. There is a record of an earlier house and there is Byrd's diary which records, in 1709, that he had workmen manufacturing brick, and that five years later stonecutters from Williamsburg were erecting the library chimney. There is also the record in 1729 of a letter telling a Mr. Spencer in London that Byrd intended "In a year or two . . . to set about building a very good house." The house that evolved from these notes and plans is regarded as not only a good but a great piece of Georgian architecture, a beautifully proportioned house that gives the onlooker the feeling of "its growing from its low meadow by the river."

The façade of Westover facing the river is the most impressive one of the several great mansions along the James. It sits on a large, level bluff about seventy-five yards from the river, behind a row of large tulip poplars over a hundred years old. The central structure, standing three and a half stories above the basement with a vast steep hipped roof and a range of dormers, is flanked on the west by a separate building which was originally the kitchen and is believed to be older than the residence, dating from 1709 or earlier. The eastern wing once contained the famous Byrd library which was burned during the Civil War when McClellan and his Union army camped here and the house was used as headquarters for General Pope. But the dominant element of this façade is the central section's elaborate doorway at the top of gray stone pyramid steps. It is framed by detailed pilasters of the Composite order supporting a broken ogee pediment with pineapple finial.

The approach to the house from the land, or north, side is made through a pair of splendid wrought-iron gates beneath a scrolled overthrow with the initials of William Byrd interwoven in its intricate design and hung from ten-foot brick piers each surmounted by a magnificent lead falcon perched on a ball. No such entrance gates are known to exist anywhere else in America, and they are only the central element of a screen extending across the entire forecourt composed of a series of piers with finials in the form of pineapples, urns and balls, the finest group of carved stone finials in the country.

According to the diaries of William Byrd II,
the exquisite black and white marble mantel
in the great drawing room came from Italy.
(Photo: John T. Hill)

The plan of Westover is a departure from the standard central-hall-with-four-equal-rooms plan because the center hall is slightly off center. Thus the main drawing room and dining room on the east side of the hall were substantially larger than the nursery and chamber to the west, although the latter two rooms are now combined as one and known as the long dining room. Although there are no original Byrd family furnishings in the house, the first floor contains only pieces made in the eighteenth century or earlier.

The hall is paneled with a molded chair rail and full cornice. The staircase — with mahogany balustrade and stringer, molded handrail and spirally turned balusters — after a long initial run, ascends to the third floor, an accomplishment duplicated only in the mansion at Shirley. But it is the plaster ceiling that is unique and a superb example of its period, following the French rococo style popular in mid-Georgian England. It is bordered by a rod-and-ribbon band which is interrupted at the corners and center of each side by large scrolled ornaments with foliage, masks and vases. This border encloses a large center panel of four swags of fruit and flowers, edged with reverse curve scrolls, leaves and flowers. The valuable tapestry chairs are part of a set also found in the drawing room.

The great drawing room in the southeast corner is the most imposing room in the house. Like all first-floor rooms it is paneled to the ceiling and its ceiling plasterwork is more extensive than the hall's, although not quite as pleasing. Along the south wall is a row of imposing tall windows with window seats, paneled jambs and molded frames. The draperies and sofa are red silk damask. It is, however, the great marble mantelpiece that gives this room distinction. Composed of black marble extensively decorated with white marble, it is probably the most monumental marble mantel of its period in the country. The architrave is ornamented with white marble carved in egg and dart design. Above this is an oblong mirror beneath a swag of fruit and flowers which is surrounded by white marble carved in a pattern of grapes and leaves. The entire piece is capped by a white marble pediment. According to Byrd's diaries, this mantel came from Italy and it was remodeled around the turn of the century when some of its present features were added to replace elements stolen or destroyed during the Civil War.

The dining room ceiling and paneling are relatively simple. The eighteenth-century Austrian chairs are covered with red cut-velvet which contrasts with the blue silk damask draperies and Bokhara rugs. The simplicity of the ceiling and paneling is matched by the two mantels of gray marble and gray-veined white marble.

It is, however, the four mantels on the second floor, all probably made in London, which together constitute a group that has been described as the finest such suite in America. The mantel in the northeast chamber is of painted Portland stone. On each side are tall consoles, scrolled and feathered with acanthus and ornamented with cords and tassels, which are believed to be unique among the many fine masonry mantels in Virginia. The other three second-floor mantels are of painted wood. Each has admirable qualities, but the one in the southwest room is probably unprecedented in this country.

Its paneled pilasters feature high-relief carving of flowers and leaves issuing from scrolled and carved consoles. They support a frieze filled with full-relief scrolled foliage in the style of Grinling Gibbons, the remarkable late seventeenth- and early eighteenth-century English carver and designer.

William Byrd left behind, at his death, his magnificent library, 179,423 acres of land in plantations scattered from Westover to the Alleghenies, hundreds of slaves, herds of cattle, squadrons of horses, and sloops enough to transport produce down the river to where the great ships lay. But his most permanent legacy, in addition to Westover, are his secret diaries which have come into public domain. Byrd had learned shorthand developed in the seventeenth century from William Mason, the most famous stenographer of his day, who taught art in London and who wrote a book called *A Pen Pluck't from an Eagle's Wing*. Byrd's diaries are painstakingly detailed and disarmingly honest. They add up to one of the most valuable reports of plantation life before the Revolutionary War and justify its author being called the "first man of letters in North America."

When William Byrd III's widow died in 1814, her son Thomas Taylor Byrd, who was accused of "loving England better than his own country" and of having "the appearance and manners of an English nobleman," moved away to settle in the Shenandoah Valley. Westover changed hands and eventually was bought by Mr. Richard Crane whose daughter Mrs. Bruce Crane Fisher lives there now.

The tomb of William Byrd II, Virginia's "most ornamental gentleman," stands in Westover's gardens. (Photo: courtesy Virginia State Chamber of Commerce)

141

Charles City County, Virginia
BERKELEY

The Stuff of History

Benjamin Harrison IV, whose great-grandmother could only afford to leave her granddaughter "the horse colt that sucks on the black mare," was the family's first college student. Accompanied by a servant, he went off to William & Mary to study rhetoric, logic and ethics, physics, metaphysics and mathematics, and he went home, perhaps inspired by the building at Williamsburg, to create one of the first of the "home-houses" of Virginia.

Home for Ben Harrison was Berkeley, a plantation that is by origin, incident and association as well as architecture, the stuff of history. It was built on a site that was part of a grant made in 1619 by King James I to the Berkely Company, where Captain John Woodlief and his thirty-eight Berkely Hundred settlers rowed ashore from the small ship *Margaret* in 1619. It was bought by Benjamin Harrison II in 1691 and it was his son, Benjamin Harrison III, who nurtured the estate to triumphant prosperity. It is said that he was a man who had worked eight hours by noon each day, that he started the nation's first shipbuilding industry and that he fitted his ships with everything from split peas to cannons. He built warehouses for tobacco, outbuildings for tanning hides, carding wool, baking bread, and forging iron. At his death in 1710 his twenty-thousand-acre estate, inherited by his son and namesake at the age of ten, was described as being "exceeded in splendor only by that of the Royal Governor."

Benjamin Harrison IV was married at the age of twenty-two to the heiress Anne Carter, the daughter of Virginia's wealthiest planter. Together they planned the beautifully balanced brick mansion that has presided over the Berkeley plantation since they carved their initials in stone on the west wall of the house in 1726. The architect who was probably responsible for the design was a young Scotsman, Rob Wilson, who managed to leave debtors' prison in England with Harrison's help. The new house was built on a slight elevation nearly a quarter of a mile back from the river, made with three-foot-thick walls, hand-hewn heart pine floors and a full brick basement to serve as a wine cellar.

Two and a half stories high, Berkeley's heroic pediment roof, said to be Virginia's first, was inspired by an illustration in James Gibb's *Book of Architecture,* that of his church at Derby. The pediment roof was a significant utilitarian advance over the hip because it provided useful end rooms in the attic without dormers (although Berkeley has three dormers on each of the fronts) and ventilation where it was needed. The main house is flanked by two smaller, well-proportioned, two-story buildings that are in line with the big house. To the east is the Bachelor's House where William Henry Harrison and his brothers and sisters attended school. On the west is the kitchen and servants' quarters, connected to the main house by a brick passageway known as the Whistle Hole because of the practice of having servants whistle as they carried meals along the way so they could not sample the food.

The twelve-foot-wide central hall is divided in the middle by a wide elliptical arch supported by fluted pilasters. The view through this arch out beyond the open door facing the boxwood garden and the river is one of the most charming in

Above: Berkeley's pediment-roofed mansion has presided over the plantation since 1726. (Photo: courtesy Va. State Chamber of Commerce)

Opposite: Mottled-gray marble facing of fireplace remains from early times in south end of Great Room. (Photo: Walter Miller)

143

Virginia. A choice piece in the hall is the Chippendale cherry linen press.

Very little of the original interior trim and paneling remains at Berkeley. About 1790 Benjamin Harrison VI had simpler then-fashionable paneling installed in place of the original, but the woodwork is elaborate enough. In the hall the chair rails are eleven inches wide, hand-tooled to give a fluted effect. All the woodwork is painted white.

The only interior finish that is undoubtedly from the early period is the fine mottled-gray marble facing of the two back-to-back fireplaces on the east chimney. These fireplaces open on the north and south parts of the Great Room which are connected on each side of the chimney by an arched alcove, its curves gracefully proportioned with fluted pilasters and beaded keystones.

Some sense of the delightful times in Berkeley's past is evoked by the exquisite little Musicians' Balcony, the only one in Virginia, on the second landing. It is placed so that music emanating from it could be heard in all the large rooms in the house. This sense of cultivation and taste perhaps reaches its culmination in the imposing and colorful dining room. A portrait of Benjamin Harrison IV over the mantel looks down upon a room filled with an abundance of blue and white Chinese porcelain, old English silver, a lovely Waterford glass chandelier from Ireland, a fine set of Hepplewhite chairs, a three-section dining table (the middle section with double gatelegs) and an eighteenth-century walnut corner cupboard from an old house in Petersburg, Virginia. Directly across from the fireplace is the finest piece in the house — a gentleman's chest, circa 1725, of rare curly cherry wood.

During the Civil War, Berkeley became a camping ground for General McClellan and over 100,000 Union troops, after they withdrew from Malvern Hill. It was during this period in 1862 that General Daniel Butterfield composed the world-famous bugle call, "Taps." However, this was not Berkeley's first brush with war: During the American Revolution Benedict Arnold encamped there and the British burned family portraits, shot cattle and carried off forty slaves. It almost seems as though Berkeley's historical pedigree is endless. Benjamin V, who signed the Declaration of Independence and had the honor of reading its preamble before Congress, was a tall, powerfully built, aristocratic gentleman who fancied silver-buttoned silk coats, silk knee breeches, and blue white wigs, and, according to John Adams, he was "an indolent, luxurious heavy gentleman . . . of no use in Congress or Committee." However, he was Governor of Virginia for three terms, and his son William first was governor of the Northwest Territory and then ninth President of the United States. William Henry Harrison wrote his inaugural address at Berkeley in the room where he was born. His grandson John Scott Harrison represented his district in the National House of Representatives and his grandson, in turn, was Benjamin Harrison, the twenty-third President of the United States. Probably because this Harrison won his office on the Republican ticket, his Virginia family considered him the black sheep of the family. In return he is reputed to have said, "The Virginia Harrisons are all like potatoes, by now the best of

them are long underground," although he did visit his ancestral home while he was President.

Among the more than 100,000 Union soldiers encamped at Berkeley in 1862 was a drummer boy, not yet fourteen, John Jamieson, who had recently moved from Scotland to Long Island. Forty-five years later Jamieson, who built docks, bridges and the base of the Statue of Liberty, purchased Berkeley as a farm and for a place of retirement. He was never able to live there, but his son, Malcolm Jamieson, later restored it and furnished it with eighteenth-century antiques, many from Westover, with the other treasures and opened the first floor to the public so that they can glimpse the way a remarkable American family lived in its prime.

Above: Chippendale cherry linen press stands opposite scroll-back settee with shell-carved Drake feet. (Photo: Walter Miller)

Stratford, Virginia
STRATFORD HALL

Home of the Celebrated Lees of Virginia

The complaint against the family who lived in Stratford Hall was "a very extraordinary thing indeed." The Lees' greatest fault, John Adams said, was having "more men of merit . . . than any other family" and he worried that if the Lees failed the "American Cause," he did not know "what family or what person will stand the test."

The tests were as varied as they were numerous. Seven generations of Lees produced soldiers, diplomats, congressmen, senators, governors, liberals and iconoclasts, the most celebrated of all Lees being General Robert E. Lee. Even by today's standards they would have to be considered an international family. Two generations before Thomas Lee built the Lees' ancestral home, Stratford Hall, there was Thomas's grandfather, Richard Lee I, who left England for Virginia in the summer of 1639 and who served at Jamestown, the capital of the Colony of Virginia, as Attorney General, Secretary of State and member of the Governor's Council. There was Thomas's father, Richard Lee II, who had returned to England for his schooling and became a language student and a bibliophile. And there was Thomas who built the severely symmetrical home on 1,400 acres bordering the Potomac with the fortune in pounds sterling left to his wife, Hannah Ludwell,

Above: Stratford Hall's raised first floor reminds critics of an Italian villa. (Photos: courtesy Robt. E. Lee Memorial Foundation) *Opposite:* The Great Hall has its original paneling and hardware, and is considered the most beautiful early paneled room in Virginia.

146

by her two grandfathers.

The house that Thomas Lee built, where six of his eleven children were born, was certainly different from the colonial mansions of the early Georgian period, and, in fact, eludes any classical category. Its raised main floor, which contains the major rooms, reminds critics of an Italian villa, while its massive proportions and two groups of four massed chimneys connected by arches over each projecting wing suggest the influence of Sir John Vanbrugh's Blenheim Palace. Basically not a subtle design, its H-shaped outline is similar to that of the Virginia capitol building in Williamsburg which Lee often saw during his thirty years as Burgess for Westmoreland and member of the Governor's Council. The eighteen-room house has thick brick walls, as do each of the four dependencies beyond the corners of the house — the brick coming from the plantation's native clays and the mortar made by burning sea shells scooped from the Potomac, some of the work performed by indentured servants. On the ground floor the walls are laid in large bricks in Flemish bond, while the main floor has smaller pink-red bricks, resulting in a visible contrast. The structure's two recessed courts at north and south contain identical centered doorways on the main floor, reached by a long tapering stairway with Portland stone steps and heavy stone balustrades. The south doorway is the main entrance, although both doors open directly into the Great Hall.

The Great Hall is considered the most ambitious and most beautiful early paneled room in Virginia, if not in the colonies. A room of elaborate moldings, it is also a room of elaborate views, opening on a grassy forecourt to the south, and a spacious lawn to the north, beyond which may be seen, nearly a mile away, the wide Potomac. Queen Anne mirrors and a settee of the same period, scroll-footed armchairs in Spanish style, and a seventeenth-century flock by William Clement in pure William and Mary style dress the room deservingly.

A second room of extraordinary interest on the main floor is the bedroom filled with delightful red, patterned toile fabric, called the Mother's Room. This is the southeast bedroom in which two signers of the Declaration of Independence and Robert E. Lee, among other family members, were born, and the room is engagingly and reverently kept to this day. The Adam mantel is typical of the style of 1800. Oyster-white walls and mahogany graining on paneled doors provide a harmonious setting for the stately canopied four-poster.

In the northwest section of the house is the elegant parlor, sometimes called the Light Horse Harry Lee Parlor, and its adjoining closet. Light Horse Harry, who owned the portrait of Lafayette by Charles Willson Peale over the mantel, redecorated the room about 1800 with a new mantel, and paneled wainscot in late eighteenth-century style. The most notable pieces here are an exquisite Sheraton-style Salem secretary with a fall-front writing flap and a Philadelphia side table and drapery-back chairs.

Completing the west wing is the library, resting place of a collection of old books on Lee family history and other Americana. Of the numerous fine pieces here, the most outstanding is an English Chippendale mahogany desk and mirror, whose delicate brown combines superbly with the two gold Queen Anne easy chairs, the auburn curtains and pale green woodwork. An English Queen Anne walnut desk and bookcase complete the furnishings. To the sides of the Chip-

Of the numerous fine pieces in the library, the most outstanding is an English mahogany desk. (Photo: courtesy Lee Memorial Found.)

The Mother's Room on the first floor has red, patterned toile fabric. Two signers of the Declaration of Independence and Robert E. Lee were born in this room. (Photo: Walter Miller)

pendale desk are companion portraits of Philip Ludwell II, and his wife Hannah Harrison, parents of Hannah, first mistress of Stratford.

The builder of Stratford, Thomas Lee, was as familiar to activity in significant places as both his grandfathers and his father had been and as his sons and their offspring would continue to be for the century to come. In 1711, at the age of twenty-one, he was appointed resident attorney for Lady Catherine Fairfax and for ten years thereafter exercised in her name the prerogatives of the Crown of England with respect to the granting of lands and the collection of quitrents in all the territory between the Potomac and Rappahannock rivers, some six million acres. As President of the Governor's Council, Thomas Lee was from 1749 to 1750 the President and Commander in Chief of Virginia, the highest political position a Virginian could hold before the Revolution. He conducted Virginia's negotiations with the Iroquois at Lancaster in 1744. The resulting treaty gave Virginia all of the Iroquois lands west of the Blue Ridge and south of the Potomac and the Ohio, a move which unlocked the Ohio Basin to English settlement.

The six surviving sons of Thomas Lee and his wife, Hannah

The dining room is furnished primarily with early eighteenth-century English pieces. In the adjoining closet is a portrait of Queen Caroline. (Photo: courtesy Lee Memorial Found.)

Ludwell, were reared at Stratford and were remarkably wide-ranging in their interests and success. Philip raised tobacco and bred thoroughbred horses at Stratford while serving as a member of the Council at Williamsburg, just as his father, grandfather and great-grandfather had. Thomas was described as the most popular man in Virginia and served as Burgess from Stafford County, member of the Revolutionary conventions and judge of the General Court, the new state's supreme court. Richard Henry, a fiery orator dubbed the "Cicero of America," opposed slavery vigorously in his maiden speech as Burgess from Westmoreland, later spoke and acted against the hated Stamp Act. "Among the many leagues that are formed," he asked, "why may not one be made for the purpose of protecting the rights of humanity?" In the Continental Congress he proposed the historic motion that "these United Colonies are, and of right ought to be, free and independent states." Both Richard Henry and his brother Francis Lightfoot signed the vital document.

Francis was one of the Revolutionary inner circle at Williamsburg, along with Patrick Henry, Richard Henry Lee and Thomas Jefferson. As chairman of a congressional committee and in overt violation of the constitutional law of that time, he

150

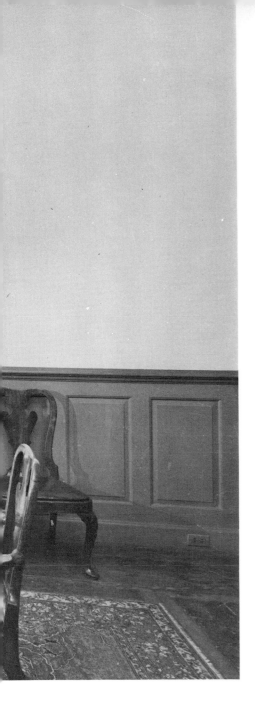

authorized the Continental Commissary to levy supply requisitions on the inhabitants of Pennsylvania, thereby saving the army at Valley Forge. William was a successful tobacco merchant in London where he was elected alderman in 1775 as an expression of the city's opposition to the American policy of the Tory minister. Later he served the Congress in Europe. Arthur, a doctor of medicine from the University of Edinburgh, practiced briefly at Williamsburg, but later went to London where he studied law and became the preeminent pamphleteer of the Revolution. Still later, he secretly obtained the original grant of French military supplies for the Continental Army, which made possible the victory at Saratoga.

It is Henry Lee — a Princeton graduate, class of 1773 — who is one of the most appealing and tragic residents of Stratford. The reputation he founded during his exploits as the captain of a company of light dragoons earned him the nickname "Light Horse Harry" and it was he who eulogized Washington at his death as "first in war, first in peace, and first in the hearts of his countrymen." At the close of the Revolution, Harry married his second cousin, Matilda Lee, the heiress of Stratford. He later became a member of the Continental Congress, Governor of Virginia and a member of the Federal Congress at the time of Washington's death. After Matilda's death, Henry Lee married Anne Hill Carter of Shirley, and it was their fourth son Robert Edward who was to become general of the Confederate army and college president. Henry Lee was a brave soldier but he was imprudent in the management of his finances and eventually found himself in prison for debt. Anne refused to leave Stratford until Henry was released, and then, at her insistence, they moved to Alexandria.

Stratford's fortunes took a more optimistic turn with the reappearance of Robert's half brother, Henry, who brought money and slaves due to a fortuitous marriage, to the plantation. The death of a small daughter, who tumbled down the staircase, affected Mrs. Lee so deeply that she became an opium addict. Henry sought consolation with Mrs. Lee's sister, a scandal that brought him the nickname "Black Horse Harry." After selling the house to a friend, he and his wife moved to Tennessee where he became a political writer for General Andrew Jackson.

Stratford fell steadily out of fortune until 1929 when the Robert E. Lee Memorial Foundation bought the plantation and the remaining 1,204 acres for $240,000. Luckily, drawings and other records have provided a basis for its faithful and affectionate restoration. Many of the authentic Lee possessions (auctioned during time of crisis) have returned to Stratford.

The dependencies, the kitchen, servants' quarters, schoolhouse and smokehouse and counting house are restored. Livestock graze the fields, boxwood hedges frame carefully tended gardens. The silver shines, the woods glow and Stratford Hall is almost exactly the way Thomas Lee's grandson, Thomas Lee Shippen, described it to his parents after his visit in 1790: "Stratford, the seat of my forefathers, is a place of which too much cannot be said, whether you consider the venerable magnificence of its buildings, the happy disposition of its grounds, or the extent and variety of its prospects. . . ."

151

Mount Vernon, Virginia
MOUNT VERNON

Washington's Lavish Country Seat

The evening he left for New England, the newly appointed Commander in Chief of the Continental Army, George Washington, wrote to his wife Martha: "I should enjoy more real happiness in one month with you at home than I have the most distant prospect of finding abroad, if my stay were to be seven times seven years." Home to Washington was Mount Vernon, where "a glass of wine and a bit of mutton are always ready" and Mount Vernon was where he hoped to find "more happiness in retirement" than he had ever experienced "amidst a wide and bustling world."

George Washington's great-grandfather John shared with one Nicholas Spencer, a five-thousand-acre tract of land between the Potomac and the Rappahannock rivers, granted by Thomas, Lord Culpeper, in 1674. The Washington property, known for generations as the Hunting Creek Plantation, was renamed by George's elder half-brother Lawrence, when he settled there in 1743, after Admiral Edward Vernon with whom he had served in the Caribbean. At their father Augustine's death, George spent time at Mount Vernon which he in turn inherited when Lawrence's widow released the property to him in 1754, two years after Lawrence's death. Washington, whose father had owned six plantations in all, had grown up riding over the land, helping manage the slaves, and learning how to grow tobacco, raise stock and survey land. At the age of fourteen Washington could plot and measure the fields for his neighbors and family and at the age of twenty he was able to manage Mount Vernon efficiently and economically.

Above: The high-columned piazza stretching across Mount Vernon's river front is believed to be unique for its period. *Opposite:* The Palladian window in the Banquet Hall is decorated with Adamesque ornament. (All photos: courtesy Mt. Vernon Ladies' Assoc.)

Left: The farm gate as it was in 1858 is faithfully depicted in this drawing.

Below: The reds and oranges of the draperies and bed hangings in the downstairs bedroom contrast strikingly with brownish-green walls.

On December 14, 1799, General Washington
died in this unadorned canopy bed which
he had ordered made in Philadelphia.

Washington loved the life at Mount Vernon and the plantation prospered until he became one of the wealthiest planters anywhere in Virginia. His 2,126 acres burgeoned into 8,000 acres and he developed an interest in soil conservation, crop rotation, grew a peach and an apple orchard, grafted cherry, pear and plum trees and raised Madeira grapes and Mississippi pecans. He liked afternoon tea on the veranda in summer, enjoyed picnics and clambakes, rode by coach to Alexandria for the fancy balls, to Williamsburg during "public times" and to both towns for plays. One visitor to Mount Vernon reported that the general "breaks all his own horses, . . . is an excellent and bold horseman, and leaping the highest fences he'd catch'd nothing."

Mount Vernon was a bustling principality from 1786 to 1789 when Washington lived there after resigning his commission at Annapolis in 1783 and before he became President. This New World version of the English country seat was modest by British comparison but not without style. There were about 90 people in residence and 140 more on four tributary farms. A visitor wrote after twelve June days at Mount Vernon, "The whole plantation, the garden, and the rest prove well that a man born with natural taste may guess a beauty without having ever seen its model. The general never left America; but when one sees his house and his home and his garden it seems as if he had copied the best samples of the grand homesteads of England."

The original house at Mount Vernon was one and a half stories high with four small rooms on the first floor and only eight rooms in all. In anticipation of Washington's marriage to Martha Custis in 1759 and while Washington was absent on military duty, the house was raised to two and a half stories, the four dependencies connected to the main house by "pallisades" surmounting low brick walls. Then, in 1773, there is a record of Washington being absorbed in plans for enlarging Mount Vernon and of his ordering materials from England to carry them out. Washington wrote that he was "very much engaged in raising one of the additions to my house, which I think (perhaps it is fancy) goes on better whilst I am present

Right: The most valuable piece in the library, Washington's Philadelphia Hepplewhite secretary-desk, was returned to the house in 1797.

Below: It was in the library that Washington wrote his many letters which were so influential in the movement for establishing a Federal Government.

than in my absence." Which seems not a bit boastful in light of one friend's observation: "It's astonishing with what niceness he [Washington] directs everything in the building way, condescending even to measure things himself, that all may be perfectly uniform."

Details concerning china, silver and landscaping, as well as furniture and architecture, occupied Washington throughout his married life. Even when Washington was away from Mount Vernon, he was briefed on the smallest details concerning its enlargement. Letters from Lund Washington, a kinsman and manager of Mount Vernon, told him that the stucco man he shared with Washington's sister and brother-in-law, the Fielding Lewises, was painfully slow. Lund wrote that the man "thinks he shall be four week in the dining room," but despairing weeks later, he wrote again saying, "God knows when we will get it done."

George Washington had "heartily" wished that the election to the Presidency did not "fall" on him. "If I should conceive myself in a manner constrained to accept, I call Heaven to witness that this very act would be the greatest sacrifice of my personal feelings and wishes that I ever have been called upon to make." While Washington was in office, he managed to visit Mount Vernon fifteen times, from several days' stay to several months'. He returned home in 1797, free at last to enjoy the classic pursuits of an affluent country squire, and spent the next two and half years at his plantation until his death in 1799, at the age of sixty-six. He was fond of dancing, fond of cards, happy to have visitors, friends and relatives surrounding him, and fascinated by the prospect of improving the breed of his favorite hounds.

In 1858 the Mount Vernon Ladies' Association acquired the two-hundred-acre tract, now grown to five hundred acres, including the mansion, wharf and subsidiary buildings and went to work restoring and refurnishing the house. Today, most of the first floor and master's bedroom as well as other rooms on the second and third floors are filled with original treasures.

Perhaps the most impressive aspect of the Mount Vernon mansion is the remarkable order of its appearance, both in itself and in relation to the site and the other buildings. The red roof has a large cupola in the center and a chimney at the end of each gable, marking the limits of the house before the additions of the 1770's. There are three entrance doors on each front, the central doors, originally the only doors, both with pediments. The central roof pediment facing the bowling green on the west side, added in 1778, extends over four of the second-floor windows. It is flanked by two small dormers, while the river front has three dormers without the roof pediment. But the most impressive aspect of the exterior is on the river front — the high-columned piazza stretching the length of the house and believed to be unique for its period. Another unusual exterior feature is less apparent: The wood siding has been "rusticated" by beveling, painting it white and then applying sand to give it the appearance of stone.

A broad central hall extends the full width of the house, from the entrance on the west side to the piazza overlooking the river. It affords access through pedimented doorways to four rooms — to the left, as one enters from the bowling green, are the west parlor and little parlor, to the right, the dining room and downstairs bedroom. Only the hall, west parlor and downstairs bedroom are paneled. Because of ventilation this hall is the coolest area in the house and during the warm months much of the informal social life of the Washingtons was centered here.

Because of its Adamesque ceiling, fine paneling and two Ionic doorways, the west parlor is one of the most elegant rooms. The splendidly detailed mantel and overmantel are surmounted by a broken serpentine pediment containing a carved and brightly painted depiction of the family coat of arms. Music was an ever-present and cherished part of plantation life in eighteenth-century Virginia and the little parlor contains the harpsichord Washington bought during his Presidency for Nelly Custis, Martha Washington's granddaughter. Over the harpsichord are duplicate prints of the marine scenes listed for this room by Washington's executors.

Across from the little parlor is the downstairs bedroom where overnight guests frequently stayed and which is an example of a feature common to Virginia plantation homes. The muted brownish-green, fully paneled walls provide a striking color contrast to the dominant reds and oranges of the hangings of the canopy bed, draperies and carpet. Directly accessible from this bedroom is the dining room whose mantel, overmantel, cornice and ceiling are the most elaborately detailed in the house. The mantel is derived from a plate in *British Architect* by Abraham Swan, published in 1745, the magnificent rococo ornamentation covering the entire frieze being almost identical with Swan's design. The whole face of each frieze bracket is covered with a broad acanthus leaf, and forming a console on each side of the fireplace, below the break in the jamb, graceful acanthus leaves flower from a shell. On the dining table, which is contemporary with the house but not original, is a mirrored plateau purchased in France by Gouverneur Morris for Washington's use during his Presidency; the classical bisque group on the plateau was also provided by Morris. The nine Chippendale ladder-back side chairs are original, as are the andirons, crystal candelabra, punch bowl and tea caddy.

The high-ceilinged Banquet Hall on the north end of the mansion is a rectangular room thirty-one feet long, with coved ceiling, and is the largest room in the house. Washington called it the New Room because it was the principal part of the addition built during the Revolution, although the interior was not finished until after the war because of the difficulty in finding craftsmen skilled enough to execute the ceiling decoration and woodwork. It has outside entrances on both sides and its largest window is the justly famous Palladian window on the north wall. Here the paneled piers that divide and flank the three sections of the window are decorated with thin pendants of Adamesque ornament both above and below the chair rail, and festoons grace the entablature frieze. The arch over the high central section of the window extends into the cove, also strung with festoons punctuated with medallions. On the south wall, flanked by doorways to the parlors, is an inlaid marble mantel, unique in Virginia, with freestanding Ionic columns supporting a frieze with bas-reliefs. It was a gift to Washington in 1785 from an English admirer, Samuel Vaughn. The Worcester porcelain vases on the mantel were also gifts from Vaughn.

At the south end of the mansion is another addition that corresponds to the north one except for the Palladian window.

The cupola in the center of the roof and the wide central pediment facing the bowling green on the west side help give the mansion its remarkable orderliness.

The principal room is the library which was completed, except for the glass-enclosed bookcases, before Washington left for the Second Continental Congress in May 1775. It was here during the years immediately following the war that Washington wrote his many letters which so profoundly influenced the move toward a Federal Government. It was also from here that he managed the estate. The wrought-iron chest and the terrestial globe near the window are original Washington possessions, but the most valuable piece is the secretary-desk that was brought back from Philadelphia in 1797 when he retired from the Presidency.

There are five bedrooms directly accessible from the upstairs hall. At the head of the central stairway is the Blue Bedroom, so called because of the color of its woodwork. Adjoining it is the Lafayette Bedroom, named for its most renowned occupant. The little room beside the attic stairway was used by George Washington Parke Custis, Martha Washington's youngest grandson, and the Nelly Custis Room, adjoining the Yellow Bedroom, was named for her youngest granddaughter, who lived at Mount Vernon from early childhood until after she married Lawrence Lewis, Washington's nephew, in 1799.

General Washington's Bedroom, directly above the library in the south addition, is reached by a narrow stairway in the southeast corner. The walls, ceiling, curtains, bedhangings and bedspread all are white, the simple woodwork off-white. Mrs. Washington's little writing desk is French, purchased from the first French Minister to this country. Over it is a charming portrait of another of Mrs. Washington's granddaughters, Martha Parke Custis, painted at Mount Vernon in 1785 by Robert Edge Pine. A companion portrait of Martha's sister Nelly hangs near the fireplace. Washington had the unadorned canopy bed made in Philadelphia and it was here that he died on December 14, 1799. The day before, he had become ill after being caught in a snowfall while riding over his beloved estate and making plans for future improvements of the grounds. He thought no place "more pleasantly situated" than Mount Vernon. A twentieth-century visitor can amplify: nor more pleasantly preserved.

Charlottesville, Virginia

MONTICELLO

Jefferson's Graceful Palladian Mansion

It cost Thomas Jefferson 180 bushels of wheat and 24 bushels of corn to have his contractor Mr. Moore level the 250 square feet of mountain out of which the statesman created a work of art called Monticello. The first plantation to be embedded in the mountains and the first plantation to have an Italian name ("little mountain" was the English translation), Monticello reflected the cosmopolitan tastes of the tall, sinewy horseman and one-time student at William and Mary who candidly admitted "architecture is my delight, and putting up and pulling down, one of my favorite amusements."

From early manhood (he was twenty-four years old when he began to plan Monticello) until his dying day at the age of eighty-three, Jefferson put up and pulled down Monticello, heightening its roofs, adding rooms, as fascinated by the exterior as the interior, as intrigued with Doric columns as cabinetmakers' carvings. Although occupied for some six years by a law practice, lawyers "whose trade it is to question everything, yield nothing, and talk by the hour" bored him. As a member of the Virginia House of Burgesses and later the Continental Congress, he hated the "morbid rage of debate." His other accomplishments include the writing of *A Summary View of the Rights of America,* which was largely the heart and soul of the Declaration of Independence, and serving as Governor of Virginia, Minister to France, Secretary of State in George Washington's cabinet, Vice President and twice as President of the United States. Yet this astonishing man found time to study architecture and he took pleasure, while in Europe, in spending "whole hours . . . like a lover at his mistress," gazing at the classical Maison Carree at Nîmes. Also, he considered himself "nourished with the remains of Roman grandeur" he encountered on the way to Nîmes from Lyons and "violently smitten with the Hotel de Salm" a beautifully made small house he studied when he went to the Tuileries almost daily during his days in Paris.

It was after his return in 1789 from five years in Europe — first assisting Benjamin Franklin and John Adams in negotiating commercial treaties with European states and then succeeding Benjamin Franklin as Minister to France — that Jefferson was determined to alter Monticello, to refine its

Opposite: Monticello represents the distillation of all Jefferson's studies and exposure to fine architecture. (All photos: Jefferson Memorial Foundation)

Jefferson hung his finest paintings in the parlor and in 1809 reported forty-eight pictures here.

design, to finish the house that had deteriorated during the neglect of the eight-year period of war and work in Europe.

The final version of Monticello represents the distillation of all of Jefferson's early studies and later exposure to fine architecture. The son of a civil engineer, he continually drew and redrew its plans, clearly influenced by the works of three visionary architects — James Gibbs, Robert Morris and the sixteenth-century Venetian, Andrea Palladio, who was admired for villas that were a "combination of grandeur and agricultural utility." Palladio's synthesis of domestic Roman architecture, his symmetrical compositions complete with dome, rotunda and portico were often connected to the farm buildings by colonnaded walks. Set in the glorious Venetian landscape, these summer residences, designed to be working farms as well, seemed to encompass all that Jefferson envisioned for Monticello. He admitted to finding equal pleasure in the land as well as in stone and plaster: "no occupation . . . so delightful as the culture of the earth ... and no culture comparable to that of the garden."

Throughout all those years when Jefferson explored ideas about regulating suffrage, limiting the acquisition of public lands, arranging the Louisiana Purchase and steering Lewis and Clark toward the Pacific and while he drew the plans and changes for Monticello, he cultivated the farm that was "originally as rich as any highlands in the world, but much worried by Indian corn and tobacco," though "very strong and remarkably friendly to wheat and rye." Jefferson never ceased experimenting with varieties and rotation of crops, kept meticulous meteorological tables and sent abroad for different kinds of grasses, trees, rice and olives.

Monticello's evolution is a fascinating study in the growth of the needs and taste, pleasures and interests of Thomas Jefferson. Jottings of his plans and new ideas date from 1767, but it wasn't until November of 1770 that Jefferson moved to his mountain where a one room building "like the cobbler's" served him "for parlour, for kitchen and hall, for bed-chamber and study too." Jefferson had hoped to get "more elbow room" and, in fact, needed it rather crucially by the first day of 1772 when he married a twenty-three-year-old widow named Martha Wayles Skelton. Jefferson worried throughout the years of the Revolution about the completion of his home, and when it was finished in its first version, it was described as "one large square pavilion, the entrance of which is by two porticoes, ornamented with pillars" and crowned by a peaked roof, as it turned out, a temporary façade.

Ten years after its initial completion, Jefferson planned changes for Monticello, influenced by his years abroad and the French return to Roman classicism under Louis XVI. Monticello, as a result, was reduced in height, enlarged in depth and a mezzanine, skylights and alcove bedrooms were added. In 1794 Jefferson wrote of "living in a brick kiln, for my house in its present state, is nothing better." But work did come to an end, or very nearly so, and the house was in satisfactory condition in 1809, though the railings on the terraces were not completed until 1824 and six cases of chimney "pilas" arrived in 1825, the year before he died. Monticello had, by that time, lost its peak roof and its great staircase and instead was crowned with a dome and connected by covered passages to servants' rooms, the kitchen, an office, coach house and icehouse, all designed with a rare sense of proportion and compactness. The perfectionist with a dream, the inventor who apparently loved challenge, Jefferson described the interior of Monticello with pride: "The internal of the house contains specimens of all the different orders except the composite which is not introduced. The Hall is in the Ionic, the Dining Room is in the Doric, the Parlor is in the Corinthian, and the Dome in the Attic."

Though Monticello is Jefferson's triumphal work of architecture, he must also be recognized for helping to redesign Pennsylvania Avenue in Washington, D.C., for creating the University of Virginia which was conceived as an "academical village rather than one large building," for designing Christ Church in Charlottesville and for helping friends with designs for private dwellings. Unfortunately, Jefferson was as gracious as he was talented and as many as fifty friends

stayed at Monticello, filling the house for months, filling his stables with their horses and emptying his cellars of the fine French wines he so enjoyed serving. Jefferson had left the President's office in debt for about $20,000 and maintenance of Monticello was another drastic drain. A national subscription in 1826 raised about $16,500, enough to keep him going somewhat peacefully until his death a few months later. Then, all had to be relinquished and Jefferson's daughter, her husband and children had to sell his furniture, silver, paintings and beloved Monticello itself.

A druggist named James Turner Barclay bought the house and 552 acres for $7,000 to start a silk worm culture, and five years later, Monticello was resold for $2,500 to Uriah Phillips Levy, a naval officer in whose family it remained for eighty-nine years. But Monticello did not come into its own again until it was finally bought by the Thomas Jefferson Memorial Foundation in 1923. Over this last half-century, with painstaking research, loans, gifts and donations, Monticello has been restored to perfection.

Beneath the great portico on the east front facing the Southwest Mountains is the tall, completely glass-paned double entrance door surmounted with a fanlight and flanked on each side by a window of identical size and shape rising from floor level. Partly surrounded by a balustraded balcony, the large square entrance hall has blue walls trimmed in white and a fine frieze with a winged beast as primary motif, that is, like all interior frieze designs at Monticello, from Desgodetz's

Above: Made in Philadelphia by Peter Strunk to Jefferson's design, the seven-day calendar clock above the entrance hall door is run by Revolutionary War cannon ball weights.

Opposite above: All the furniture in Jefferson's Bedroom is original. The statesman died in this room in this bed on July 4, 1826.

Opposite below: The book room in the library suite holds the large ceremonial chair Jefferson used when he was Vice President.

The blue walls of the dining room match the graceful Wedgwood medallions set in the mantel. The table is Chippendale.

Les Edifices Antiques de Rome. Above the door is one of the most curious items to be found anywhere, a large seven-day calendar clock. Thought to have been made in Philadelphia to Jefferson's design, it is run by Revolutionary War ball weights. On the north wall the weights control the striking of the copper gong on the roof each hour, moving slowly down the wall as the hour is struck. On the opposite wall, where the names of each day of the week except Saturday are indicated at regular intervals, the location of the top weight indicates what day it is and the time of day. Because of lack of space the Saturday mark is in the basement.

No stairway is to be seen from the entrance hall. Jefferson had two identical ones, only twenty-four inches wide, inobtrusively placed in the north and south halls, or "lateral passages," as he called them, that extend from the entrance hall toward the northern and southern ends of the house. The stairways lead to the six rooms on the second floor and four

rooms on the third floor, including the dome room, none of which are open to the public.

The door to Jefferson's Bedroom, in the southern part of the house just off the entrance hall, was seldom opened by anyone other than Jefferson himself when he lived here because inside was his sanctuary, a marvel of light and color and ingenuity. The skylight is as high as the ceilings of the parlor or dining room. The cream-colored walls and beige woodwork provide a neutral background for the draperies and bedspread after his own design. Their color is thought to be close to his idea of "crimson red." All the furniture here is original, including Jefferson's red leather-covered revolving chair which, together with a small table and padded bench, form a kind of chaise lounge that Jefferson assembled to allow him to write in a semi-recumbent position. The small circular Chippendale table with missing feet is the only piece to survive from Shadwell, Jefferson's birthplace. The bed, in an alcove open on both sides, was where Jefferson died July 4, 1826, the same day his long-time friend and sometime opponent, John Adams, died in Quincy, Massachusetts.

On the south side, Jefferson's Bedroom opens onto the library suite "cabinet" which is connected to the book room where Jefferson had six thousand books that eventually became the nucleus of the Library of Congress — the books here now are duplicates. The architect's table is believed to be where he made the plans for the University of Virginia. Beyond the glass doors on the south is the glass-enclosed piazza, called by Jefferson the greenhouse or workshop, that projects from the south side of the house under a full pediment.

Directly to the west of the entrance hall and providing the entrance from the west front portico is the large, unique parlor in the form of a semi-octagon. The squares of the parquet floor are cherry, the border beechwood. Jefferson's family musicales took place here and it also served as his picture gallery. In 1809 forty-eight paintings hung here and five of them, Italian, English and American works, still do.

The door at the north end of the parlor opens into the dining room with its blue walls matching the Wedgwood medallions set in the mantel. The Chippendale dining table, believed to have been a gift to Jefferson from his former law teacher, George Wythe, holds a charming glass epergne surmounted by a fruit basket. Projecting from the north end of the dining room is the cozy semi-octagonal tea room which can be closed off by sliding glass doors. Across the north passage is the north octagonal room, or Madison Room, the only room with wallpaper. The present paper, in a Lattice and Treillage pattern, is the reproduction of the one Jefferson purchased in Paris. Between this room and the entrance hall is the north square room, the only other guest room on the first floor. To the other side of the entrance hall is the south square room, once occupied by Jefferson's daughter and her husband.

Sitting serenely on its mountaintop, Monticello has made Jefferson's words prophetic: "With what majesty do we there ride above the storms!" And triumph over them besides.

Fredericksburg, Virginia
KENMORE

English Manor House by the Rappahannock

When Betty Washington, the "mannerly maid," married her cousin Fielding Lewis, the young widower and gentleman justice from Spotsylvania County, she brought the promise of a dowry of four hundred pounds sterling and two female slaves when she turned eighteen the following year, as well as a tea chest complete with six silver spoons, strainer and tongs, both green tea and Bohea and a sugar box full of sugar "ready broke." She also brought warm ties with her brother George who was the very one to help the couple when they decided to buy land "joyning" to the town of Fredericksburg, on which to build a new home, just two years and two children after their marriage.

Brother George at twenty was a young man of vague formal education but wide experience as a land surveyor and it was he who studied the 861 acres on February 26, 1752, that the Lewises bought for 861 pounds, "Current Money of Virginia," including "Gardens, Meadows, Commons, Pastures, Feedings, Trees . . . and watercourses." Of the area, it was said that "Heaven and earth never agreed better to frame a place for man's habitation." Brother George also helped to select the site for the new home — a gentle green hill sloping down into the Rappahannock River surrounded by a thicket of red, white and black oaks, and gums and hickories.

Work began on the house now known as Kenmore almost immediately, and the design was not unfamiliar to those who knew the English manor houses of the same vintage. Robert Adam's father William had put together a book of Georgian design called *Vitruvius Scoticus* which Fielding Lewis may well have studied. There may even have been an architect named John Ariss called in on the job, the very one who advertised in the *Maryland Gazette* in 1751 that he did "Buildings of all Sorts and Dimensions . . . in the neatest manner . . . either of the Ancient or Modern Order. . . ." Kenmore rose to two stories, and although its exterior is excessively plain, it is a fine example of mid-eighteenth-century Tidewater Virginia architecture. Flanked by dependencies on the north and south, the red brick dwelling is topped by a relatively flat-pitched gable roof with a pair of high chimneys on each end. The brickwork is Flemish bond, with a three-course brick belt defining the second story. Set into the façade are nine windows which are six lights high on the first floor and five on the second, a common characteristic of

Above: Kenmore is a fine example of mid-eighteenth-century Tidewater Virginia architecture. (All photos: Louis H. Frohman) *Opposite:* Nothing in the house surpasses the magnificent plaster relief overmantel in the drawing room which depicts an Aesop fable.

Above: The plaster relief ceiling of the library has plant symbols for the four seasons: palms for spring, grapes for summer, acorns for fall and mistletoe for winter.

Below: The elaborately carved mantel in the dining room has the Washington crest of swan and crown in a design of leafy scrolls.

houses of this period. Delicate rectangular fanlights are placed over the doors on both the east and west sides, while the east or garden side is further distinguished by a charming portico with four white columns.

Kenmore and Mount Vernon, whose mistresses, Sister Lewis and Sister Washington, were on affectionate terms, shared a carpenter and a stucco man. The plaster relief ceilings and overmantels of Kenmore were executed in later years and are called "the glory of the house." Kenmore in all its glory was planted in tobacco, corn and waving grain with cattle grazing in the fields and sheep in the distance. Betty Washington was thought to be the "dearest and best of women, . . . the most majestic looking woman, and so strikingly like the brother, that it was a matter of frolic to throw a cloak around her, and placing a military hat on her head, such was her amazing resemblance that on her appearance battalions would have presented arms and senates risen to do honor to the chief." She ran the plantation with Rachel, the cook, Bill, the house servant and a washerwoman named Hetty. Pompey was the blacksmith and there were ropemakers, a plow boy, a cooper named Scipio and forty-two slaves.

Fielding Lewis was a gentleman of "fortune and character," a land developer (working with his brother-in-law George to cultivate lands in the Shenandoah Valley), and a leader in the industrial development of the town and its surrounding territory. He served in the House of Burgesses and nine years in the Virginian Assembly during the crucial pre-Revolutionary period. In some ways, Fielding is an unsung hero of the American Revolution, for in the end, his devotion to its cause cost him fortune and plantation alike. Lewis was fifty years old at the beginning of the Revolution. He was chief commissioner of the gun factory, carrying out details of military and naval preparation in Fredericksburg. He superintended the building and outfitting of vessels for the navy, supplying saltpeter, sulphur, powder, lead, salt, flour, bacon, and clothes for the cause and, though he did not go into actual battle, he provided for the sick and wounded.

Lewis was considered "a most zealous partisan in behalf of his country," and took "a warm and decided part in opposition to the tyrannical measures of Great Britain." A man of order and of admirable disposition, it was said he "ever stood high" in the affections of George Washington and of his fellow citizens. Unfortunately, the order and happiness of his life were destroyed when the money he had advanced for the building and maintenance of the gun factory shrank his fortune, leaving him at the end of his life a ruined man financially. Bitterly he wrote the treasurer of Virginia, "Can it be expected that the State can be well served when its best friends are used in the manner I have been treated?"

Colonel Fielding Lewis was fifty-six years old when he died in 1781. Within eighteen days after his wife Betty's death sixteen years later, 1,100 acres of Kenmore were sold (the 861 original acres having been added to through the years). It was not until 1930 that devoted citizens of Fredericksburg went to work restoring the Lewis home and acquiring on loan from the Metropolitan Museum of Art superb and appropriate pieces of furniture. In this, the original inventory made in 1782, shortly after Lewis's death, proved an invaluable guide.

The authenticity of the restoration is admirable in detail —
even the ceilings, overmantels, woodwork, floors (except one)
and the color of the walls are all true to the original state.

Portraits of the Lewises are in place and a hunt board
originally owned by Betty's mother Mary, who lived in a small
cottage down the walk from the main house, stands against
one dining room wall. A trunk which belonged to Betty is at
the foot of the canopied Chippendale bed in the Lewises'
bedroom, and her highly prized tea chest is beside the
fireplace in the Mary Washington Bedroom. A gift from her
uncle, Joseph Ball, who wrote, "As soon as you get your chest
you may sit down and drink a Dish of Tea," it was delivered by
Major George Washington.

But it is for its magnificent decorative details, primarily in
plasterwork, that Kenmore is renowned. The plaster relief
ceiling of the library is outstanding with its plant symbols for
the four seasons — palms for spring, grapes for summer,
acorns for fall and mistletoe for winter. The ceiling of the
drawing room is also masterful but perhaps nothing in the
house surpasses the plaster relief overmantel in this room. Its
design — Aesop's fable of the fox and crow — is believed to
have been suggested by George Washington.

The grounds of Kenmore have not been neglected either.
Betty Washington's gardens have been re-created using her
favorite pansies and sweet William, lilacs and phlox and lilies
of the valley, and very possibly they have been made even
more delightful than they were while she was alive and
tending these same gardens.

A trunk which belonged to Betty Lewis
is at the foot of the canopied Chippendale
bed in the Lewises' bedroom.

Richmond, Virginia
WHITE HOUSE OF THE CONFEDERACY

A Rebellious Nation's Executive Mansion

It was only the accident of war that brought the President of the Confederate States to live in the house built by the affluent president of the Bank of Virginia. Jefferson Davis, whose father was a Revolutionary soldier and a friend of Thomas Jefferson, was inaugurated for the second time (the first ceremony took place the year before in Montgomery, Alabama) on February 22, 1862, in Richmond, Virginia, and went to live, with his wife Varina and their four children, in the "old Brockenbrough house" on East Clay Street. The mansion, now called "The White House of the Confederacy," had been designed by Robert Mills, an architect known for his work on the Monumental Church, for Dr. John Brockenbrough. Brockenbrough's one claim to national fame seems to have been his serving jury duty during Aaron Burr's trial in 1807.

Locally, the Doctor, who had no record of practicing medicine, was admired for his courtly manner and his imposing figure, which he wrapped in a sable-lined cloak brought from Russia that hooked together with a gold clasp engraved with his name. Dr. Brockenbrough's house pleased Mrs. Jefferson Davis. She wrote that she "felt at home walking through the old-fashioned terraced gardens or the large airy rooms in the seclusion of family life." The high ceilings, wide windows, curved staircases pleased her, while the Carrara marble mantels had delighted the children who insisted on kissing the

Above: The small front porch of the White House of the Confederacy is original. (Photo: courtesy Confederate Museum)

Left: A large two-story portico on the garden side of the mansion provides a cool place to sit or walk on summer evenings. *Below:* The Carrara mantel in the parlor depicts Aurora bringing the dawn. (All remaining photos: Keller Color, courtesy Confederate Museum)

The elliptical entrance hall has two original black-painted plaster statues representing Comedy and Tragedy.

sculptured faces of Hebe and Diana. Altogether, the Brockenbrough mansion which had been bought by the City of Richmond for $35,000 was a comfortable setting for a relentlessly uncomfortable drama that endured for three years and eight months and ended in tragedy.

Jefferson Davis was a thin, graceful, painfully sensitive man whose coldness and dignity irritated some, but whose "loyalty to his friends was thought to be a 'positive vice.'" Some found Davis a man of "peculiar ability," and a grave, solemn speaker. Taciturn, he did not enjoy talking; "thin-skinned," he lacked the saving evasiveness of a practical politician. Maligned, persecuted, imprisoned and tortured, Davis in the last years of his life was thought to have "sincerely aimed at strengthening and unifying the country." Whatever the consequences, Davis remained true to his beliefs. As he explained to a friend, late in his life, "My father was a revolutionary soldier, and, as you can see by the name he gave me, a friend of Thomas Jefferson, and an adherent to the states' rights doctrine. I grew up in that faith, and could no more conscientiously have abandoned it, than I could have deserted a friend when surrounded by foes."

Davis graduated from the United States Military Academy in 1828, served in the House of Representatives, was chairman of the committee on military affairs for the U.S. Senate, was a defeated candidate for governor and was colonel of the First Mississippi Infantry during the Mexican War. There are historians who think of his four years as Secretary of War under Franklin Pierce as the apogee of his career, a time when he enlarged the army, directed surveys for a railroad to the Pacific and was responsible for improvements at West Point. Davis argued that Congress had no right to deny admission to the Union to any territory because of the existence or nonexistence of slavery, but it was not until the election of Lincoln that Jefferson Davis felt circumstances justified withdrawal from the Union.

Davis, convinced that the South in self-protection had to exercise its right of secession, left the Senate early in 1861, became commander of his own state troops and was unanimously chosen by Congress as provisional President of the Confederate States. He did not order military operations to be opened at Charleston, South Carolina, in April 1861, until he was convinced that the Lincoln administration had sent an armed expedition to revictual and reinforce the garrison at Fort Sumter.

Jefferson Davis's time in Richmond was haunted by war, fire, death in numbers, yet one of his biographers concludes that Davis "was perhaps the only political chief in history who successfully organized a new nation in the course of pursuing a mighty war." As a leader of a new nation there was on one hand the opportunity to entertain one's friends and constituents as well as the absolute necessity of fighting one's enemies. On the one hand, jelly cake, claret and champagne at dinner and after-theatre parties; on the other, the sense of imminent disaster and the belief that parties were "too careless for such

terrible times . . . all out of place in battle-scarred Richmond."
On the one hand, Mrs. Davis dressed in silks, on the other,
prepared for escape, and not having any transportation in one
crucial moment, she and her sister tried to wear as many
clothes as they could manage. Mrs. Davis recalled later that
she piled on "seven petticoats, 3 chemises, 2 pair of stockings
and six pair buckled round her legs by her garter."

By May 1864, there was such an "immense deal of suffering"
that servants walking along the streets were pressed into
nursing the wounded. One year later Richmond was evacuated
and executive officers were removed to Danville, Virginia, and
then to Greensboro, North Carolina, and finally to Charlotte,
South Carolina. Just before capitulation, Mrs. Davis, whose
five-year-old son had fallen to his death from the banister in
the Richmond mansion, and who had recently given birth to a
daughter, wrote of her husband being "in a state of anxiety,
which he does not express" but which she could not "help
feel." Just before the capture Davis wrote this moving note to
his wife: "This is not the fate to which I invited you when the
future was rose-colored to us both." And she answered, "It is

The only furnished bedroom in the mansion
was used by the Davises and contains a
Louis XV-style bed with recessed tester.

surely not the fate to which you invited me in brighter days, but you must remember that you did not invite me to a great Hero's home, but to that of a plain farmer. I have shared all your triumphs, been the *only* beneficiary of them, now I am but claiming the privilege for the first time of being all to you now that these pleasures have passed for me.''

After the fall of Richmond, troops of the Union armies occupied the White House of the Confederacy for five years. Then there were twenty years of the mansion serving as a schoolhouse before it was acquired by the Confederate Memorial Literary Society, who have restored several of the rooms so that they appear as they might have during the occupancy of the Davises. Among their personal possessions are a pair of Dresden vases, a glass wine cooler and some decanters, and a berry bowl and silver egg boiler.

The original house, with stuccoed exteriors and slate roof, was two and a half stories, which included the high basement. Around mid-century a third story was added which disturbs the neoclassical proportions of the house and renders it more Victorian in appearance. Both the small front porch and the large two-story garden portico in back with four pairs of columns are original.

The elliptical entrance hall and the niches there and along the stairway, that ascends from the smaller side hall to the right, resemble similar features in another Mills house in Richmond, the Wickham-Valentine House, built in 1812 and still standing. The seventy-inch-high newel post is a cast-iron replica of the original mahogany one and most of the house's woodwork has been similarly reproduced. The niches on each side of the folding doors, directly across from the front door, contain black-painted plaster statues representing Comedy and Tragedy, which now include light fixtures. The folding doors lead to the large parlor, the middle room of the three principal rooms — dining room, parlor and drawing room — across the garden side of the house, an arrangement also found in the Wickham House. However, the rooms here are better lighted due to the two-story portico which may have been Brockenbrough's idea since he built one on an earlier house. This garden portico, undoubtedly the most magnificent in Richmond, helped to set the fashion for years to come. While the Davises lived here it looked out from the brow of a hill across a terraced garden, and the floor-to-ceiling windows of all three rooms still afford access to the garden portico.

The parlor is the most lavish room in the house and it contains primarily pieces which were used here between 1861 and 1865. The red damask draperies of the huge window complement and emphasize the uncommon ''grayed rose'' color of the walls that duplicates the background shade of the original curtains that hung here. The Carrara marble mantel, believed to be original, depicts Cupid and Psyche on the sides and, on the frieze, Aurora bringing the dawn. The six-piece horsehair-covered set of oval-back chairs and medallion-back sofa are from the house's Civil War period as are the rosewood carved triple-back sofa and the Belter-style chair — examples

The niches along the stairway resemble similar features in the Wickham-Valentine House, another Richmond mansion.

of the rococo revival which dominated the medley of styles found in mid-nineteenth-century America. In the midst of the horsehair set is another rococo piece, a marble-topped walnut card table with extremely incurved cabriole legs.

Although the old dining room is to the east of the parlor, the dining table used by the Davises while they were in Richmond is now in the drawing room, or west parlor. This table is supported by a pedestal and is made of rosewood with maple overlay. It was in this room that President Lincoln conferred with his generals on April 4, 1865, the day after the Confederates evacuated Richmond and five days before Lee surrendered to Grant at Appomattox Courthouse.

The only furnished bedroom is on the west side of the second floor and was used by the Davises. The most impressive piece here is the version of the Louis XV bed with recessed tester and exposed molded cornice, but the only piece from the Civil War period of the house is the huge wardrobe. The remainder of the rooms on the second and third floors contains an outstanding collection of Confederate artifacts and documents, including the sword and uniform worn by Lee when he surrendered the Army of Northern Virginia to Grant. But even these rooms retain something of the Victorian grandeur of the years when Jefferson's and Varina's future had seemed "rose-colored."

Lorton, Virginia
GUNSTON HALL

"A Cottage on the Outside, A Palace Inside"

To visit his friend George Mason at Gunston Hall, George Washington took a four-mile row in a four-oared gig down the Potomac River. Mason, with whom Washington often dined after church services at Pohick and who worked with his brothers Lawrence and Augustine on colonizing the Ohio Valley, had an "impeccably genteel" manner but radical convictions about the rights and opportunities of his fellow men. The gouty, "plump, long-nosed, brown-wigged" statesman, "with eyes at once quick and contemplative," was the "reluctant statesman" only in the sense that he preferred "the happiness of independence and a private station to the troubles and vexation of public business." Though Mason entered the Virginia House of Burgesses with Washington in 1759, he refused, although elected, to serve either in the Continental Congress or as one of the first United States Senators from Virginia. But he was the primary author of the Virginia Declaration of Rights whose opening words, "All men are by nature equally free and independent," helped label Mason as the "pen of the Revolution."

In Mason's case, the pen was mightier not only than the sword, but official office and titles as well. Mason lived comfortably and busily at Gunston Hall, which he began in 1755, helping to build and maintain a striving nation as well as a thriving plantation. Educated largely in the law library of his guardian John Mercer, a gentleman justice of the county court at Fairfax, George Mason wrote the Non-Importation Resolutions in protest against taxation without representation and summarized the grievances of the American colonies

Above: Gunston Hall's unique hexagonal river porch looks out on the eighteenth-century pattern of the restored South Garden. (Photo: courtesy Gunston Hall) *Opposite top:* The Palladian Drawing Room is ornamented with lavish carvings, pilasters and pediments. (Photo: Louis H. Frohman) *Opposite bottom:* The dining room shows a Chinese Chippendale influence in its window carvings and furnishings. (Photo: courtesy Gunston Hall)

Mason drafted the Virginia Declaration of Rights at the small table in the Little Sitting Room. At left is a magnificent Rhode Island desk. (Photos: courtesy Gunston Hall)

against the mother country, after the British had closed the Port of Boston, in a document called the Fairfax Resolves. He also wrote with James Madison the Presidential inaugural oath and headed the committee that designed the Great Seal of Virginia with its motto "Sic Semper Tyrannis" (Ever Thus to Tyrants).

After the Revolution, Mason served as delegate to the Constitutional Convention of 1787, but he refused to sign the Constitution because it did not provide for the abolition of slavery or safeguard sufficiently the rights of the individual. He was bitter that the new Republic did not immediately outlaw the slave trade as "diabolical in itself and disgraceful to mankind." A man of his word and philosophy, Mason, the author of the Non-Importation Resolutions, refused to have a stick of English furniture made after that date of 1769 in any of his rooms at Gunston Hall. Typically, and in meticulous detail, Mason supervised the architecture and the interior of his home as he had the architecture and content of his nation's constitution. The result was a simple, transitional story-and-a-half structure, important on its exterior for its quoins and handsome porches.

"When I built my house I was at pains to measure all the lime and sand as my mortar was made up and always had two beds, one for outside-work . . . one for inside-work." The contents of mortar were "no slight consideration" since mortar was "apt to nourish and harbour those pernicious little vermin the Cockroaches," and Mason had seen brick houses "so infested with these devils that a man had better have lived in a barne. . . ." When the exterior was completed, Gunston Hall was put into the talented hands of William Buckland of Oxford, England, "a complete Master of the Carpenter's & Joiner's Business both in Theory & Practice." It was Buckland with his "tour de force of woodworking," that has "outrivaled any Colonial mansion before or since," that distinguishes Mason's house. Gunston Hall has since been described as a "cottage on the outside, a palace inside."

The Palladian Drawing Room is the most noble room in the house, ornamented with lavish carvings, pilasters and pediments. The silver tea set displayed in this room is one of four ordered by Mason for his daughters from J. Denzilow in 1783. The dining room is definitely under Chinese Chippendale influence, both in its carvings that festoon the windows and rim the ceiling and in the furnishings, though these are American-made. One of the most gracious rooms in the house is also one of the most memorable historically. In what is called the Little Sitting Room, Mason drafted the Virginia Declaration of Rights. A folding ladder, to reach to the top library shelves, was sent by his friend Thomas Jefferson who thought Mason "of the first order of greatness."

George Mason, a statesman's statesman, at his death in 1792 willed his children "on a father's blessing never to let the motives of private interest or ambition induce them to betray, nor the terrors of poverty and disgrace, or the fear of danger or of death, deter them from asserting the liberty of their country." Mason's plantation suffered in the early years of the nineteenth century when tobacco crops lost their value and Gunston Hall grew wheat, raised cattle, operated large fisheries, but was finally put up for sale by the last Mason owners in 1866.

Over the years, Gunston Hall has passed through several hands, among them Colonel Edward Daniels, a Northern officer who had admired the house during the Civil War and bought it in 1872, and Paul Kester, a playwright and author. The last private owners, Mr. and Mrs. Louis Hertle of Chicago, helped to restore Gunston Hall and re-create its gardens and in 1932 deeded the estate to the Commonwealth of Virginia to be managed and supervised by a Board of Regents named from The National Society of the Colonial Dames of America. The Board's attempts to furnish the house as nearly as possible as George Mason would have known it have been difficult because of the absence of an inventory of furnishings. However, through gifts and purchases of original Mason pieces and through the acquisition of furniture made-during Mason's lifetime, the Board has achieved its goal. Posterity is George Mason's chief beneficiary, for in addition to inheriting one of Virginia's finest buildings from him, generations have gained an awareness of the man who valued personal rights in terms of the Union, not of himself alone.

The Masons' bed chamber on the ground floor was the center of domestic activity. Sugar, spices and herbs were kept in one of the cupboards next to the fireplace.

Yorktown, Virginia
MOORE HOUSE

The Revolution Ended Here

Above: The Revolution virtually ended at Moore House with Cornwallis's surrender of his army to Washington. *Opposite above:* The Articles of Capitulation may well have been drafted on the small mahogany tilt-top tea table in the Surrender Room. *Opposite below:* The Family Parlor has a Windsor chair believed to have been in the house in 1781. (Photos: courtesy Colonial National Historical Park)

A simple frame house in Yorktown, Virginia, was the setting for a momentous milestone in American history. Around noontime on Wednesday, October 17, 1781, the British Major General and Marquess, Charles Cornwallis, surrendered his army, a step that marked the beginning of the end of British resistance to the American revolutionaries. A drummer boy carried a flag of truce to General George Washington and a crucial message: "Sir, I propose a cessation of hostilities for 24 hours and that two officers may be appointed by each side, to meet at Mr. Moore's house, to settle terms for the surrender of the posts of York and Gloucester." Washington's reply was a two-hour grant in which the British commander could submit proposals in writing and by 4:30 p.m. Washington, feeling "there would be no great difficulty in arranging the terms," ordered hostilities to be suspended for the night and arrangements made "to digest the terms of surrender into 'form'."

On the afternoon of October 18, Colonel John Laurens, a Swiss-educated officer of Washington's army, wearing a buff and blue uniform, joined by the French officer Vicomte de Noailles in white and gold, waited in the Moore House for the arrival of the red-coated British commissioners and the beginning of the final, wrenching negotiations. Cornwallis had commanded the British forces in South Carolina in 1780 and the next year defeated General Nathanael Greene at Guilford

Pine cupboard in the southwest corner of the dining room came from an eighteenth-century room in Fanshaw-Old Hall, Wakefield, England. (Photo: Country Beautiful)

Court House. When Washington heard that Cornwallis was fortifying Yorktown, he left four thousand men to guard the fort on the Hudson and headed for Virginia. On September 28, the allied army, sailing from the head of the Chesapeake, disembarked near Williamsburg and marched on toward Yorktown. Sixteen thousand strong, they overwhelmed Cornwallis, who abandoned his posts, tried an escape by water which was ruined by a storm and two days later surrendered his army of 7,073 officers and men.

The afternoon that Laurens and de Noailles waited in the Moore House they had no idea that negotiations would last into the night. While basic issues were more or less decided before the meeting, the details were nettlesome. There was friction over the fate of American deserters who had enlisted in the British army, over whether servants who were not soldiers would be allowed to attend to their masters, whether proper hospitalization would be provided for the sick and wounded and whether wagons would be furnished to carry the baggage of the officers "attending on the soldiers, and to surgeons when travelling on account of the sick, attending the hospitals at the public expense." The bargaining lasted deep into the evening and in the end Washington was not pleased with the results. "The business was so procrastinated by those on their side," he said, "that Laurens and de Noailles could do no more than make a 'rough draft' of the Articles under consideration."

The next day, Washington took charge and by the afternoon of the nineteenth, the British had formally surrendered. Among the arrangements agreed on was that the garrison of York would march out "with shouldered arms, colors cased, and drums beating a British or German march." At last the Articles of Capitulation were signed. "Done in the trenches before York Town in Virginia October 19, 1781: G. Washington, Le Comte de Rochambeau, Le Comte de Barras, *en mon nom et celui de* Comte de Grasse." Two years later, the War of Independence was officially and legally terminated by the Treaty of Paris.

Just why Cornwallis suggested the Moore House is not completely clear. It was hardly a heroic setting. A frame house, a story and a half high with a hipped gambrel roof, it may have been chosen because it was back of the American lines, technically not in their encampment area and had not suffered damage during the siege. Besides, it was a convenient distance from town and directly on the river — a place familiar to the British who had covered the ground thoroughly and fought a skirmish near it. It may possibly have been used by the British as temporary quarter, or perhaps Cornwallis preferred that the meeting not take place in Yorktown. Whatever, the Moore plantation is on history's map.

Most architects date the Moore House no later than 1725. It was probably bought by Augustine Moore in 1768 as a going plantation, built originally by Lawrence Smith when he came to live in York. In 1768 Augustine Moore, for 1,250 pounds plus other obligations, contracted for the plantation of five hundred acres. Later, in 1789, it passed on to a series of other owners, went through a traumatic period during the Civil War, when it was "much frequented . . . by the sharpshooters, the orchard beyond offering fair opportunities to advance to the front unobserved. Stealing among the trees, purple with the

The boy's bedroom on the second floor is being
furnished by the Virginia Society of
the Daughters of the American Revolution.
(Photo: courtesy Colonial National Hist. Park)

bloom of the peach, the riflemen would proceed, at the first
glimpse of dawn, while yet the mist hung in the air, to take a
position, they would not have to leave till night extended her
friendly cover."

In later years the "old wooden house" served as a shelter
for transient Negro farmers, survived a Victorian façade, and
in 1931, 150 years after the Siege of Yorktown, the Moore
House acquired a protector, the National Park Service. A true
restoration began and the Moore House was transformed back
into a plantation dwelling of the late colonial and revolutionary periods.

A wide central entrance hall runs the length of the house. In
the family parlor at the rear is a Windsor chair believed to
have been in the house in 1781. At the front of the house in the
dining room are some Moore family pieces, including some
silver and Chinese porcelain plates. Across from this room is
the room known as the Surrender Room, where it is thought
the Articles of Capitulation were drafted. It contains a corner
fireplace and a few other Moore pieces, but its principal feature
is the mahogany American Chippendale tilt-top tea table on
which the commissioners may well have worked.

The Moore House is, in its quiet and comfortable modesty,
an appropriate reminder of another crucial time in the history
of our United States.

185

Loudoun County, Virginia
OAK HILL

Monroe's Palladian Country Seat

James Monroe openly admitted to Thomas Jefferson that "whatever I am at present in the opinion of others, or whatever I may be in future, has greatly arisen from your friendship. My plan of life is now fixed." Monroe was speaking broadly. Jefferson was not only the architect of Monroe's political future but of his dwelling places, first Ash Lawn, near Jefferson's Monticello, and then his splendid retirement home, Oak Hill. Monroe's maternal uncle, Judge Joseph Jones, had wisely advised the twenty-two-year-old graduate of William & Mary to work for Jefferson rather than to follow William Wythe's law lectures. "You do well to cultivate his friendship," Uncle Joseph told his nephew who was to be the nation's fifth President, "and while you continue to deserve his esteem he will not withdraw his countenance."

On the contrary, Jefferson valued his discreet, courteous follower and admirer and thought him a man "whose soul might be turned wrong side outwards without discovering a blemish." When Monroe bought eight hundred acres of land in Charlottesville, he asked Jefferson's assistance in building a "cabin-castle" at Ash Lawn and Jefferson agreed to oversee the construction while Monroe was in Paris. Jefferson was delighted at the prospect of this close neighbor. "I find friendship to be like wine, raw when new, ripened with age, the true old man's milk and restorative cordial."

It was in 1806, when Monroe, at the thrust of his career, was

Above: One of the South's truly great mansions, Oak Hill has massive thirty-foot Doric columns on the south portico. (All photos: Howard Allen)

Opposite top: The comfortable living room is lighted by windows that look out on the large Italian terraced garden.

Opposite bottom: The Zuber "El Dorado" wallpaper in the dining room depicts flora and fauna of the different continents.

Minister to Great Britain and Envoy Extraordinary to Spain, that he inherited from his Uncle Judge Jones the rolling farmlands in Leesburg, Loudoun County, to which he would eventually retire. The bulk of Monroe's work remained between the time he took possession of this tract of land — originally owned by King Carter and sold by George Carter to Monroe's uncle — which Monroe called Oak Hill, and the time he could move into the completed Palladian house in 1823. This imposing dwelling was the handiwork of an extraordinary combination of talents, those of Jefferson and James Hoban, the original architect of the first home of the Presidents of the United States, which came to be known as the White House.

James Monroe — whose father Spence Monroe was apprenticed as a carpenter in the days when "it was possible to be a carpenter and a gentleman at the same time" — grew up on the edge of a neighborhood of sixty thousand-acre estates manned by a hundred Negroes or more, where house parties and balls, horse racing and cockfighting, drinking and hunting kept the great landowners and their families amused. The Monroes' two-storied frame house, "within a stone's throw . . . of a virgin forest," was a simple one that "showed plainly the unskilled art of the craftsmanship of the labor of the period." While the Lees and the Carters dined in formal rooms, the Monroes ate in their living room in which the fireplace was "conspicuous with its pots and pans hanging on cranes over a slow wood fire." While the Carters and Lees, the Masons and the Harrisons were tutored in plantation schoolrooms before, in many cases, going on to study at the English universities, Monroe went off to Parson Campbell's with books under one arm, and a gun slung over the other to be taught by "a disciplinarian of the sternest type," whose pupils "in their various subsequent careers . . . were noted for solidity of character."

None more than James Monroe who was to be admired for his "direct simplicity," his "approachable mien," as a man "unwearied in the pursuit of truth and right, patient of inquiry, patient of contradiction, courteous even in the collision of sentiment, sound in its ultimate judgments, and firm in its final conclusions." Monroe's public service began when he served as second lieutenant in the Third Virginia Army, and ended with his second term in the White House. In the years between he served as a delegate and a U. S. Senator, a diplomat in France, Spain and England, took a leading role in the purchase of Louisiana and Florida, served both as Secretary of State and Secretary of War in James Madison's cabinet and produced the Monroe Doctrine, affirming faith in the American way of life and independence from Europe.

Monroe was fifty-nine at the time of his first inauguration. It was said that "few persons ever knew him intimately who did not love him. There was a downrightness, a manliness, a crystal-like integrity in his conduct, which constantly grew upon his associates." His wife did not fare so affectionately. The former Elizabeth Kortwright, a chronic invalid, "regal and staunch" was "immediately and definitely unpopular" because she rearranged protocol, abandoned first calls on wives of visiting dignitaries and otherwise streamlined White House etiquette. In the end it was said she did outlive her "spasm of unpopularity." Though Monroe was thought to be more at home riding through the countryside than in the formal drawing room, and though the Monroes' dinners were thought

to be "dull," lasting barely later than 9 p.m., their linens were admired and so were the hickory wood fires and for one visitor at least they entertained with elegance, in "French style a little Americanized." Monroe may have preferred simple clothes and simple pursuits but he also had a predilection for fine furnishings and beautiful surroundings. He bought furniture and silverware in Europe for the White House and asked Congress to grant enough money to furnish it "in a style befitting an executive mansion, . . ." and that each article be selected with an idea of "fitness" for the President's home. He defended his purchases as "wise," though the cost was "high."

At the end of the second term the Monroes were at last free to retire to their awesome country seat with its high Doric columns and its sweeping horizons curved with the Blue Ridge Mountains on one side, the Sugar Loaf on the other, to enjoy their two daughters and their families, receive esteemed visitors such as Adams and Lafayette and to brood over

The white marble mantel in the east drawing room is one of two sent by Lafayette to Monroe, his "earliest and best" friend.

The secretary in the west drawing room holds a mug presented to Monroe by the British government at the time of the promulgation of the Monroe Doctrine.

mounting debts. Tragically, for Monroe as for Jefferson and for George Mason, "poverty was the badge of all his honors" and his last years were consumed with efforts to reclaim back expenses, such as money paid to free the Revolutionary pamphleteer Tom Paine from a Paris prison. "It is my wish that all matters of account and claim between my country and myself be settled with that strict regard to justice which is observed in settlements between individuals in private life," he petitioned before Congress.

In 1825, Monroe advertised his estate and slaves at Ash Lawn for sale, along with 3,500 acres, and in 1831, a year after his wife's death, he was forced to transfer his property in Loudoun County to his daughter. "It is very distressing to me to sell my property in Loudoun, for besides parting with all I have in the State, I indulged a hope, if I could retain it, that I might be able occasionally to visit it, and meet my friends . . . there." Monroe moved to New York to live with his daughter and son-in-law, the Postmaster General of New York, and died in 1831.

Presently owned by Mrs. Thomas N. DeLashmutt, Oak Hill has changed somewhat since the Monroes lived here, but this red brick house remains one of the South's truly great mansions. Standing on a hill, surrounded by old trees, including many planted by Monroe — one for each state in the Union — it easily dominates the immediate countryside. The rather plain facade of the north, or entrance, side almost has the look of an urban dwelling, but the impressive, high south portico with customary fanlight beautifully reflects the Greek temple that inspired it, except for the column in the center, clearly a non-classic feature. The massive Doric columns stand thirty feet high.

A pair of chimneys is at each end of the two-and-a-half-story central portion of the mansion, Monroe's original structure. In 1922, the then owner, Frank C. Littleton, enlarged the two wings laterally and vertically, concealing a new second story by setting it back from the outer walls. Pillared porches were added at the end of each extended wing; a small porch on the entrance side was removed; and a large Italian terraced garden was added to the south side below the great portico. Some of the interior woodwork was changed and, in 1949, ornate new trim was installed in the library.

The broad entrance hall — especially graceful with a fanlight the breadth of the double entrance doors flanked by narrow windows — is one room-length deep and intersects a narrower central hall running perpendicular to it. Across the north side of the house are several small rooms, with the pantry at the west end of the horizontal central hall and the master bedroom at the other end. The principal rooms — twin drawing rooms in the center, flanked by the dining and living rooms — have the benefit of the garden view.

Oak Hill has acquired some interesting furnishings with historic association with Washington, Madison, Monroe and Jefferson. The identical white marble mantels sent by Lafayette to his "earliest and best" friend for the handsome twin drawing rooms are in fine repair. The "Roman-style" pilasters support a frieze in the "Grecian style," a flower-and-stem motif centered with a palmette. Beside the fireplace in the west drawing room is a fine highly carved, pierced-slat triple-back settee in the Chippendale style. Set against the lavender walls and white woodwork of these two rooms, are two marble

This Dolley Madison tester bed has its original hangings. The acanthus leaf carving is a typical Regency motif.

busts that belonged to Monroe and a straight-back chair with its original horsehair seat that belonged to George Washington at Mount Vernon. The floor-to-ceiling windows here, with inside paneled shutters, provide a fine view out through the south portico and can be used for passage onto this porch.

The stately dining room, perhaps the most admirable room in the house, has been altered since Monroe's time. Now thirty-four feet in length, it has "El Dorado" wallpaper, made by Zuber in France several decades ago, showing flora and fauna of different continents. The west end of the room is dominated by a large Chippendale breakfront. The dining room is thought to have been used by Monroe as his office and the place where he drafted the Monroe Doctrine. The master bedroom, across from the dining room, is completely furnished in heavy Regency-style pieces which once belonged to James Madison when he lived at his estate, Montpelier, in Orange County, Virginia. The Dolley Madison tester bed, with its original hangings, lacks ornamentation except for the large acanthus leaves — a typical Regency motif — atop the massive footposts and the carved and pierced cresting on the footboard. Another Madison piece is the gold console mirror with marble shelves, in the east drawing room.

One of the few Presidential homes in private possession, Oak Hill is open every second year during Virginia's Historic Garden Week. Sadly, the Era of Good Feelings, appropriately Monroe's era, ended for its author as the era of hardship. But it is heartening to realize that Presidents today receive pensions of $25,000 plus earned civil service retirement fees as well, if for example, they have served in Congress. Meanwhile something of the gracious spirit of our fifth President and his era endures at Oak Hill.

Staunton, Virginia

WOODROW WILSON BIRTHPLACE

A Greek Revival Presbyterian Manse

When Thomas Woodrow Wilson's grandfather came to visit him in the manse of the First Presbyterian Church in Staunton, Virginia, he pronounced the plump and "extraordinarily quiet" baby "dignified enough to be Moderator of the General Assembly." The dignified baby who grew up to be the dignified twenty-eighth President of the United States was the son and grandson of Presbyterian ministers, and the atmosphere of the manse and the church across the yard, and the character of the disciplined and devout people who lived in the gracious columned house for the first year of Tommy Wilson's life molded him forever.

While both parents, Jessie Woodrow and Joseph Ruggles Wilson, were of undeviating Scotch Presbyterian ancestry, they were spectacularly different in appearance and personality. Jessie Wilson was a "sallow, undervitalized woman of thirty" when Tommy was born. She had a "long thin face, a long nose," was silent and solemn. Her father, the Reverend Thomas Woodrow, in pursuit of a livelihood, was the first member of the family to leave Scotland, serving as minister of a church in Carlisle, England, before settling in Brookville, Canada, and then in Chillicothe, Ohio. His wife barely survived the crossing of the ocean so it was Jessie who kept house, raised the other seven children and read the Bible until she married. Though she leaves a pale impression, solemn and dutiful, her son wrote later "I remember how I clung to her (a laughed-at 'mama's boy') 'till I was a great big fellow but love of the best womanhood came to me and entered my heart through those apron strings." There were also sisters — Marion, six years older, and Anne, two years older — and all the Wilson women tended to "coddle" Tommy who was a frail boy with stomach problems that seemed to haunt him always. The Wilsons moved to Georgia a year after he was born.

Wilson's father, it was said, had two great passions, "words and his son Tommy." And in turn, Tommy adored his "incomparable father," admired his face and figure. The Reverend Wilson made word games up with his son, juggling synonyms, similes, phrases, policing his speech and altogether making him a "class of one" for the former Professor of Rhetoric at Jefferson College. It was by training and inheritance, not by accident, that in public office he had wrapped the true heart of the nation in a "spangled shroud of rhetoric." Wilson had practiced in his father's pulpit lecturing to an imaginary congregation on Patrick Henry and Nathanial Webster, and it was in 1874 at Princeton University that he had read about that "Christian statesman," the British Prime Minister William Ewart Gladstone, in the *English Gentleman's Magazine* and decided on the course of his life's work. The article was called "The Orator," and Wilson, who was active in organizing the Liberal Debating Club society at college, wrote

Opposite top: The Greek Revival facade of the Wilson manse reflects quiet stateliness. (All photos: courtesy Va. State Chamber of Commerce) *Opposite bottom:* Victorian garden has been restored to include gazebo, on right, and bow-knot flower beds in boxwood borders.

Deep red brocade drapes and rich oriental rug furnish the otherwise pale-colored front parlor where Jessie Woodrow's guitar rests.

Portrait of Ellen Axson Wilson, once in the White House, now hangs in the spacious upstairs hallway which has original flooring.

an article for the newspaper on oratory stating that "the greatest and truest model for all orators is Demosthenes." His goal settled, Wilson wrote on some of his visiting cards, "Thomas Woodrow Wilson, Senator from Virginia."

Woodrow Wilson, who dropped his first name just about the time he finished studying at the law school of the University of Virginia, did graduate work at Johns Hopkins University, taught at Bryn Mawr College, Wesleyan University and Princeton, and was considered a distinguished historian and political scientist of his day. He was president of Princeton University in 1902 but resigned in a bitter controversy over the construction of a graduate college in 1910. Wilson went on to become Governor of New Jersey, and was elected President in 1912, at a time when the nation's difficult relations with Mexico were overshadowed by the crisis of the outbreak of World War I. During his first term, Wilson fought for a neutral stand on the warring nations. After reelection he hoped to mediate between them but German submarine warfare precipitated his taking a more radical position, and 1917 saw Wilson's decision to enter the war to make the world "safe for democracy." Wilson outlined "Fourteen Points" for peace settlement, worked for a new world society at the Paris Peace Conference and his disappointments over failure to achieve his objectives in the Treaty of Versailles seemed mitigated only by his abiding religious faith that he was "guided by an intelligent power outside himself." He believed in "Divine Providence" he told a friend. "If I did not I would go crazy."

The house in Staunton where the family listened to the Reverend Wilson pray five times daily, where he read the Bible twice during the day and where he led them in hymns at night has been turned into a museum which reflects very specifically the main interests of the Wilson family. The restoration of the house was begun in 1938 when the Woodrow Wilson Birthplace Foundation acquired it. Three years later it was dedicated by President Franklin D. Roosevelt. The street front of this late Greek Revival brick house, built in 1846 by the master builder John Fifer, is a modest one with two small columns and two stories. As with a number of houses in this hilly section of Virginia, however, the slope allows the house an extra story on the garden front, and this has been designed with a stately four-column, two-story porch and garden-level kitchen and dining room.

The interior is perhaps what one would expect of a residence for an earnest Presbyterian minister and his family — honest and comfortable if somewhat austere. A wide central hall runs to the rear of the house and affords a splendid view of the garden. To the left of the entrance is the room where Woodrow Wilson was born and behind it is the nursery. Across from the birth room is the front parlor, probably the most attractive room in the house. The wood mantel and walls are painted a soft gray-green, contrasting with the dark red brocade draperies and the red and beige oriental rug. Jessie Woodrow's guitar and the President's violin are displayed here. Directly behind the front parlor is the rear parlor containing Wilson's graceful drop-leaf mahogany table which he used at Princeton and a velvet tapestry depicting George Washington which he bought in France.

One of the first things one should see is the family Bible in the second-floor study which records the birth: "in Staunton, Virginia on the 28th December 1856, at 12-3/4 o'clock at night, *Thomas Woodrow* and baptized April, 1857 by the Reverend J. D. Smith of Charlottesville." The bookcase here is one Wilson bought with the first money he ever earned by selling a book, *Congressional Government*. The rocker, upholstered in red velvet with mahogany trim, belonged to his father and is in excellent condition.

Both the Little Museum Room, which holds Wilson's roll-top and typewriter desks, and the rear bedroom upstairs provide an excellent view of the garden. The portrait of Ellen Axson Wilson, the first Mrs. Wilson, that hung in the White House now hangs in the spacious upstairs hall. One of the two memorable dresses at Staunton is hers — one designed and made by her to wear during the Princeton presidential festivities. The other dress, owned by the second Mrs. Wilson, Edith Bolling Galt, came from Worth in Paris to wear at parties given at the signing of the peace treaty ending World War I. It was the second Mrs. Wilson who enriched Staunton by donating a number of personal possessions and treasures, including the sample pieces of White House china by Lennox used during Wilson's administration (he was the first President to use American-made china in the White House) and citations from Rome for Wilson's contribution to world peace and from Carlisle, England, his mother's birthplace, making her son an honorary citizen.

One of the most charming aspects of the house in Staunton is the restored Victorian garden where the boxwood has been clipped in a bowknot design, planted with seasonal flowers and laced with brick walks. This in juxtaposition with the simple crib in the nursery and the Pierce Arrow automobile out in back of the garden, one of the White House fleet, seems very succinctly to indicate the scope of Wilson's life. Altogether a sentimental tribute to the man Lincoln Steffens thought "the most perfect example we have produced of the culture which has failed and is dying out."

Mahogany drop-leaf table, with turned, leaf-carved legs tapering to peg feet, was Wilson's. Tapestry depicts George Washington.

When he left the White House, Wilson bought the prized Pierce Arrow vestibule sedan from the government's official fleet.

Brandenburg, Kentucky
BUCKNER HOUSE

Headquarters of a Confederate Raider

"Our little town is still in an uproar. No man or family feels safe in life or property," Robert Buckner wrote in 1862 to his daughter who was at college in Louisville. His letter reflected the imminent disaster of the Civil War and the choice to be made, as well as the price to be paid. "I was yesterday arrested by orders of a tyrant captain with pistols and other weapons . . . and was compeled to take the oath or be sent to Camp Chase and there I would have died, being so old and feeble as I am. . . . This adoo and all our troubles are brought on us by wicked & malicious neighbors claiming to be Union men and I am sorry to say nearly all are members of the Methodist Church."

Colonel Buckner, an officer in the War of 1812, was writing from his home in Brandenburg, Kentucky, one of the busiest ports between Louisville and Owensboro on the Ohio River. Brandenburg had a population of about eight hundred in 1860 and these citizens had set aside $1,000 for building a school on a grant of six thousand acres. The Methodist and Baptist churches flourished, and the small river town prosperously shipped tobacco, corn and hay as well as fruit from the nearly 100,000 acres known as "Fruit Ridge." The apples in this region were said to provide the ingredients for the "finest apple brandy in the world," and the brewing of this liquor was considered a "traditional household art." Brandenburg also claimed grain mills and a textile mill and what was said to be the oldest gas field west of the Alleghenies, first developed in 1858 but not used commercially until thirty years later.

At the crest of Brandenburg's prosperity, in 1855, when many handsome houses rose on the hills of the countryside, the Buckner family bought their twenty-three-year-old house with its sweeping view of the Ohio River and proceeded to remodel it. Retaining its low, rather sleek lines (for those

Above: The Buckner House is built of yellow poplar, a native Kentucky tree, and is hammered together with square nails.
Opposite: Two mahogany-veneer love seats flank the parlor fireplace just as they did a century ago. (All photos: Country Beautiful)

times), they added a west wing, augmenting floor space to include five rooms downstairs and five upstairs. Built of yellow poplar, a native Kentucky tree, hammered together with square nails, and furnished with mahogany veneer-framed settees, it was altogether a genteel and comfortable home for those times in Kentucky. Today, the neat modest two-story house with gable roof and a chimney at either end of the main section gives the appearance of a story and a half. Above a spacious square-columned front porch which reaches the roof line are three dormers, two of them with double six-over-six-light half-windows, the third, a dog-house dormer between the other two, with a handsome fan window. The illusion that the house is a story and a half can best be dispelled by seeing that the second-floor windows on each end of the main section begin substantially below the roof and the dormers. The main part of the house is faced with the same hand-grooved weather boarding it had over a century ago, now painted white. Four large windows in the front façade and three smaller ones in the addition have shutters the same dark shade of green as the clipped shrubbery along the front of the house.

Colonel Buckner was justified in regretting the division in his Brandenburg "parradice." Shortly, his home was to serve as headquarters for the Confederate raider, John Hunt Morgan, who had a cannon set up on Buckner's cherished lawn to protect Marvin's Landing below. Brigadier General Morgan, who had organized the Lexington Rifles in 1857, was a dauntless, controversial ladies' man and military leader, a "thorn to his enemies," not so much for his brilliance as for his courage and ruthless determination and his willingness to shoot, plunder, burn or rob to suit his goals. He was eventually suspended from command over the Mount Sterling bank robbery, and the issue of whether the funds that he and his associates seized were used for private gain or the Confederate cause remains unsettled. Morgan's exploits in Brandenburg make the Buckner House significant, particularly for Civil War buffs.

On July 8, 1863, Morgan rode into Brandenburg, intending to cross the Ohio River into Indiana. He arrived with two thousand men who managed, according to witnesses, to roll three barrels of whiskey out on the sidewalk, "to fill their canteens . . . until soon 150 gallons of high-powered whiskey was well distributed among the men of grey. . . ." A music teacher, Miss Carrie Doyle, noted that one of Morgan's men "climbed on the piano and walked back and forth upon the keys." Morgan himself and his staff rode straight up the west hill of Brandenburg to Colonel Buckner's residence and set up their guns. Shortly, he was bombarded from the Indiana shores by Colonel John Timberlake and his three hundred Union men as well as from a small river gunboat, the *Springfield*, which, "like an angry beauty of the coal pits, sidled a little toward the town, and commenced to scold." The fighting lasted more than an hour before finally the last boatload of "Johnnies invaded the land of 'The Yank'." Morgan ordered two steamers, the *Alice Dean* and the *John B. McCombs,* burned once they had served his purpose of ferrying his raiders across the river.

Though Morgan did succeed in crossing the Ohio River he was closely pursued by the Union forces as he moved north

Opposite: One feature of the house that was not altered during restoration is the circular stairway, a rarity in Kentucky.

A fine Johnson press-on-press and a cherry corner cupboard are among the best pieces in the dining room.

through Indiana. When his men were caught on July 19, most of them surrendered in sheer exhaustion, having ridden fifty to sixty miles a day in hopes of escaping their followers. Morgan dashed on, but when he was encircled in New Lisbon, Ohio, on July 26, he, too, surrendered. Though his raid had destroyed his division and only punished the Federal soldiers slightly, Morgan did save East Tennessee for the Confederacy for several months by preoccupying Union soldiers with his own capture. He was imprisoned in the Ohio State Penitentiary, escaped, and took up headquarters at the home of a Mrs. Catherine Williams in Greenville, Tennessee. It was her Union soldier son who is said to have reported Morgan's presence and to have precipitated his being shot while he walked in his white nightshirt in the wet garden. He fell on his face "into a clump of gooseberry bushes," dead.

The highway marker on the lower end of Main Street in Brandenburg reads "MORGAN — ON TO OHIO" and tells his story succinctly. Another reminder of the drama on the Ohio River is the Buckner residence which was sold to James R. Watts and his wife in October 1953, after the death of Buckner's granddaughter. The house and grounds were in great disrepair at the time, and it took the Wattses nearly ten months to restore the property. They reversed the front and back, making the north, or river side, the back and the street side the entrance. Doors and windows were transferred from the river side to the street side, a porch was substituted for two lean-to rooms, a large kitchen-family room with a river view was added in the back and several pieces of original furniture that had been auctioned were found, bought and returned to their proper place. Two features of the house that the Wattses fortunately did not alter are the wide central hall and a graceful circular stairway, a rarity in Kentucky. The carved woodwork in the hall and throughout the house is painted white, while the floors are of a soft reddish wood thought to be Pennsylvania pine floated down the Ohio and unloaded at the house's landing.

By far the most worthy pieces of furniture in the house are found in the dining room to the left and the parlor to the right of the hall. Both these rooms convey a sense of gentility, even luxury, especially the dining room which has a magnificent mahogany sideboard styled after the Federal furniture of Duncan Phyfe. Four reeded half-posts separate three doors in the lower section, while an extended overhang above holds three drawers. Over the sideboard is an oval mirror with carved gold edging. In the center stands a graceful three-section mahogany table, also in the Duncan Phyfe style, with a crotch mahogany trim around the under edging. The center section has six legs and two drop leaves, while the end sections have four legs and one drop leaf and diagonal corners above the two end legs. The chairs are hand-carved mahogany rose-backs. Also here are a fine Johnson press-on-press, a cherry corner cupboard, and a pale maroon rug that adds a desirable touch of color.

In the parlor across the hall are two mahogany-veneer love seats with bead design and gold velvet upholstery, flanking the fireplace exactly as they did over a century ago when General Morgan sat in them. Also original, the round three-legged rosewood table facing the love seats was cut down from a standard height parlor table to make a coffee table. Behind the love seats, a spool whatnot and a finely worked inlaid bookcase hold Mr. Watts's valuable collection of bisque figurines and early American milk glass, while two Dresden porcelain candelabra decorate the carved white wooden mantel. Three gavels made from the wood of the sunken *Alice Dean* and a dish from the steamer's dining room are mementos of the time before "the Lincolnites" had "the run of several families, . . ." before gentlemen had been "dragged to prisons in Ohio," before Brandenburg and Colonel Robert Buckner's life had been turned into an "uproar."

The mahogany sideboard is styled after the Federal furniture of Duncan Phyfe. The mirror has carved gold edging.

201

Lexington, Kentucky
ASHLAND

Regal Brick Home of Henry Clay

"I had rather be right than be President." Henry Clay's own words poignantly describe his life in politics. Though he was never President, but almost always a strong candidate in all the campaigns between 1824 and 1848, he did succeed in being right, at least a good deal of the time. The self-made Virginian was tall, gray-eyed, his mouth "a long and deep horizontal cut," his voice, the voice "of an actor" (his years reciting aloud in his father's barn hadn't been wasted), and from the age of twenty-two to his death at seventy-five, he importantly influenced the course of a young nation from his platforms in Kentucky and in Washington.

Clay, who had studied law with George Wythe, the teacher of Jefferson and Marshall, after being admitted to the bar, followed his mother and step-father to Versailles, Kentucky, and later to Lexington, where he built his personal fortune and his public reputation with breathtaking efficiency. So pronounced was his success that one colleague considered him "quite a young man — an orator — and a republican of the first fire," while another, considerably less enchanted, said Clay preferred "the fame of popular talents to the steady fame of the bar. . . ."

At twenty-two Clay was elected to a constitutional convention in Kentucky; at twenty-six to the Kentucky legislature; at twenty-nine, under age, he was appointed to an unexpired term in the U.S. Senate. Between 1811 and 1852 he served fourteen years in the House of Representatives and fourteen more in the Senate, his terms in Congress interrupted by four years as Secretary of State in John Quincy Adams's cabinet. Clay fought dramatically for federal financing that would help establish transportation to bind the East and West

Right: The dome-ceilinged library is beautifully paneled in light and dark walnut.

Opposite: The deeply carved cornice of shield and bracket design is found in both the dining and drawing rooms. It is similar to that in the Hall of the Marshalls in the Tuileries.

together, and made an impassioned speech in favor of Greek independence. He worked for sounder domestic banking procedures, for tariffs to build up industries in time of war, and, with John Calhoun, he championed the War of 1812 with Great Britain, asking, "Is the rod of Britain to be forever suspended over our head?"

Clay's position on the subject of slavery brought about the Compromise of 1850 and the controversy over whether Clay was a great humanitarian or a practical politician — or just a timid one. At twenty-two he believed Kentucky's new constitution ought to contain an emancipation clause and he congratulated the South American republics on having abolished slavery. But threats of the Southern states to destroy the Union led him to his precarious position which resulted in "the abolitionists renouncing him as slave-holder, and the slave-holder as an abolitionist. . . ." Lukewarm toward recognizing the independence of Texas because it might increase slave territory, yet torn by the fact that the South was on the point of secession, Clay's Compromise of 1850 admitted California as a free state, organized Utah and New Mexico as territories without reference to the issue of slavery. Clay was known as the "Great Compromiser" probably because he believed that "all legislation, all government, all society is founded upon the principle of mutual concession, politeness, comity, courtesy . . . I bow to you because you bow to me. . . ."

On the subject of his home, however, Clay bowed to no one. He bought his land a mile and a half east of Lexington from where you could view, across the rolling bluegrass meadows, the spire of Christ Church and the cupola of Fayette courthouse. Court records show he made his first purchase on

This bedroom has ash-wood furniture made from trees that grew at Ashland. The handsome wallpaper is "Antique Baroque."

October 11, 1806, paying 1,000 pounds current money of Kentucky for 123 acres, "building up to close to five hundred acres in all, the poor Baptist minister's son evolving into a landed gentleman, a many-acred squire, acquiring more slaves, more stock, and paying with four other men, $5,500 for a race horse named Buzzard." He asked Benjamin Latrobe, the man Jefferson had hired to complete the capitol building, and who would eventually design the naval hero, Stephen Decatur's house, to design part of the home where he lived for forty years. He asked Major Pierre Charles L'Enfant, the French engineer who had served in the Revolutionary War, the planner of Washington, to lay out his own parks and walks.

Clay had married Lucretia Hart in 1799, the cousin of Thomas Hart Benton, a young woman of "good sense," who was "discreet, kind, a good manager and a devoted mother." She was said to be a "thousand times better pleased sitting in the room with all her children round her, and a pile of work by her side, than in the most brilliant drawing room...." and at their parties she "decked" herself out with flowers, drank punch, ate sugar plums and cakes and oranges, and played the piano for them.

Clay's attachment to his children brought him happiness and, in time, great tragedy. One suffered insanity, another, Henry Clay, Jr., was killed in the controversial Mexican War: "If I could derive any consolation from the fall of my beloved son on the bloody field of Buena Vista it would be from the fact that, if he were to die, I know he preferred to meet death on the field of battle, in the service of his country. The consolation would be greater, if I did not believe that this Mexican War was unnecessary and of an aggressive character."

Clay, who admitted he had "always paid peculiar homage to the fickle goddess . . . poker and brag and whist, . . ." whom some considered "no lawyer, and no reasoner," who once danced on a dining table sixty feet long "amidst the loud applause of his companions, and to a crashing accompaniment of shivered glass and china," and a bill for $120, found peace at Ashland. To his son Henry Clay, Jr., he wrote, "I am getting so much attached to the pursuits of my farm — I consider life as so uncertain, and public affairs so full of vexation, that I have become more indifferent than I ever expected to be in regard to public life."

Clay's will, made on July 10, 1851, the year before his death, provided specifically for guidance regarding the Ashland slaves. All children of his slaves born after January 1, 1850, were to become free, the males at twenty-eight, the females at twenty-five. For three years before arrival at the age of freedom they were to receive wages "at the fair value of their services, to defray the expense of transporting them to one of the African colonies. . . ."

After Clay died in 1852, his son James purchased Ashland from the estate. Because the house was deemed unsafe, it was torn down and rebuilt. Completed in 1857, the new building used some of the materials of the old and largely followed its plan, although some details were altered. Window headings were arched, quoins were added at the corner and cornices made heavier. Clay's great-granddaughter Nanette McDowell Bullock left part of her estate to the Henry Clay Memorial Foundation, so that it could buy this regal house and open it to the public in 1950. Today Ashland stands on twenty acres, its balanced proportions intact, its red brick covered with vines.

The central two-story structure with gable roof is flanked by a single-story wing on each side. The central entrance consists of a projecting bay with colonetted doorway and fanlight and a tall, triple-sashed window on each side. The end pavilion of each wing projects forward to slightly beyond the line of the entrance bay. The triple-arched front window of each pavilion has a little wrought-iron balcony which echoes a somewhat larger balcony in front of the attractive Palladian window above the entrance bay.

Inside, the décor is typically Victorian although perhaps more tastefully restrained than usual. The octagonal-shaped entrance hall, with ash woodwork, creates a rather majestic feeling. To the left is the parlor dominated by the pink onyx mantel, one of Ashland's eleven Italian carved marble mantels; to the right the staircase hall. Straight ahead are entrances to the mansion's two most elaborate and impressive rooms: the drawing room on the left, the octagonal-shaped dining room on the right. The long dining table is made up of separate tables which belonged to Ann Clay McDowell, Clay's granddaughter, and which are fitted together. The table is placed lengthwise in the room so that one end of it faces out the large window overlooking the broad terrace in back, added when the house was rebuilt. The hangings at this window are handsome dark red velvet curtains with gold trim that were stored in Ashland's attic for forty years and rehung when Ashland was opened to the public. Perhaps the principal feature of this room, as well as of the drawing room, is the ornate, deeply carved cornice of shield and bracket design, similar to that in the Hall of the Marshalls in the Tuileries. It gives a sense of the Napoleonic revival but not of being done by a French hand. Worthy of attention is a charming silver service, a wedding gift to Ann McDowell, depicting tea leaves on the teapot, coffee beans on the coffee pot and sugar cane on the sugar bowl.

The drawing room is directly accessible from the dining room through a wide arched opening with sliding doors and handsomely molded woodwork. Gold dominates this spacious room. The two pairs of gold brocatelle draperies were brought by Clay from Lyons, France, in 1814, after he had signed the Treaty of Ghent ending the War of 1812. Several pieces of the furniture are upholstered with gold-color materials, including the gold Empire Madame Recamier sofa, also imported from France by Clay in 1814. The involved carving on the keystone of the Carrara marble mantel depicts the four seasons, with the bird of spring preeminent. Off the drawing room is the dome-ceilinged library, beautifully paneled in light and dark walnut. After dinner Clay would frequently retire to this room with a guest to play a game of chess on the round, pedestal-based Renaissance gaming table that had been a gift to him while in France. The skirt has plain carved medallions and

Clay's rose-colored conversation chair and the Louis XV architectural bed are two significant pieces in the colorful family bedroom.

acorn pendant finials. The four slender, turned columns have four supports with cyma-scrolled feet. A portrait of Clay by Matthew Jouett, a Kentucky artist, hangs here.

The upstairs hall is furnished with a Belter love seat and chairs and the Palladian window is hung with deep rose-colored velvet draperies and Swiss embroidered lace curtains. There are five bedrooms. The family bedroom — a colorful chamber with red and white patterned carpet and green and gold figured wallpaper — has Clay's conversation chair, another room his fire screen. A third contains ash-wood furniture made from trees that grew at Ashland. But the Henry Clay Bedroom is the treasure trove of Clay items, with the silk quilt made for him by the "ladies of Philadelphia" in 1844, his well-worn deerskin trunk which he used on his stagecoach trip between Washington and Lexington and the coat he wore when he signed the Treaty of Ghent, along with a hat box he used.

It was these things at Ashland and the innumerable intangible pleasures connected with them that held Clay there for forty years and caused him to say, "After all that I have seen, Kentucky is still my favorite country. There, amidst my dear family, I shall find happiness in a degree to be met nowhere else."

Hermitage, Tennessee
THE HERMITAGE

Jackson's Pillared Mansion

Andrew Jackson, "wide-awake" and "not scared with trifles," "prompt, frank, ardent" to some, was a "most uncivilized unchristian man" to others. He was, for the record, district attorney, a judge, senator, duelist, shot, major general and military governor of the Territory of Florida (owned by the Spanish but used by the British), advisor in the framing of the Constitution of Tennessee, irreconcilable opponent of George Washington, and defender of Aaron Burr, and seventh President of the United States. He was also a leader of a "middle-class democracy" and an extensive landowner who acquired "large tracts when large tracts could be bought for a horse or a cow bell, and held them till the torrent of emigration made them valuable." What he was *not* was "a plain cultivator of the soil," which was what he called himself; nor could he label, accurately anyway, his pillared mansion The Hermitage, "just a farm," which he did.

Jackson changed homes six times, the last three being Poplar Grove, Hunter's Hill, and finally, in 1801, a tract of 650 acres of fertile and rolling land approximately twelve miles from Nashville, bought for $800 a square mile. This was The Hermitage, from whose vantage point he was to spend his last twenty-five years enjoying the life "of a country gentleman and first member of his society." "The man of the people" was definitely a man of affairs. He operated a cotton gin, had an "occasional fling at the highly lucrative business of slave trading," bred and raced horses. His ownership of the remarkable horse named Truxton made Jackson a leader of the turf "for some years."

A two-story block house, one of a number of cabins, was General Jackson's first dwelling on Hermitage farm. The mansion was not built until 1819. Jackson was said to have been "abundantly" satisfied with this little group of houses, and that he built the Hermitage mansion "solely as a testimonial of his regard for his wife." Jackson's wife Rachel Donelson Robards, "the best story-teller, the best dancer, the sprightliest companion, the most dashing horsewoman in the western country," was a divorcée whose mother-in-law had sided with her when her husband Lewis Robards had sued her for adultery. Jackson and Rachel Robards had married in the

Above: The front portico of The Hermitage is supported by six fluted columns with cast-iron capitals. *Opposite:* The entrance hall wallpaper depicts Telemachus landing on the island of Calypso during his travels in search of his father Ulysses. (All photos: courtesy Ladies' Hermitage Association)

The two elaborately carved mahogany chairs in the front parlor were a gift from the Khedive of Egypt to President Jackson.

summer of 1791 and learned in December 1793 that due to a legal oversight, the divorce had not been granted. At the suggestion of Jackson's devoted friend Judge John Overton, "so as to prevent all future caviling on the subject," the couple was remarried in January 1794, and lived together in a marriage that was "one of the very happiest ever contracted." Jackson, however, was touchy about his marriage. His temper, with regard to other causes of offense, was tinder; with respect to this, it was gunpowder. On the other hand, he remained Mr. Jackson, never "General," and she was either Mrs. Jackson or "wife" and together they made an outsider feel "not a guest merely, but a *family*." "Put down in your book," said a neighbor, "that the general was the prince of hospitality; not because he entertained a great many people; but because the poor, belated peddlar was as welcome as the President of the United States, and made so much at his ease that he felt as though he had got home."

Jackson's advice to his ward, Andrew J. Hutchins, reflects his own thoughts on wifely qualifications. "Seek a wife, one who will aid you in your exertions in making a competency and will take care of it when made, for you will find it easier to spend two thousand dollars than to make five hundred." Jackson was speaking from heartfelt experience because his wife made his home a contented one. She was short and stout while the general was tall and slender, and though she spelled badly and her grammar was poor, her anecdotes were vivid and firsthand — she could remember her father and his friend Daniel Boone's escapes and attacks by Indians. And it was said the sight of the couple dancing a reel together "would shake to pieces the frequenters of modern ball-rooms."

Rachel died in 1828, leaving a heartbroken husband but a successful candidate for Presidential office, defeating John Quincy Adams with the help of his "Let the People Rule" slogan. When Jackson arrived in Washington it was half expected by some that he would be carrying a "tomahawk and a scalping knife between his teeth." What they failed to realize was that his personal tastes ran to hand-printed wallpapers from Paris, and that he could place an order of $1,500 worth of cut glass for his private collection.

Meanwhile, Jackson was adding to The Hermitage — the wings, in 1831, and a new, detached kitchen, a smokehouse and a tomb. Radically damaged by fire in 1834, the roof and much of the interior were rebuilt at the cost of $6,500. This time the proportions were more spacious and Sarah, the wife of his adopted son Andrew Jackson, Jr., who served as hostess both at the White House and at The Hermitage, was sent off to Philadelphia to buy $2,203.77 worth of furniture from seven different stores. Sarah was free to choose as she liked, bearing one thing in mind: The bedposts were to be plain "to make cleaning a simpler matter."

The general died in 1845, and by 1856, Andrew, Jr., had sold five hundred acres worth for $48,000. His widow and her sister lived on, and of their collective sons who joined the Confederate Army, only one, Colonel Andrew Jackson III, survived. Together along with Andrew IV they are buried in the Hermitage garden, along with the general and his wife.

Because of the devotion of the Ladies' Hermitage Associ-

For thirty years the Hermitage library was, according to some, "the political center of the United States."

James Monroe, Martin Van Buren and James K. Polk are among the Presidents who have dined at this table. The silver tray was given to Jackson by Sam Houston.

ation, Hermitage's 625 acres are now operated as a grass and beef cattle farm. The cedars the general helped to plant line the curved driveway planned by his friend, the painter Ralph W.E. Earl. Virtually all the furnishings are original although they have had a worrisome time, having traveled to Cincinnati and eventually back.

The front portico is supported by six fluted columns with cast-iron capitals. The entrance hall wallpaper was printed by duFour in Paris and the twenty-five strips represent the legend of the landing of Telemachus on the island of Calypso during his travels in search of his father Ulysses. They were ordered by Jackson in 1835, and the mahogany sofas, Brussels stair carpet, pier table and graceful chandelier are its fitting companions. The front parlor is a classic of its time, furnished with an Italian marble mantel, gilded overmantel, a Japanese clock inlaid with enamel, an autograph album inlaid with mother-of-pearl and a mahogany whatnot. The two elaborately carved mahogany chairs were a gift from the Khedive of Egypt to Jackson when he was President. The lace curtains are reproductions of the originals made by Salmon Frères of Paris, and the lavish crimson brocatel draperies, so typical of affluent Victorian times, are exact reproductions by Scalamandré of the originals. Jackson was painted by several renowned artists of his day and there are three portraits in this room, one by Ralph Earl and another by G.P.A. Healy, who was commissioned to do the portrait by Louis Philippe. Another version of this is in the Louvre.

The back parlor, furnished in similar style, has two special mementos — a mahogany center table, the only piece remaining of the set presented to General and Mrs. Jackson when they visited New Orleans after the battle there which made Jackson a national hero, and a clock which is one of the few relics at The Hermitage that was there while Mrs. Jackson was still alive.

Jackson's ground-floor bedroom is just as it was the day he died in its canopy bed. Personal items include his tobacco box, leather hat box, hair and clothes brushes with a strawberry

design on the back and a French china teapot or *veilleuse* with a place for a candle at the bottom.

But perhaps the room that is most expressive of the interests of Jackson is his office, or library, as it is also called. For thirty years it was, according to some, the "political center of the United States." It certainly was a center of Democratic Party affairs and it does have an air of successful business taking place, and of Jackson being there in fact as well as spirit. His bust by Hiram Powers is an honest piece of sculpture, his portrait astride the white horse Sam Patch was presented to Jackson by the citizens of Pennsylvania. Jackson's bound copies of the *Globe Democrat*, published at Washington, D.C., while he was President, are invaluable as are the other bound newspapers of Jackson's time.

Hermitage includes a most special guest room on the second floor, the Brides' Room where relatives and friends spent their honeymoons. It is filled with special private delights such as the handwoven bedspread and the silk quilt made by the granddaughter of Jackson's neighbor, Josiah Nichol. If the library is the most politically significant room, the dining room on the second floor is certainly the most historical — intangibly anyway — having seated at one time Presidents from James Monroe to James Polk to Franklin D. Roosevelt, ten in all, at least, and other honored men such as General Sam Houston and the Marquis de Lafayette, who, judging from the extent of his travels and his social life, must have been the most popular extra man of his time.

Altogether, The Hermitage is an affectionate tribute to an ornery statesman and prosperous planter and decidedly refutes Jackson's claim of being "just a farm."

Above: General Jackson's ground-floor bedroom is just as it was the day he died in its bed. The bed hangings and draperies are exact reproductions of those used originally.

Below: A most special guest room on the second floor is the Brides' Room, where relatives and friends spent their honeymoons.

New Bern, North Carolina
TRYON PALACE

Monument to a Governor's Vanity

When the two shrewd Swiss adventurers, Christopher de-Graffenried and Ludwig Mitchell, also known as Lewis Mitchess, were engaged by the Canton of Bern to find a tract of land in the "English America," it was widely believed that North Carolina was an auspicious investment. The Swiss needed to find a republic where some of their people might settle since their own tiny country was bursting with refugees, with Protestants persecuted during the Reformation, with Huguenots escaping from France after the revocation of the Edict of Nantes, with the Dutch fleeing the Spanish in the Netherlands. At one point it seemed as though every well-to-do family in the Canton of Zurich quartered one or more of the homeless by order of their government. When deGraffenried did manage to buy a large body of land in North Carolina, he was made a Baron, and for the sum of five and a half pounds each person, offered to arrange transportation from England, not only for the Swiss, but for German Palatines. The new settlers landed in Virginia and then traveled by land across the south to settle on a "tongue" of land between the Neuse and Trent rivers. It was here they soon founded the small city of New Bern, a name that might have been especially consoling to the new Swiss-Americans.

In the swift eighteen months after their arrival around 1710, the Swiss managed to build their homes, set up wheelworks on the brooklets, to construct a water mill, in fact, to make "more progress in that length of time than the English inhabitants made in several years." There were Indian massacres to cope

Above: Tryon Palace was described as the continent's finest government house when completed in 1770. *Opposite:* The lavish State Dining Room includes an Adam-Chippendale three-part dining table and Turkish carpet. (All photos: courtesy Tryon Palace)

Early portrait by Gainsborough (far wall) and architectural seascape by Claude Lorrain over mantel enhance the library.

with and with them, repeated destruction, but still, by November 1723, New Bern, the second town to be established in North Carolina, was declared a township, covering 250 acres, and soon made its capital. By 1766 the American colonial governor sought quarters suitable to his eminent position which to William Tryon, or at least to his wife, a wealthy Londoner named Margaret Wake, meant nothing short of a palace. Tryon had been commissioned a lieutenant of the first regiment of footguards and in 1757 he was promoted to a captaincy with the army rank of lieutenant colonel. Tryon's appointment as Lieutenant Governor of North Carolina under Governor Arthur Dobbs (and his succession on Dobbs' death) may have been the result of Tryon's wife's connections: Wills Hill, Margaret Wake Tryon's cousin, later Earl of Hillsborough, was first commissioner of trade and plantations, a helpful position, as one historian suggests.

Whether it was family connections or whatever, the Tryons had certain standards in mind for their new house. Despite the lack of funds it was thought that, "Policy, perserverance, cajolery, covert threats . . . finally secured, in two separate sums, 15,000 pounds from a province scarcely able to raise the ordinary expenses of government." By 1767, with "heavy and intolerable taxation," a square of six acres was condemned and selected, bounded by Eden, Metcalf and Pollock streets and the Trent River. Bricks were imported from England, John Hawks, an English "master builder," was hired as architect for the sum of 300 pounds and a contract was signed on January 9, 1767, to build what was called "the palace." It was finished in December 1770. It had cost $80,000 and Tryon was charged with "gratifying his vanity," with building an "elegant monument of his taste and political influence at the expense of the interest of the province, and of his personal honor, in changing the plan of a province-house to that of a Palace."

The palace was two stories high, connected by colonnades to separate buildings, on the right a stable, on the left a kitchen and servants' hall. Tryon did not have long to enjoy his palace. He had some years earlier refused to allow meetings of the colonial assembly to take place, thereby preventing North Carolina from sending representatives to the Stamp Act Congress in 1765, and with the support of a certain law-abiding element, he had suppressed the Regulator uprising provoked partly by excessive taxation. Six months after the completion of the palace, in June 1771, Tryon was transferred to New York to act as governor, nominally at least, though his actual authority did not extend beyond the British lines. In 1777 he became commander of a troop of loyalists and in 1779 invaded Connecticut and burned Fairfield and Norwalk. By 1780 he was home in England.

Tryon's palace outlasted its builder, who died in 1788, by ten years only. By 1792 it was "much out of repair" and one of its halls was used for a school and another for a dancing room, and Washington's horses occupied the stable at one point. By 1798 the main building was gone, burnt to ashes.

The present and splendid reincarnation of Tryon Palace is the product of loving dedication, scholarship and a generous fortune. The Tryon Palace Commission, a state agency, has supervised the restoration from original drawings, and the sum of $3,500,000 was supplied by the late Mrs. James Edwin Latham as a memorial to her son Edward who died at Fort

GEORGIVS III REX

CARLOTTA REGINA

The old Siena marble mantel in the
Council Chamber is flanked by portraits of
King George III and Queen Charlotte.

Thomas, Kentucky, in 1918, while serving in World War I. Aided by an inventory Governor Tryon drafted and the fifty-four exquisite English antiques Mrs. Latham donated to the state before her death in 1951, Tryon Palace has become a treasury of peerless English and American antiques.

The beautifully landscaped grounds around the palace have several gardens elegantly designed in the eighteenth-century English manner, along with two, two-story dependencies, connected with the palace by a series of curved colonnades, and five garden buildings, also in eighteenth-century style. The approach to the palace is as impressive as any in the nation, through stately wrought-iron and gilt gates, taken from a 1741 London house, up a broad, tree-lined walkway to an inner wrought-iron and wooden gate with brick pillars and sentry boxes, opening into the spacious entrance courtyard with oval walk, the dependencies at each end and the palace directly ahead. This two-story red brick structure has a hipped roof with four chimneys and an eaves parapet extending from both sides of the white-painted pavilion pediment featuring a huge carving in color and gilt of George III's royal coat of arms above the main entrance. There is a brick pediment on

The parlor features suite of George II carved mahogany chairs and card table by royal cabinetmaker William Vile.

the waterfront side.

The entrance hall has an inlaid marble floor in a geometric pattern and the four marble statues in the wall niches represent continents. To the left is the striking library paneled in ochre-grained wood, matching the color of the paint on artifacts found in the palace ruins. The early Spanish Savonnerie rug depicts the rampant lion of León. The draperies are Genoese silk-cut velvet in a range of shades from apricot to wine red. At the mahogany desk, circa 1760, is a rare roundabout chair inlaid with bone.

The largest room is the Council Chamber, which was also used as the ballroom, accessible from the library or the staircase hall immediately beyond the entrance hall. Beneath two superb cut-glass chandeliers, this grand and colorful room has a seventeenth-century Isphahan carpet and a stately old Siena marble mantel flanked by large portraits of George III and Queen Charlotte. Under the portraits are eight George II side chairs such as might have been used when a ball was held here. At one end of the room, under a portrait of George I, is a fine Gothic Chippendale table. Between the windows hung with eighteenth-century red silk damask are a pair of pier glasses made about 1720 by the renowned John Gumley. In the center of the room is the almost throne-like governor's master chair at a Chippendale table-desk. To provide for council members there are a pair of Townsend-Goddard mahogany drop-leaf tables surrounded by twelve Gothic Chippendale elbow chairs.

At the rear of the house, between the Council Chamber and parlor, is the State Dining Room, second only to the Council Chamber in lavishness. The grayish-green dado and white

walls and ceiling provide the ideal background for the brightly colored 1770 Turkish Savonnerie carpet of English-strapwork design and the blue-veined marble fireplace surround, surmounted by a painted, Adam-style frieze with carved swags and ribbons. Above, within a gold-outlined and crossetted panel, is a portrait of Mary, Queen of Scots. One of the glories of the room is the eight-branched English cut-glass chandelier, circa 1740, that hangs above the Adam-Chippendale mahogany three-part dining table with a silver epergne centerpiece made in London in 1751. The parlor features a suite of George II mahogany chairs covered with Soho tapestry; a card table by William Vile, a prominent cabinetmaker to George III; a mirror with Chinoiserie painting on glass; and a handsome silver kettle and stand, made about 1734.

According to English custom, the family quarters were on the second floor, and the outstanding rooms here are the drawing and supper rooms. The latter is dominated by a great Chinoiserie mirror above the needlework sofa, while the drawing room contains a number of choice items from the Latham collection: a pair of inlaid hare and fruitwood tables surmounted by carved and gilt Chippendale mirrors, a Chippendale mahogany secretary and a pair of Raeburn open-arm chairs. The Alcove Bedroom and Mrs. Tryon's dressing room have appropriately feminine colors with soft pink, Wedgwood blue and white predominant.

The elegant style and the beauty of these rooms reflect a sovereign regard for grandeur. One of the mottos on the elaborately carved and emblazoned royal coat of arms over the entrance door seems to set the mood: *Dieu et mon doit*, "God and my right."

Clemson, South Carolina
FORT HILL

John Calhoun's Porticoed Mansion

Fort Hill and the surrounding 1,100-acre plantation, which John Caldwell Calhoun purchased in 1825 while Vice President, witnessed internal battles possibly as fierce as any Calhoun fought in Washington, D.C., over his doctrine of states' rights. The original four-room portion had been built about 1803 by the Reverend James McElhenny and was called Clergy Hall. Calhoun named it Fort Hill because during the American Revolution it had been the site of a small fort.

Calhoun, who had studied law at Litchfield, Connecticut, was six feet two inches tall, with a mass of springy dark hair "which seemed to rear almost erect when the fire was in him," and was said to be a "lion even in the neighborhood of his own house." Born in Abbeville, on the South Carolina frontier, in the first frame house in Long Cane Settlement, he was taught by his father, a Scotch-Irishman from Donegal who became a

surveyor, legislator and county judge, that life was a "struggle against evil." A member of what was sometimes called the "frontier farming class," at twenty-nine Calhoun married a cousin, wealthy Floride Bonneau, ten years his junior, with more aristocratic family claims. Floride was a beautiful and provocative young woman who, with the obvious exception of Mary Todd Lincoln, could be rated the most baffling and stormy figure among all the wives of America's historical figures.

The battles at Fort Hill were due primarily to Floride's obsessive desire endlessly to "improve" the mansion — whether because she hated being left behind to raise her seven children while her husband was serving as Vice President, then U.S. Senator, then Secretary of State, or whether out of boredom or simply because she enjoyed designing new rooms, remains a mystery. The legend was that every time Calhoun went to Washington, Floride added a room, that carpenters hammered and shingled for more than twenty years, much to her husband's consternation. In time, Fort Hill evolved from an "overgrown farmhouse with little architectural distinction," to a many-winged, many-columned mansion of fourteen rooms.

There were other intimations of personal skirmishes at Fort Hill. Calhoun took great pleasure in his precisely designed garden which Floride willfully proceeded to rearrange, replanting the entire area with the help of servants while her husband slept. There is a dented silver pitcher, talk of shattered family china, talk of a note Calhoun had to write, petitioning for admittance to his plantation office which he had been locked out of by Floride. The engagement of a house-

Opposite: Fort Hill has a central entrance portico supported by four Doric columns and two-story porches with similar columns on the east and south. (Photo: Dean Stone) *Above:* The brass floor candelabra on either side of the English spinet in the parlor came from Dumbarton Oaks, Calhoun's Washington home. (Photo: Country Beautiful)

Perhaps the mansion's most gracious room is the State Dining Room, furnished with a Duncan Phyfe mahogany table. (Photo: Dean Stone)

keeper Calhoun thought a "happy change." After a feud between Floride and her son Andrew had been resolved, Calhoun wrote his daughter, "I trust the former unpleasant state of things has passed, not to return, and wish to see harmony all around."

Calhoun, who spent hours in solitary thought, had "an imperfect acquaintance with human nature" and was "baffled by those inferior to himself." A complicated personality, "a genius who made demands," Calhoun scorned doctors and medicine and, when he was well past sixty, he took three- or four-mile daily walks in the heat of Washington. He was said to have the "grace of a younger man," and a "courtesy that might have come from generations of old aristocracy." In fact, one political opponent complained that he had been treated with such kindness, consideration and courtesy by Calhoun that he "could not hate him as much as I wanted to do."

Calhoun entered Congress when Henry Clay was Speaker of the House of Representatives; historians claim "no two members were more influential in precipitating the War of 1812." Calhoun, Secretary of War in James Monroe's cabinet, in 1817, was twice elected Vice President, first under John Quincy Adams, and, in 1828, under Andrew Jackson, but he resigned to serve in the Senate. Calhoun declined to be a candidate for the Presidency in 1844, but did serve as Secretary of State that year under President Tyler. After Tyler left office he returned to the Senate until his death in 1850. Calhoun, an ardent critic of Jackson, attacked the spoils system and opposed the removal of Government deposits from the United States Bank and believed that the Government, under the Constitution, should prevent any interference with slavery in the territories. Kindly to his own slaves, he was a staunch believer in "states' rights" on behalf of the conservative slave-holding interests of the South.

A man of "stainless integrity," a Spartan in an age of heavy eating and drinking, whose one indulgence seems to have been snuff ("When Calhoun took snuff," it was said, "South Carolina sneezed."), Calhoun took his greatest pleasure in Fort Hill, even with all the problems it caused him. "After all," he told a friend, "there is no life like a farmer's life, and no pursuit like that of agriculture." He planted figs, melons, pear trees, mulberries, tried cattle breeding, crossing a dark, red, humpbacked "sacred cow" to the swamp cattle of the marshlands. He was said to have been the first to successfully attempt a grape culture in his part of the country, and he experimented with silkworms, subjecting his family to an invasion of cocoons that dropped "unheralded from the shelves of every closet, barn, storehouse, and outbuilding on the plantation," resulting in three silk suits for Calhoun.

John Calhoun died in Washington in 1850 and thirty-three years later his son-in-law, Thomas Green Clemson, declared his wish to establish a "scientific institution upon the Fort Hill place, ..." Today, that institution is known as Clemson University. The fourteen-room, two-story white frame house with a gable roof has a large central entrance portico supported by four Doric columns and two-story porches with similar columns on the east and south. It is maintained by Clemson University and the South Carolina Division of United Daughters of the Confederacy with faithful attention to its

A svelte Duncan Phyfe-style sofa in the parlor has an elaborately carved black mahogany frame upholstered in horsehair. (Photo: courtesy Clemson University)

The four-poster bed in the master bedroom is thought to have been used by Lafayette when he visited the Calhouns at Dumbarton Oaks. (Photos: courtesy Clemson University)

furnishings, including several pieces with special fascination for historians. The garden provides an attractive background for the plantation house and the surrounding English boxwoods, holly trees and tulip poplars are remarkable in their size.

Calhoun's desk, pier table and banjo clock are in the central hall and to the left of the entrance door is the large State Dining Room, perhaps the mansion's most gracious room. Furnished with a Duncan Phyfe African mahogany table with twelve matching chairs, Calhoun silver in a fiddle-thread colonial pattern and a steel engraving of Calhoun himself over the mantle, the dining room has gold velveteen drapes, complemented by the russet-brown figured wallpaper. The staunch sideboard was a present from Clay to Calhoun after Calhoun had spoken in defense of the Constitution of the United States. It was made from the mahogany that paneled the officers' quarters of the old frigate *Constitution* after it was condemned as unseaworthy and partially dismantled and before Oliver Wendell Holmes wrote the poem "Old Ironsides" which helped to save the vessel from being totally demolished.

Across the hall are the smaller, pine-paneled family dining room, the only paneled room in Fort Hill, and a bedroom. The mahogany sideboard in the family dining room holds a pair of knife boxes elaborately inlaid with satinwood, and one wall of this room is taken up with glass-enclosed cabinets containing mementos of the Calhoun and Clemson families, such as the Japanese dagger in carved ivory case which the Emperor of Japan gave Calhoun while he was Secretary of State.

A side hall, entered from the high-columned porch on the east ell, leads past the parlor, the scene of many memorable festivities over the years, including the wedding of Anna

Marie Calhoun and Thomas Green Clemson in 1838 which attracted national interest. Thomas Clemson's sister had married George Washington's nephew Samuel, and two pieces of furniture he had inherited from Mount Vernon stand in the Fort Hill parlor — a wood chair and a svelte Duncan Phyfe-style sofa with elaborately carved black mahogany frame upholstered in black horsehair. The parlor also includes a small English spinet that is a memento of Mrs. Calhoun's girlhood and a carved chair and footstool covered in crimson velvet, presented to Thomas Clemson by King Leopold I of Belgium. An autographed copy of the song, "Hills of Home," lies on the piano — its lyrics were written by Calhoun's great-granddaughter Floride.

The eight bedrooms in the house have an astonishing variety of furnishings, including a Napoleonic bed Clemson brought from Europe, a maple pineapple-design bed with handwoven coverlet, Clemson's own seven-foot walnut bed which was necessary to accommodate his six-foot-six-inch height and, in the master bedroom, the heavy-posted mahogany tester bed thought to have been used by Lafayette in 1825 when he visited the Calhouns at their home in Washington, D.C., Dumbarton Oaks.

Calhoun's efforts to prevent the South from seceding from the Union and to make peace between the opposing forces, were crystalized in a speech he was too ill to make. Read by another, it was said to have postponed the Civil War. Today, Calhoun is honored for his attempted peacemaking in North and South alike: Yale's Calhoun College is named for the statesman who entered the university as a junior and graduated with honors in 1804, and Clemson University's Fort Hill is his other loyally maintained memorial.

The kitchen's massive fireplace and Dutch oven holds heavy iron cooking vessels. The sturdy pine table has baking utensils.

DeSoto County, Louisiana
LAND'S END

Cypress Columns in the Deep South

In many ways "Land's End," the name of Henry Marshall's home, marked not only the end of a stretch of territory (it was sixteen miles short of the Louisiana border) but the end of an era. Born in South Carolina of Irish descent, Marshall was educated at Union College in Schenectady, New York, and was a colonel in the South Carolina militia. He made his reputation in northwest Louisiana as a planter, a slaveholding aristocrat, one of six men from his state to help frame the Constitution of the Confederacy and an ardent member of the Confederate Congress from Louisiana. Admired for the "urbanity and modest self-respect which ever mark the character of a gentleman," Marshall was said to be "typical of his class and he and it were swept away."

Marshall had moved west from South Carolina to find cheaper and more plentiful land. It was customary early in the nineteenth century to farm land as long as it was profitable, then to acquire new land and begin all over again; fertilization and crop rotation were not widely practiced. In 1833, land values and speculation were erratic because of the banking situation and President Andrew Jackson's decree directing the Secretary of the Treasury to forbid government deposits in the Second Bank of the United States. As a result, the bank, deprived of these deposits, collapsed and the state banks issued notes in large quantities, regardless of their ability to redeem them with gold or silver.

Chaotic speculation resulted and prices of everything, in-

Above: The most striking feature of the exterior of Land's End is the one-story gallery with its fluted cypress columns. (All photos: Country Beautiful)

Opposite: The parlor's dark blue velvet draperies and red damask-covered rosewood sofa contrast dramatically with white walls.

The harp-shaped Chickering grand piano in the parlor was made between 1845 and 1850. Portrait is of Mrs. Henry Marshall, for whom the Land's End house was built.

cluding land, soared. Faced with huge land prices which he would not or could not afford in his native state, Marshall set out by ox-drawn wagon for Louisiana, at that time one of the westernmost states in the Union. Beginning in 1835, and until his death in 1864, he acquired ten thousand acres of land, 201 slaves, and produced ten thousand bushels of corn per year. By 1857 he was prosperous enough to hire Mr. Robbins, the designer of many of the affluent neighboring plantation houses, to build the Marshall family's new mansion.

The Greek Revival dwelling has fluted Ionic columns of cypress, eleven- to thirteen-foot ceilings, and a sweeping staircase leading to four bedrooms and two dressing rooms on the second floor, and to two more bedrooms on the third floor — room enough to accommodate Mrs. Marshall, her parents, six daughters and three sons. As construction proceeded, Marshall toured the continent with three of his daughters, acquiring engravings, bric-a-brac, furniture and carpets, from the continent as well as from New York, while keeping in touch with the details of his new home even to the matter of the proper dimensions of the windows.

When it was finished, Land's End crowned Marshall's property which had grown to the size of a village, studded with fifty log houses in the slave quarters, each with its own spring of

water, with barns, smokehouses, all encircled by profitable groomed land. By 1861 Marshall was concentrating on state and national affairs, particularly the Constitution of the Confederate States of America, adopted on March 11 of that year. In drafting this document the hope was "to form a permanent federal government, establish justice, insure domestic tranquility and secure the blessings of liberty to ourselves and our posterity. . . ." This intriguing document established a six-year term for the president and did not permit his reelection and allowed cabinet officers to sit on the floor of Congress. Two passages on slavery are pertinent: "The importation of Negroes of the African race from any foreign country other than the slave-holding states or territories of the United States of America, is hereby forbidden; and congress is required to pass such laws as shall effectually prevent the same." The other: "Congress shall also have power to prohibit the introduction of slaves from any state not a member of, or territory not belonging to, this Confederacy."

Marshall, at the peak of his prosperity, in 1861, was wealthy enough to equip a regiment for his cousin Maxcy Gregg, a general at the Battle of Fredericksburg. Three years later, and three months before his death in 1864, he was appointed by the governor, along with two others, to "investigate and

At the foot of this carved rosewood bed is a cradle that can be rocked automatically by winding a clock spring in one end.

furnish relief to planters who had suffered loss by reason of the recent incursion of the enemy." Tragically, he could not repair his own losses due to the Civil War. Two of his sons died, one in 1863 while on leave from the Confederate Army, the other in 1864 while a Union prisoner of war; within that same year he was gone and Land's End was turned into a military hospital, its carpets and draperies cut up and used as blankets for those wounded in the Battle of Mansfield.

The original matching wings that extended from the rear of the house were demolished in 1926, as was a detached kitchen in 1950, but otherwise Land's End has remained intact and in the hands of the same family for seven generations and is owned today by Colonel Henry F. Means, USAF (Ret.), a direct descendant. As a result, the two-and-a-half-story clapboard house with gable roof is filled with original pieces. Beyond the one-story gallery with the fluted cypress columns extending across the entire front, is a central hall running the length of the house. The woodwork here is heart pine painted and grained to simulate oak and the original plank floor is pine. Overhead in the ceiling is a plaster of Paris medallion with an embedded hook that once held a chain by which an oil chandelier could be lowered for lighting. The music cabinet holds volumes of music that belonged to various daughters in the family and the Empire tilt-top table came from an old house in Natchez, Mississippi.

To the left is the main parlor, the most impressive room at Land's End. As they are throughout the house, the walls are white, as is the woodwork in this particular room, except for the oak-simulated doors. In dramatic contrast are the dark blue velvet draperies and matching upholstered rosewood chairs and the red damask-covered rosewood sofa. Originally the draperies and the rosewood set, purchased for Land's End in 1859, were all covered in a beige and blue damask that wound up over the wounded; only the tiebacks are visible now. The baseboard has been painted to imitate the handsome but simple black, tan-veined Italian marble mantel which is original with the house. The harp-shaped Chickering grand was made between 1845 and 1850.

Across the hall is the dining room that was originally the second, less formal, parlor. Here, as in the hall, the woodwork, as well as the door, is painted to simulate oak. Original pieces include the card table, syllabub set and the cut glass and silver on the Victorian sideboards. The small, horizontal marble clock on the mantel was purchased in France in 1859 by Henry Marshall.

Immediately inside the rear entrance door to the right is a graceful staircase that sweeps up to the second floor. The hall here has an unusual rustic summer chair which was made for Colonel Marshall's father-in-law of sage grass, oak strips and deer thongs. The rosewood set in the southwest bedroom includes a half-tester bed, nine-feet high, with pierced cresting on the headboard and half-tester and a typically mid-Victorian serpentine-arched footboard, molded at the top and flanked by downswept cyma curves. At the foot of the bed is a walnut and mahogany cradle, original with the house, that can be rocked automatically by winding a clock spring in one end. The clustered-column tester bed in the southeast bedroom, also

nine feet in height, is an original piece and is covered with an enchanting quilt made about 1833 by Mrs. Marshall's mother. The cream background is appliqued with flowers, birds and butterflies in rose, green and blue, the green echoing the color of the small upholstered love seat with serpentine-arched and crested top rail. The northeast room serves as a documents room, containing items with which Henry Marshall was historically associated, such as copies of the Ordinance of Secession, the Confederate Constitution and early maps and newspapers. There is a fourth bedroom with a cherry-wood spool bed and two dressing rooms on the second floor and two more bedrooms on the third floor.

Everywhere at Land's End the past is evoked, for the mansion is still surrounded by ancient trees and sheep can still occasionally be seen grazing over the lawn where there are time-worn ruts of the stagecoach road that once connected this important plantation to Shreveport and other towns. Henry Marshall's Confederacy has not survived, but he and his descendants have bequeathed to us a valuable glimpse of another time and place.

The clustered-column tester bed in the southeast bedroom is covered with a handmade quilt that has appliqued flowers and butterflies.

San Juan, Puerto Rico
LA FORTALEZA

Sixteenth-Century Palace of Governors

Above: Two-story pilasters and Isabelline motifs in the frieze enhance La Fortaleza's stucco and stone façade. *Opposite top:* A Genoese marble floor and gilt-framed mirrors dignify the Reception Room décor. *Opposite bottom:* A maroon carpet bearing the seal of the commonwealth and the coat of arms of Ponce de León covers the marble floor in the State Dining Room. (All photos: courtesy La Fortaleza)

It was obvious that Puerto Rico, the "rich port," so named by Juan Ponce de León, who searched less successfully for youth than for new territory, was desirable and needed the protection of a fort. Christopher Columbus had discovered the island "as lovely as an orchard" on his second voyage to the New World, on November 19, 1493, and named it San Juan Bautista, in honor of Prince Juan, heir to the Spanish throne. Fifteen years later Ponce de León renamed the island "Puerto Rico," called its bay "San Juan," and became the island's first governor.

The island's population was a tangle of Africans, French, Dutch and English, vulnerable to the attacks of pirates who, in 1528, had destroyed the second most important town next to San Juan, San Germán. The Spanish had two choices: to abandon or to fortify. In 1533 they began to build a series of forts in San Juan harbor, the first of which was simply called La Fortaleza, the fortress. Its circular stone tower came to be called the "Tower of Homage," a name born out of the customary loyalty oath governors took there in times of danger. One of its two vaulted rooms was the chapel, and behind it four thick stone walls enclosed a patio. But La Fortaleza, it was soon discovered, was not the answer; its site was ineffective and three larger and more efficient fortresses rose, the Morro Castle, San Cristobal and San Gerónimo.

Meanwhile, during the first century of Spanish occupation, Puerto Rico's gold mines produced some four million dollars worth of gold, and this was more than enough to attract adventurers from across the ocean. Silver, lead and copper and marble deposits were among the other reasons for the risks taken by Sir Francis Drake, by George Clifford, Earl of Cumberland, and by the Dutch commander, Boudewijn Hendrick, who installed himself in La Fortaleza in 1625. When his attempt to capture the island was thwarted, Hendrick withdrew, burning San Juan to the ground and damaging the fortress so severely that its reconstruction was not begun until fifteen years later. Drake's attempt to capture Puerto Rico for his Queen Elizabeth is a fiery and frustrating tale of war. On the night of November 23, 1594, Drake led a party of twenty-five boats, manned by fifty or sixty men each, into the port of

San Juan and set fire to several Spanish frigates which "burned furiously." The entire port was lit by the fire. According to one account, it was "a fine sight to see how the frigates fought and how capitally they were backed by the artillery of the forts," including that installed in La Fortaleza.

Less than a week later, the battle was over and the enemy, "who up to this time has never met with any resistance at sea," had had "his head broken. . . ." Many of Drake's men were wounded, about four hundred had perished, including one of the leaders, John Hawkins, and two millions worth of gold, silver and cochineal were saved — wealth that might otherwise have helped Queen Elizabeth to "equip and maintain a force" to give the island "further trouble." Puerto Rico's defenders were proudest of all of the "spirit which our people have shown, and the renown which they have won, proving the inferiority of the enemy. . . ."

Since November 27, 1822, La Fortaleza has served in another official but more pleasant role: as a palace for its governors. As the executive residence of Puerto Rico, it was enlarged by Count de Mirasol, governor in 1846, to its present palatial twenty-two-room size. While retaining the basic patio, the count practically reconstructed the entire building, adorning its austere façade with six, two-story pilasters and a frieze using motifs of the Isabelline era, enlarging the main entrance, laying the floors and main staircase in marble tiles from Genoa. Today, the façade encompasses a ground floor of stone and two stories above it faced with stucco. The horizontal line of the building's flat roof is paralleled by a narrow balcony with iron grillwork that runs across the entire front between the ground floor and the first floor above, where the major rooms are. A wide, arched entrance with a massive wooden door leads into the front patio which is surrounded on the two upper floors by state rooms, including an open gallery and corridor on the first floor. To the left, the main staircase leading to the Grand Reception Room sets the overall tone of lavish décor: Tuscan-style banisters and steps of valuable dark Puerto Rican ausubo wood have risers embellished with nineteenth-century azulejos, rich-colored enameled earthenware tiles made in Catalonia.

The Grand Reception Room at the top of the staircase is dominated by a massive center table with highly carved, incurved legs and large nineteenth-century gilt-framed mirrors. On the walls are portraits of Luis Muñoz Rivera and Eugenio María de Hostos, two famous Puerto Rican patriots,

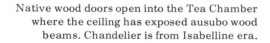

Native wood doors open into the Tea Chamber where the ceiling has exposed ausubo wood beams. Chandelier is from Isabelline era.

and George Washington and Simón Bolivar. In the corridor outside the reception room stands an antique mahogany clock that is especially meaningful: It purposely maintains a broken face, marred symbolically in 1897 by the sword of the last Spanish governor, to mark the last minute of Spanish rule in the New World.

The open corridor leads to the largest room in La Fortaleza, the State Dining Room, where the long heavy ausubo table seats sixteen. The Genoese marble floor is almost completely covered by a dark maroon carpet bearing the seal of the commonwealth and the coat of arms of Ponce de León. Standing on each of the three sideboards is a crystal fruit bowl with the Seal of Spain, said to have been gifts from Queen Isabella.

Perhaps the most dazzling room in the mansion, however, is the Hall of Mirrors, adjoining the dining room. Ten mirrors in all, framed in burnished gilt topped by ribboned flower garlands, reflect a pair of marble-topped pier tables and a set of handsome, richly upholstered armchairs in the Adam style. Twelve Corinthian columns and sedate gold draperies on the windows and doors give the room a further air of formality. As in the other state rooms, the doors here are of native wood with joined panels that fold in the middle and back to the sides. The floor is tiled with white and gray marble.

The result of over a century of additions, alterations and restorations, La Fortaleza today is a mosaic of almost countless materials and styles — Canarias stone, Italian marble, stucco, stained glass, Spanish-style furniture, Arabian windows, classical stonework. And the processes of change are still evident: Following research prepared by the Institute of Culture of Puerto Rico, present Governor Luis A. Ferré and his daughter Rosarito are directing a general restoration that will make La Fortaleza both a more comfortable executive mansion and a more authentic fortress.

Ten mirrors framed in burnished gilt reflect Corinthian columns and richly upholstered Adam-style chairs in the Hall of Mirrors.

237

Mentor, Ohio

LAWNFIELD

"The Gothic Sentiment Prevailing"

The visitor who arrived in Mentor, Ohio, twenty-six miles from Cleveland, traveled over flat land dotted with houses "every hundred rods or so," little farms, orchards and gardens before he reached his destination, Lawnfield. This was the home of the newly elected twentieth President of the United States, General Garfield, the "big man of the place." Garfield had bought his land in two parcels, 120 acres first and then 40 acres, had hired an architect from Cleveland to redo the existing building which he found "too small and barren of conveniences." After the decision was made to raise the roof to two and a half stories, and enlarge the building till it stood sixty feet by fifty feet deep, Garfield wrote to the architect from Washington on March 6, 1880: "These plans must stand as above, unless otherwise ordered hereafter. If any part of them is impracticable, inform me soon and suggest change." Lawnfield that year grew to twenty-six rooms at an expenditure of between $3,500 and $4,000, was painted white with a "Turkish" red roof, its style, the visitor said, was "composite, the Gothic sentiment prevailing."

Garfield had bought the property in the fall of 1876 when he was forty-five years old and the incumbent representative (for the eighth time) to the U. S. Congress from Ohio. He was tired of "tossing" about in watering places in summer "at great expense" with his wife, Lucretia Rudolph, the mother of his seven children, and he paid for his property on five or six years' time, at $115 an acre.

He was, to the visitor, a "large, well-fed, hale, ruddy, brown-bearded man weighing about 220 pounds, with blue eyes, military face, erect figure and shoulders, large back and thighs, and broad chest, and evidently bred in the country on a farm." He had, in fact, been born in a log cabin in the frontier town of Orange, Cuyahoga County, Ohio, and left home at sixteen. He had worked as a canal boatman, studied at Western Reserve Eclectic Institute at Hiram, and after graduation from Williams College in 1856, he had been professor of

Above: Lawnfield's style was described as "composite, the Gothic sentiment prevailing." *Opposite above:* A Victorian Gothic armchair of oak is beside the reception hall fireplace. *Opposite below:* The large window on the south side adds much to the parlor's attractiveness.

ancient languages and literature back in Hiram where the next year saw him Hiram's president.

Garfield, who had worked as a carpenter, and was drawn to the church, made his name in political life with his ardent and eloquent stand against slavery. At the secession of the cotton states and the call for 75,000 troops, he offered his services to the governor, rose from lieutenant colonel to brigadier general with the 42nd Ohio Volunteers, served as chief of staff in the Army of the Cumberland in 1863, and finally resigned his commission to take his seat in Congress. Garfield was a member of the radical wing of the Republican Party, advocating the confiscation of Confederate property. In a blazing scandal he was accused of corruption which was never proven, but with energetic campaigning and "village-to-village canvas" he overcame demands for resignation and managed in 1876 to be re-elected for the eighth time to represent his district. In 1880, he was elected to the Senate and the quarreling Republicans, in an "anything to beat Grant" effort, managed to unite on the candidacy of Garfield and defeat the other two candidates, James G. Blaine and General Sherman.

Following the custom of the time, Garfield did not travel during the subsequent months, but he initiated what has been called the first "front porch" Presidential campaign. One of Lawnfield's small farm outbuildings, still to be seen there, was equipped with telegraph wires and adapted as his campaign headquarters. Here he received reports from around the country and consulted with party leaders, and from the same porch he regularly delivered his graceful speeches to the thousands of visitors who came to Lawnfield during the late summer and fall of 1880, including many delegations sent by the party.

Though his campaign was threatened by abusive accusations of his having received $329 as a stock dividend, and though the forged "Morey letter" made him seem prejudiced against the Chinese, he won the election and immediately became a widely beloved and profoundly respected President. Writing in the *Cincinnati Enquirer,* George Alfred Townsend reported that Garfield's "large brain, with room for play of thought and long application, rises high above the clear, discerning, enjoying eyes." He thought Garfield "never indifferent, never vindictive," and "on a broad scale a schoolmaster of the range of Gladstone, of Agassiz, of Gallatin." Since John Quincy Adams, "no President has had Garfield's scholarship." He was thought to be the "ablest public speaker in the country, and the most serious and instructive man on the stump" but during recess of Congress, he worked like a field hand "restoring his mind by resting it."

While going about his farm, Garfield wore a soft slouch hat with a broad brim and tucked his trousers into a pair of cowhide boots. Early in the morning he would mount his horse or walk about his place or plow or make hay, and his taste for "improvements" led him to farm scientifically. Occasionally, he was invited to speak at the Disciples' Church which he attended and before the Murphy Temperance Society where he said he was "not a believer in total abstinence," but cautioned against the evil of "immoderate drinking."

While he was President, Garfield answered every civil letter he received, sometimes ninety in a single morning, and leafed through two hundred newspapers. He was admired for his "genius of labor." Because of his oratorical talents, Garfield was able to make the dreary palatable, and sympathetically

The charming fireplace in the dining room is faced with colored tiles that are copies of Audubon prints of birds and flowers.

but firmly he urged his fellow men to face the problems of the day. "I am aware that financial subjects are dull and uninviting in comparison with those heroic themes which have absorbed the attention of Congress for the last five years," he told those witnesses who had endured the Civil War. "But to these questions we must come, and to their solution Congress, political parties and all thoughtful citizens must give their best efforts. . . ."

Tragically, there were not many years left for Garfield who found his "worst days of darkness . . . greatly alleviated by throwing myself with all my energy into some work relating to others." On July 3, 1881, just four fleeting months after his inauguration, Garfield, who was on his way to celebrate his twenty-fifth reunion at Williams, was shot by Charles J. Guitea, a disappointed office seeker, and lay dying until his final breath two months later. The catastrophic event is movingly reported in letters of Mrs. James G. Blaine whose husband had driven Garfield to the station the morning of the shooting and received news of it in the middle of her breakfast with her children. She drove to the White House and was standing with a friend in the hall "when a dozen men bore him above their heads, stretched on a mattress, and as he saw us and held us with his eye, he kissed his hand to us — I thought I should die; and when they brought him into his chamber and had laid him on the bed, he turned his eyes to me, beckoned, and when I went to him, pulled me down, kissed me again and again, and said, 'Whatever happens I want you to promise to look out for Crete' [Lucretia, his wife]. 'Don't leave me until Crete comes.' I took my old bonnet off and just stayed." About six o'clock Mrs. Garfield came, "frail, fatigued, desperate, but firm and quiet and full of purpose to save. . . ." But he could not be saved.

The Lake County Historical Society has made Lawnfield available to the public. Standing midst numerous tall elm trees, the L-shaped, high-gabled house retains its white color, but green shutters have been added to it and a slate roof has replaced the red one. The front porch, which originally extend-

Garfield's brief term as President is recalled in the dining room where the buffet holds two silver pots from the White House tea service.

President Garfield used the silk hat and hat box when tràveling. The secretary was in his office at the Eclectic Institute in Hiram.

ed across the entire front of the house, now reaches only halfway, the result of Mrs. Garfield's attempt to brighten up the parlor. The austere but comfortable interior was maintained by Lucretia Rudolph Garfield, the wife whose husband thought her "one of the coolest and best-balanced."

Lawnfield's spacious reception hall is hung with a number of portraits, including one of Falstaff, indicating Garfield's literary interests. It was painted by an artist friend of Garfield's from the President's impressions of that favorite Shakesperian character. Garfield was a member of the Washington Literary Society and had a scholarly interest in English literature as well as in the works of Goethe. The German author's portrait hangs over one of twin banquet tables with an elaborate silver centerpiece that was used in the White House. Another indication of the "Gothic sentiment" prevailing is the stately Victorian Gothic armchair of oak beside the fireplace and two matching side chairs.

The large parlor, perhaps the most attractive room in the house, holds a Follansbee portrait of a grave-eyed Mrs. Garfield, painted from life in 1908, as well as her daughter's thirteenth birthday present, an upright piano with sheet music scrolled with Mollie Garfield's initials. But probably what most enhances this room's appearance is the large window on the south side which floods the room with light and the beautiful carpet with celadon-green medallion on gray-green background, laid during the 1885 remodeling.

Garfield's brief term as President is again recalled in the dining room where the buffet holds two silver pots from the White House tea service, along with two pieces from Mrs. Garfield's green Wedgwood, and the table is set with White House china. Charming and unusual is the fireplace faced with brightly colored tiles that are copies of Audubon prints of birds and flowers. An attractive curiosity is the chandelier in this room which shows three stages of lighting — originally kerosene was used in the center, gas lamps rim the outside and the entire piece has now been electrified.

The house's most noteworthy woodwork is found in the Memorial Library on the second floor. Requiring three years to complete, the white oak was hand-carved when Mrs. Garfield had the room built to house the President's books. The double wedding ceremony of Garfield's daughter Mollie to his secretary Joseph Stanley-Brown and his son Harry Augustus to Belle Mason took place in the library's bow window, and guests dined later on innumerable courses while listening to the orchestra's numberless waltzes.

One is also reminded of the sadness in the Garfields' lives by nostalgic portraits of two of their children in Mrs. Garfield's bedroom — of Edward Garfield, who died in childhood of undetermined causes, and of Eliza Arabella, known affectionately as "Little Trot," who died of diphtheria at the age of four. But evidence of hope and ongoing life are also here. The cradle at the foot of the bed was made of poplar by Zebulon Rudolph for his daughter Lucretia in 1832. It has served every generation since, and even today, Garfield children are brought to lie in it and their names are printed on the bottom along with those of their many forebears.

Zebulon Rudolph, Mrs. Garfield's father, came to live with the Garfields in 1879 and remained until he died eighteen years later. His bedroom contains richly grained wild cherry furniture, including a built-in chest of drawers. The furniture in Mollie's bedroom is japanned to look like ebony and there is a little cast-iron stove because it is the only bedroom without a fireplace. The President's bedroom has its original wallpaper, chandelier and oriental rug, and the hatbox at the foot of the bed still has his silk hat inside. His upstairs study contains his desk and his favorite tufted leather reading chair; one visitor called it the "General's snuggery." Its simplicity and studious atmosphere seem to convey the essence of this rather brilliant man who was tragically prevented from exercising his abilities in his country's most prestigious and difficult job.

Mrs. Garfield's bedroom displays a nostalgic portrait of her daughter Eliza Arabella, who died at the age of four.

Vincennes, Indiana
GROUSELAND

William Henry Harrison's Georgian Mansion

By the year 1790, the splendid Harrisons of Berkeley had suffered drastic financial reverses. This meant that the great-grandson of Benjamin Harrison II, whose twenty thousand-acre estate had been second only to the Royal Governor's, and the grandson of Anne Carter Harrison, who was the daughter of the awesomely wealthy King Carter, could not afford tuition for medical school and had to look elsewhere for his career. As it turned out, William Henry Harrison looked to the West, first to Ohio and then to Indiana, on the advice of his family friend, Governor Richard Henry Lee, and with the help of an old family acquaintance, General George Washington, Harrison entered the army as an ensign.

By September 20, 1791, when the regular army claimed only a single infantry regiment and an artillery battalion, and the military life itself was "generally despised," Harrison was one of a little company of eighty men who had traveled over rough and mountainous country, "feet swollen and calloused," and on the Ohio River via flatboards to reach Fort Washington in Cincinnati. Harrison carried a book of rhetoric and his Cicero all the way. He also bore the manner and tastes of a Virginia gentleman, which would account for the home he was to build, called Grouseland, and the "copious fund of that eloquence . . . fitted for the camp and for gaining partisans," which helped him, along with his subsequent victory at the Tippecanoe River, to be elected the country's ninth President.

William Harrison was born at Berkeley on February 9, 1773, at the time of the colonial boycott of tea and the trauma of Revolutionary rumblings. He fished and swam in Kimadges Creek and in the James River and rode horseback over the family property. His first classes, held in a small brick building on the family plantation, were halted by Benedict Arnold's raid and were continued at the Brandon School located on

Above: Grouseland was said to be the first brick mansion in Vincennes. It is Southern in conception. (All photos: Country Beautiful)

Opposite: In the parlor, the portrait of the serious, quizzical young Harrison in dress uniform is by Rembrandt Peale.

The nursery on the second floor of the
"great house" has a rocking chair
that once belonged to Francis Vigo.

another Harrison property. At fourteen he chose medicine
over law and took the two-day journey by stagecoach over to
Hampden-Sidney College in Prince Edwin County, but he left
when many Episcopalians, along with Thomas Jefferson,
thought that because of its Methodist leanings the school was
"going to nothing owing to the religious phrensy that they
have inspired into the boys . . . and which their parents have
no taste for." Harrison wound up eventually at the medical
school of the University of Pennsylvania but left when he
inherited three thousand acres of land at his father Colonel
Benjamin Harrison's death and no money with which to pay
any bills.

Harrison's promotions and recognition in the army were
bravely earned and after his first Indian campaign a fellow
officer said of him, "If he continues a military man, he will be a
second Washington." At Fort Washington Captain Harrison
met and eloped with the "dark-eyed and sedate" Anna Tuthill
Symmes whose disapproving father he attempted to reassure,
"My sword is my means of support, sir!" Harrison was also a
partner in a whiskey distillery on Deer Creek, was appointed
Land Office Registrar, and he was thinking about resigning
from the army when he was recommended because of his "fair,
indeed unblemished reputation" to be Secretary of the Northwest Territory (including the present states of Ohio, Indiana,
Illinois, Michigan and part of Minnesota). He was appointed to
the $1,200-a-year position by President John Adams and, in
1800, he became the governor.

It was to Vincennes, on the edge of a broad prairie and a
large forest on the east bank of the Wabash, that Harrison
came with one Negro servant from Berkeley. He built a home
for his family and a reputation for wisdom and understanding
in his approach to the Indians, who had in many cases
intermarried with the French and who probably comprised
four-fifths of the population of 5,640. Harrison reported to the
Secretary of War that the Indian chiefs "profess and I believe
that most of them feel a friendship for the United States . . .
but they make heavy complaints of ill-treatment on the part of
our citizens. They say that their people have been killed —
their lands settled upon — their game wantonly destroyed. . . .
Of the truth of these charges I am well convinced." But
Harrison not only befriended the Indians, he fought them, too.

One of his duties as governor was to amass land for his
country, and when the Treaty of Fort Wayne in 1809 marked
the cession of two and a half million acres of Indian territory,
Tecumseh, a Shawnee chief, denounced it and began organizing a confederation of tribes to resist, persuading the Indians
to remain on the treaty land. On November 7, 1811, Harrison
attacked an Indian village at Tippecanoe Creek, winning a
pivotal battle that many historians regard as the "opening
skirmish" in the War of 1812. Nevertheless, later in his life,
Harrison pleaded to his fellow members of the United States
Senate that they "lose no opportunity of inculcating, among
your constituents, an abhorrence of that unchristian and
detestable doctrine which would make a distinction of guilt

The Federal-style fireplace in the Harrisons' bedroom was hand-carved and conveys a sense of the affluence the family enjoyed.

between the murder of a white man and an Indian.''

Harrison's army career flourished and earned him several promotions. On March 2, 1813, as commander of all the troops in the Northwest, he was promoted to major general, and later that year he reoccupied Detroit and achieved a notable triumph at the Battle of the Thames in Canada.

After the War of 1812 Harrison entered politics and eventually was elected to the United States Senate. In 1840, as the "log cabin and hard cider" Whig candidate for President, Harrison was teamed with John Tyler, previously of the Democratic Party, for Vice President. The campaign cry, "Tippecanoe and Tyler too," successfully transformed the Virginia aristocrat into a rough-hewn general who preferred log cabins to plantations, cider to wine, and a landslide vote catapulted him into the White House where he died only a month later of pneumonia.

Harrison was just thirty-one, with the most difficult and momentous years of his period in the Northwest and Indiana

The bed in the northwest bedroom is covered with a handsome old blue and white spread that dates from 1790.

territories still ahead of him, when he started building Grouseland in the summer of 1803 on a "gentle elevation in the midst of a walnut grove." Grouseland was said to be the first brick mansion in Vincennes, more Southern than Midwestern in conception. The land was wonderfully fertile and planted with corn and tobacco, hemp and hops. When the fruit trees were in bloom and the prairie was crimson with strawberries, the scene was so moving that a friend of Mrs. Harrison's wrote, "This beautiful country, which I cannot sufficiently admire . . . would be injured by a comparison with any other."

Harrison lived there with his wife and ten children, and after Tippecanoe, the household included the daughter of his friend Thomas Randolph who had died in that battle. He enjoyed reading and smoking on the front porch and he held meetings in the walnut grove, receiving Tecumseh, among others, under the elm tree.

Grouseland's road to restoration has been a rocky one. After 1850, when it passed from the hands of the Harrison family, it

The basement warming kitchen served an auxiliary function to the main kitchen, which was located in a separate building at the rear.

was used as a granary, as a hotel, and, sporadically, as a residence. It was bought by the Vincennes Water Company in 1909 and rescued from demolition that same year by the Francis Vigo Chapter of the Daughters of the American Revolution. From 1910 onward attempts have been made to re-create Grouseland as it was originally conceived by its builder and lived in by his family.

Grouseland is reminiscent not only of the homes Harrison had known during his childhood in Virginia, but especially of his own family home, Berkeley. Georgian in its inclinations, it is two and a half stories high, encompassing thirteen rooms and four large chimneys. The smaller, distinct section to the rear was originally a separate dependency containing the servants' quarters. At some time during the Harrison occupancy the buildings were linked on both floors because of the additional space needed for the growing family.

The first floor of the main structure, the "great house," includes two handsomely proportioned rooms, one, the bow-

The walnut cannon ball post bed in the east bedroom of the dependency belonged originally to Francis Vigo.

end Council Chamber, for meetings and entertainment, the other, the dining room, for the family. The details are many and beautifully wrought — the mantels hand-carved, window glass imported from England, chair rails of polished black walnut and sashes and doors made by artisans in Chillicothe and in Pittsburgh. Many security measures are still evident. A closet under the semi-circular staircase hid records that were not uncovered until years later. The eighteen-inch outer walls of the house are slit to make portholes, the broad-silled attic windows "designed for sharp-shooters," the six-foot-high windows fitted with heavy shutters inside and out. A powder magazine in the cellar has heavy masonry walls, an arched ceiling of brick and a trap door that leads to a roof-top look-out.

In the Council Chamber, or parlor, the portrait of the serious, quizzical young Harrison in the dress uniform of the War of 1812, is by Rembrandt Peale and is a far cry from the older Harrison described by one visitor as a "small, and rather sallow-looking man, who does not exactly meet the associations that connect themselves with the name of general." The dominant colors here are yellow and blue. The glazed yellow wallpaper is bordered with blue swags, the blue matched by the brocaded stripe draperies, the yellow by the upholstery of the Martha Washington chairs. The most treasured piece in the room is Harrison's cherry pedestal table.

The dining room to the right of the hall is papered festively in the tradition of the more prosperous homes of the day and proudly claims an original family sideboard as well as the portrait of Jane Findlay Harrison, wife of William Henry Harrison II, who often served as her father-in-law's hostess at the White House. The bullet hole, said to have been fired through the window just missing Harrison while he was carrying his infant son John Scott in his arms, is a memento of the Indian troubles.

The graceful stairway, similar to those found in Virginia, has

250

cherry treads, risers and banister and leads to the second-floor hall which often functioned as a room itself, frequently serving as a sleeping space for guests. The yellow and white wallpaper with a classical arch motif is carried up from the lower hall and staircase. Much of the furniture at Grouseland was made in Indiana in the early part of the nineteenth century and its strong, simple lines are at their most appealing in the southeast bedroom, believed to have been the Harrisons' bedroom. The Federal-style fireplace, carved in Vincennes, and the charming provincial-style paper portraying hunting scenes convey an authentic sense of the homely affluence this family enjoyed. The small Windsor chair, table and blanket chest belonged to the Harrisons.

It has been said of William Henry Harrison that he was "not a great man, but he had lived in a great time, and he had been a leader in great things." And General Harrison was not the last of the family to be honored by his country. Among those who mourned his death in 1841 was his eight-year-old grandson Benjamin who was to become the twenty-third President of the United States.

The graceful stairway, similar to those found in Virginia, has cherry treads, risers and banister.

Springfield, Illinois
THE ABRAHAM LINCOLN HOME

"Here I Passed from a Young to an Old Man"

Above: Native hardwoods, white pine and hand-split hickory laths went into the Springfield home Lincoln bought in 1844. *Opposite:* Globes flank the red-patterned sofa near fireplace. (All photos: Country Beautiful)

The Lincolns bought the story-and-a-half house on Eighth and Jackson streets in Springfield from the Reverend Charles Dresser for the sum of $1,500 in the year of 1844. In the following months neighbors were likely to find Lincoln lying on his living room floor in faded trousers and loose slippers, reading by lamplight. They also noticed that he sawed his own wood, fed and curried his own horse, and also fed and milked his cow. He did plant a rose bush once but neglected it and he never planted any vines or fruit trees.

Both Abraham Lincoln and his wife Mary liked the theatre, went together often; Sunday church service was another matter entirely. Mrs. Lincoln might go twice on Sunday, but Mr. Lincoln often went straight to his office where he was partner in a law firm, first with John T. Stuart, one of Illinois' most distinguished lawyers, and then with William H. Herndon. Lincoln, whom one writer described as being "composed mostly of bones, and when walking he resembles the offspring of a happy marriage between a derrick and a windmill," was a frequent host with his wife at parties for as many as five hundred friends at a time, but where his wit really flourished was over at the drugstore among his cronies. As one indignant hostess put it whose food cooled waiting for him, Lincoln was "the laziest man there ever was, good for nothing except to tell stories."

Above: Lincoln's massive high-post bed with thick, turned posts dominates his bedroom. *Below:* Mirror at height at which Lincoln shaved hangs above cottage-style stand.

Abraham Lincoln rode to Springfield from New Salem in 1837, at the age of twenty-eight, on a borrowed horse, with only two possessions. He owned a pair of saddlebags and a license to practice law which he had been encouraged to study by his friend and law partner John T. Stuart. Lincoln's family had migrated from Kentucky, then from Indiana to the vicinity of Decatur, Illinois, the men mostly journeying on foot, the women by oxen drawn wagon, Abraham Lincoln driving them much of the way. To earn his keep, Lincoln worked in nearby New Salem at splitting rails, as a surveyor and as a clerk in the general store. In a wrestling match he bettered the town toughs, the Clary Grove Boys, and earned sufficient respect and backing to elect him to the state legislature in 1834. By 1837 he had taken a position on the issue of slavery. At the end of the legislature session that year he pronounced "the institution of slavery is founded on both injustice and bad policy; but that the promulgation of abolition doctrines tends rather to increase than to abate its evils."

Though Lincoln's political career in Springfield limped slowly at the beginning, his private life took permanent shape. After one broken engagement and another broken and mended, he married Mary Todd in 1842, worrying and confiding in his friend Joshua Fry Speed that it was "the peculiar misfortune of both you and me to dream dreams of Elysium far exceeding all that anything earthly can realize." And Mary Lincoln remains a most controversial figure. "Self-willed, even tyrannical," there are those who think her "dogmatic firmness the saving of her mystic, doubting husband." Lincoln seemed to draw strength and courage from Mary, and his affection for her was indisputable. "In this troublesome world," he wrote to her from Washington, "we are never quite satisfied. When you were here, I thought you hindered me some in attending to business; but now, having nothing but business — no variety — it has grown exceedingly tasteless to me."

Mary, who mothered Lincoln's four sons, only one of whom, Robert Todd, lived to adulthood, suffered from what must have been severe headaches. At one point when she was feeling better he wrote to her that he was afraid she would get so well "and fat, and young, as to be wanting to marry again." It was Mary who wisely talked Lincoln out of accepting the governorship of the new Territory of Oregon and it was Mary who apparently spurred him on toward the Presidency, which Lincoln thought "too big a thing for me." Apart from his own opinion, he admitted to a friend, "Mary insists that I am going to be a senator and President of the United States."

It was Lincoln, however, who recognized that "only events can make a President," and the event on which his political career revolved was the quest for the preservation of what he called the "immortal emblem of humanity — the Declaration of Independence." Lincoln grew prosperous in Springfield, was recognized as a great jury lawyer, and while he had served in the state legislature and in United States Congress for one term, from 1847 to 1849, it was the Kansas-Nebraska Act of 1854 opening the Northwestern territories to slavery that found him in Peoria making one of the pivotal speeches of his career, insisting that slavery be checked because he thought it "inhuman" and that "new free states are places for poor people to go to and better their condition." Again in 1858,

The piano was played at Lincoln's wedding in 1842. Other possessions — music box, books, stereopticon and Tad's chair — are on view in the well-restored sitting room.

accepting the Republican nomination for the Senate, he declared that "A house divided against itself cannot stand. I believe this Government cannot endure permanently half-slave and half-free." Lincoln, "while pretending no indifference to earthly honors," did claim to "something higher than an anxiety to office." At the Republican National Convention at Chicago, Lincoln was nominated on the third ballot to run for President of the United States. He won fewer than two million out of four and a half million votes; all but twenty-four thousand came from the free states. But this did give him the electoral college and the ultimate prize.

When Abraham Lincoln was leaving Springfield for the White House, he stood on the platform at the back of the train and talked to his friends and neighbors who came to wave him on his way to Washington. Tears lined his face, "so bony and sad, so quizzical and comic," as he spoke of the "sadness of this parting. To this place, and the kindness of these people, I owe everything. Here I have lived a quarter of a century, and have passed from a young to an old man. Here my children have been born, and one is buried. I now leave, not knowing when or whether ever I may return."

On May 5, 1865, Lincoln was buried in Springfield. With Lincoln's assassination, the *New York Herald* predicted "it will take a new school of historians to do justice to this

Hanging above Robert Lincoln's spool bed is an embroidered Old Glory, crafted when Wisconsin entered the Union.

eccentric addition to the world's gallery of heroes,'' and speculated about how men could ''ever be brought to comprehend the genius of a character so externally uncouth, so pathetically simple, so unfathomably penetrating, so irresolute and yet so irresistible, so bizarre, grotesque, droll, wise and perfectly beneficent in all its developments as was that of the great original thinker and statesman for whose death the whole land, even in the midst of victories unparalleled, is today draped in mourning?''

Mary Lincoln never did return to the Springfield house. Instead, she rented it for anywhere from $90 to $350 a year, and it was finally given to the State of Illinois by her son Robert, a lawyer, who had attended Phillips Exeter Academy and Harvard University. Many of the household furnishings had been dispersed through a public sale when the Lincolns went to Washington in 1861, and some sold to the tenants who seemed then to have taken them to Chicago where they were lost in the Great Fire. Eventually the home was restored through the efforts of the State of Illinois.

The house in Springfield, to which Mrs. Lincoln added a second story in 1856, with the help of a small inheritance, is sturdy, with a frame and floors of oak, the laths of hand-split hickory. Today the shutters are again painted green, the house "a Quaker tint of light brown," as it was when the Lincolns lived here. Its significant rooms are the two parlors on the north side. Here on May 19, 1860, Lincoln received the committee that formally notified him of the Republican Convention's nomination for President. The striped wallpaper, the Brussels carpet and the furniture in these rooms have been selected to reflect authentically Lincoln's Springfield years. Original pieces in the parlors are Lincoln's secretary with glass-enclosed bookcase and his mohair sofa.

After completing the ceremony notifying Lincoln of his nomination, the committee and guests were led into the sitting room to be introduced to Mrs. Lincoln. This room has been completely restored after its picture in *Leslie's Weekly* in 1861. Lincoln's horsehair rocker is here along with two others — young Tad's wicker-back and his mother's sewing chair. The Scherr piano against the wall was played at Mary's wedding and the elaborate blue and brown wallpaper is a facsimile of the paper she selected for this room. The glass medicine bottles on the mantel were found buried in the backyard of the house.

In the dining room the walnut double gateleg dining table, the tea-leaf-design dessert service on the center of the table and the English-made ironstone on the sideboard are all original with the house. Upstairs in Lincoln's bedroom are a shaving mirror, washstand, tall wardrobe and an American Empire four-drawer bureau with heavy rolled feet, all of which belonged to the President. The massive four-poster is not original, although it is appropriate for the period. The wallpaper here is the same as in the sitting room. Other valuable pieces on the second floor are the blanket chest at the foot of the bed in Mary Lincoln's bedroom, the rush-bottom chair at the end of the bed in Robert Lincoln's bedroom — both original — and the cane daybed in the children's bedroom.

The last day the Lincolns occupied the house before leaving for Washington, D.C., was an exciting one. From seven o'clock p.m. to midnight they held a grand public levee attended, according to several accounts, by thousands. The President-elect personally greeted each visitor as he entered and then passed on to the center of the parlor to be introduced to Mrs. Lincoln, festively dressed for the occasion in a simple but elegant dress of white moire antique silk with a dainty French lace collar. The next day they left the house and Springfield for the White House.

Toys made in 1859 and the Lincoln boys' marbles lie deserted in the children's room. Cane daybed fills corner to left of early Victorian chest.

St. Paul, Minnesota
ALEXANDER RAMSEY HOUSE

The Governor's Ornate Victorian Residence

The "Mansion House marking the full accomplishment of a Pennsylvania Dutch burgher" named Alexander Ramsey, is also a monument to the remarkable transformation of Minnesota in the middle of the nineteenth century. In treaties made in 1837, the Chippewa and the Sioux Indians relinquished title to the valued wedge of land between the Mississippi and St. Croix rivers. Twelve years later Congress passed a bill organizing the territory of Minnesota, and on May 27, 1849, Ramsey, its first territorial governor, arrived by steamboat in St. Paul, at the capital — "just emerging from a collection of Indian whiskey shops and birch-roofed cabins of half-breed voyageurs." The population of the territory would grow from 300 to 150,037 in a brief eight years.

It was not sheer wanderlust but diligent and clever politics that propelled Ramsey west. Ramsey, whose father had died when he was ten and who had earned his education as a carpenter and a clerk, had campaigned successfully for the United States Congress in a German-speaking district in Pennsylvania *in* Pennsylvania Dutch dialect, making much of the fact that his mother's ancestry was German. During his second term in Congress he organized "pivotal" Pennsylvania to back Zachary Taylor for President and his reward was the Minnesota territory governorship. "A hearty, heavy, hard-fisted" man, Ramsey "wasted no time on fanciful projects," was elected mayor of St. Paul in 1855 and was chosen second governor of the newly formed State of Minnesota in 1859. Before his second term ended, he was elected United States Senator, an office he held for twelve years. He continued his public service as Secretary of War in the cabinet of President Rutherford B. Hayes.

Alexander Ramsey was not only a respected public servant in his era but an esteemed real estate investor, and the area of St. Paul proved a brilliant sphere for his operations. At the instigation of General James Wilkinson and with the approval of Thomas Jefferson, in 1805, Lieutenant Zebulon M. Pike had acquired this territory for the United States from the Sioux for sixty gallons of whiskey, a handful of gifts, and somewhat later, a cash payment of $2,000. The French who settled there in 1840 built a log church dedicated to St. Paul and, when Ramsey arrived nine years later, the village was named the capital of Minnesota and incorporated as a city.

Ramsey and his family lived in a "neat white frame cottage," actually made of logs covered with board siding, then in a "handsome, spacious house," which was in turn moved from his Walnut Street property to make way in 1872 for the gray

Above: Three generations of the Ramsey family lived in the Walnut Street mansion. (All photos: Minnesota Historical Society) *Opposite:* Flanking the reception room fireplace are a pair of sleepy hollow chairs, upholstered in wool gros point.

Above: The dining room in the back wing was the scene of a dinner attended by President Rutherford B. Hayes and his wife.

Below: The staircase in the central hall, with black walnut banister, leads to five bedrooms on the second floor.

limestone "Mansion House." Ramsey's newest house, dominating the city's most prosperous and stylish neighborhood and developed from "oak scrub and swamp," was the work of many hands, talents and influences. It took the architect Monroe Scheire, the contractor John Summers and a chief carpenter, Matthew Taylor, to build the ornate three-story house with full basement, attic and mansard roof that was to serve the Ramsey family for three generations. The style of architecture has been called, rather grandly, French Renaissance, but gentle Victorian seems more appropriate.

Beyond the cavernous porch where Ramsey liked to read on summer evenings is the marble-floored vestibule. Taking up the entire left half of the first floor of the main section is the great parlor, measuring twenty by forty feet, the largest room in the house. A bay formed in the center of the west wall by three high windows overlooks the spacious, well-shaped lawn. Flanking the bay are white marble fireplaces with arched openings and intricately and deeply carved fruit and flower designs covering much of the mantel. Designed by J.F. Tostevin of St. Paul, they were never intended for anything other than decorative purposes and a fire has never been built on their hearths. This most lavish room in the house — a room that was transformed into a ballroom on short notice — has a fourteen-foot-high ceiling, as do all first-floor rooms, black walnut woodwork, Bohemian-crystal chandeliers, and a Steinway concert grand piano which Ramsey purchased.

Across the broad central hall are the reception room and library. Each has a fireplace similar to those in the large parlor, although less ornate. The opening of the one in the reception room is covered by a mirrored shield preceded by a clear glass screen framed in dark wood. Flanking the fireplace

are a pair of sleepy hollow chairs, upholstered in wool gros point by Mrs. Ramsey.

In the back wing, with the kitchen and butler's pantry, is the dining room where President Rutherford B. Hayes and his wife dined in 1878. The massive Victorian sideboard, one of many pieces the Ramseys purchased in New York when their house was completed, is surmounted by a rounded-top pediment that echoes the gently contoured tops of the principal windows and all the doors throughout the first two floors. Menus for the hearty dinners served here included wild goose, boiled mutton, asparagus, rhubarb pie as well as a "kraut dinner." A staggeringly opulent Thanksgiving dinner in 1882 entailed tomato soup, quail, white fish, roast turkey, fried oysters, celery salad, mince and oyster pies.

The staircase in the central hall, with black walnut banister, leads to the five bedrooms on the second floor which have changed very little through the years. The one called the Blue Room was daughter Marion's room for three years and then became a guest room. Here are the original horizontally paneled low bed in early Eastlake style and matching dresser with full-length mirror.

Historically, the most important room is Governor Ramsey's upstairs study-office in the rear wing which Ramsey called his "sitting room." Because it could be reached from a back stairway leading directly to an outside door, visitors, including Indians in full regalia, saw him without disturbing others in the house.

The mansion that was hailed by the *St. Paul Daily Press* as the "new and elegant residence," was willed to the Minnesota Historical Society in 1964 by Alexander Ramsey's grandchildren and is now in the last phase of a major restoration project.

Beside the butternut desk in Ramsey's study-office is a fancy-painted, gold-trimmed cuspidor in red, white and green.

261

Lincoln, Nebraska

FAIRVIEW

The Great Commoner's "Feudal Castle"

William Jennings Bryan, the Great Commoner, had a bond
with the average person that had nothing to do with political
philosophy and everything to do with private budgeting. He,
like so many others, had spent more than he planned on his
house. However, because he was a prominent personality in
the town of Lincoln, Nebraska, he had to face his problem not
with private remorse but with public explanation. In answer to
accusations that he was "milking" subscribers of his weekly
paper, *The Commoner,* in order to finance what the Republicans and the press called his "feudal castle," Bryan had to set
the record straight. His new house, Fairview, he said, was
designed to "cost about $10,000 but owing to the numerous
alterations in the plans, to the expense of delivering material
so far from town and to the recent increased expense of
building, the house cost considerably more than I anticipated
it would." Bryan had earned $34,000 from his book *The First
Battle,* a chronicle of the 1896 campaign, and he was able to
use some of the funds to withstand the extra costs he had
incurred to build a place where his children could "find fresh
air and healthy exercise," where he could indulge his "taste
for farming" and where "the friends who are passing this
midway point between the oceans can find a welcome and a
word of cheer."

If Bryan's home was controversial, its master was provocative and perplexing. Theodore Roosevelt thought him "a
personally honest and rather attractive man, a real orator and
a born demagogue, who has every crank, fool and putative
criminal in the country behind him, and a large proportion of
the ignorant honest class." Bryan, who was the losing candidate for President of the United States three different times,
was a spellbinding orator, yet it was said that "one could drive
a prairie schooner through any part of his argument and never
scrape against a fact." On the one hand, Bryan was "perfectly
attuned to the needs and aspirations of rural America,"
fighting high tariffs on manufactured goods, battling for
currency reform, opposing imperialism, advocating a federal
income tax, an eight-hour day, women's suffrage, the control

Opposite: A visitor to massive Fairview said
the house breathed an air of "open-handed
hospitality." (Photo: courtesy Nebraska State
Hist. Soc.) *Above:* The entrance hall is hung
with a portrait of a determined-looking Bryan.
(All other photos: Country Beautiful)

263

of monopolies and the strict regulation of public utilities. And though he was a confirmed pacifist, he approved of fighting Spain in 1898 to free Cuba because, he said, "Humanity demands that we should act." One of his most ardent crusades was in favor of bimetallism which he and others thought would curb the inflation then rampant. In 1873, the country had gone on the gold standard which meant that only gold was accepted for coinage at the mint. Allowing the free coinage of silver again would increase the amount of bullion being coined. The issue provoked one of Bryan's most glowing phrases: "You shall not press down upon the brow of labor this crown of thorns," he warned, "you shall not crucify mankind upon a cross of gold."

Only not all of Bryan glittered. Him name was gradually tarnished by small deeds and larger persuasions. As Secretary of State under Woodrow Wilson he refused to serve alcoholic beverages at department receptions and dinners because of his private disapproval of drinking and his convictions in other directions led him to resign when Wilson broke his policy of strict neutrality. He, of course, defended prohibition, refused to condemn the Ku Klux Klan and was thought to have "undignified associations" with the promotion of Florida real estate. But it was during the Scopes antievolution trial in Dayton, Tennessee, that Bryan was so "pitilessly exposed." Bryan maintained, among other things, that Eve was actually made from Adam's rib and that Jonah had really been swallowed by the whale. It is the opinion of one historian anyway, that "it would have been better for Bryan's reputation if he had died in 1915; instead he lived on for another decade, as amiable and well-intentioned as ever but increasingly out of touch with the rapidly changing times."

In 1893, when Bryan was thirty-three, his career, "his solid accomplishments," his fatal errors were all ahead of him. He had been born in Salem, Illinois, had studied law in Chicago, and a year after moving to Lincoln, he became active in the local Democratic organization. A month before his thirtieth birthday, he won his party's nomination to congress. He lived with his wife in a house paid for by his father-in-law in "little more than a cottage, though it boasted a second story and a cupola." But he was buying land already about three miles southeast of Lincoln, paying $250 an acre for the first five acres, figuring the scenery "is worth $100 an acre, the climate $100 and the soil $50." Crops of corn, wheat and oats grew in every direction "as far as the eye could reach"; there were thick forests along Antelope Creek which ran within a few hundred yards of the farm, and neat country homes, surrounded with shade trees, formed an "ideal landscape."

Because of an agricultural landscape of "unsurpassed beauty," Bryan chose Fairview as the name of his "suburban home," an aggressive example of the General Grant style of architecture, fussy and firmly built. One visitor, a hungry one presumably, admired Fairview for its warmth and its food. "The house is certainly a *home,* with its broad approaches, its sweeping entrance. . . ." The house breathed an air of "openhanded hospitality." "The milk was milk, indeed, the cream was *cream*; the bread was most delicious; the meat was tender — everything was neat, tasty, appetizing and home made." A

Opposite: Beside a bust of Bryan in the front parlor is an elephant table from India, an original piece that occupies the same place in the room as it did in 1908.

Below: The oak desk and chair in the library are the first Bryan used in his law office in Lincoln where he moved in 1887.

large porch was built around the southwest corner of the house, but because of the wind, due to the high elevation, the porch was barren of flowers and often chilly and uncomfortable. The interior was another matter.

The spacious entrance hall, in the center of the house, is hung with a large portrait of a determined-looking Bryan, by J. Laurie Wallace, and a smaller oil above the fireplace depicting a Philippine volcano. But it is the hall fireplace itself that is the focal point, with its yellow ochre and pink Travertine marble mantel piece streaked with deep red, white and black veins. The mantel shelf and molding above it are of golden oak. A small rectangular mirror flanked by light green marble panels is set into the marble above the shelf. Various objects of art unobtrusively decorate the hall, among them an Italian majolica oval bowl and a richly colored Japanese vase.

Of the library, the front parlor and the den, the three rooms which adjoin the entrance hall, the library reflects most personally Bryan's conservative taste. The plain oak desk is stained dark red and holds three of Bryan's literary works and four bound volumes of *The Commoner*. The desk and its chair are the first used by Bryan in his law office in Lincoln. Also here is a leather-covered armchair which dates from 1900 and was originally in *The Commoner* office.

The choicest piece in the front parlor is the walnut elephant table from India, an original Fairview piece that occupies the same place in the room as it did in 1908. Found here also is a handsome mahogany American Empire-style chair, circa 1900, and an elegant dark oak table with brass trim, also from about 1900.

Evidence that the Bryans had "traveled far and had done well" is found in the den or Curio Room with its several souvenirs from their 1905 world tour — four metal plates from India, a Japanese Imari plate, two Mexican stirrups and a brass basket. Representative of the type of objects the Bryans collected are a Chinese brass bowl, several Japanese Satsuma vases (Mrs. Bryan's favorite porcelain), a blue and white Canton bowl, circa 1800, and a fine hand-wrought silver bowl from central India. William Jennings Bryan, Jr., was largely responsible for the care and arrangement of this room.

Two other major rooms, the back bedroom and the back parlor, complete the extensive first floor. The bedroom was William, Jr.'s, and presently contains several handsome oak pieces: a golden oak bed and desk, circa 1890, and a Victorian dresser. The most noteworthy objects here are two Bryan campaign banners, one over the bed and the other on the closet door. The back parlor was used immediately after Fairview's construction as a bedroom for Mrs. Bryan's blind father and today contains an American Empire sofa and a Victorian center table, both probably original.

The Bryans spent exactly fifteen years in the home where they had intended to spend the "remainder of our days except such time as may be devoted to travel." Mrs. Bryan's arthritic condition required a move to a warmer climate and Miami was their choice. The couple deeded Fairview and part of its acreage to the Bryan Memorial Hospital. It served as a

dormitory for student nurses until 1961, and one year later members of the hospital board and the Junior League began a project of restoring the first floor and recreating the benevolent atmosphere of cluttered affluence enjoyed by Bryan and his beloved wife.

Fairview today is a pleasant memorial to a man who seemed to have enjoyed his life and who is, despite crushing criticism, thought to have lived with point and profit. Bryan was satisfied with his record: "Sometimes I have had over-sanquine friends express regret that I did not reach the Presidency. . . . But I have an answer ready for them," he said. "I have told them that they need not weep for me . . . I have been so much more interested in the securing of the things for which we have been fighting than I have been in the name of the man who held the office, that I am happy in the thought that this government, through these reforms, will be made so good that a citizen will not miss a little thing like the Presidency."

Two Bryan campaign banners are the most noteworthy objects in the first-floor back bedroom. The handsome bed is golden oak.

Nebraska City, Nebraska
ARBOR LODGE

J. Sterling Morton's Palatial Home in a Forest

"Trees are the monuments I would have. The cultivation of flowers and trees is the cultivation of the good, the beautiful and noble in man." The speaker was the editor of the Nebraska City *News,* James Sterling Morton, and before his life was over he could claim to have inspired the planting of 600 million trees and the creation of 100,000 acres of forest on the once open plains of Nebraska. He could also claim another monument. Part of the 160 acres of barren loam on which he and his wife had taken squatter's rights is today Arbor Lodge State Park, twenty-three tree-studded acres overlooking the west bank of the Missouri River and surrounding a white mansion. Some two hundred varieties of trees grow in the park, including a thousand pines Morton himself set in a grove north of the house back in 1892. In the early days the house had only four rooms, but it grew over the years to a palatial fifty-two rooms, complete with pillared porches.

Sterling Morton came to Nebraska City with his wife Caroline Joy French in 1855, seven years before the Homestead Law went into effect. Born in Adams, Jefferson County, New York, of New England ancestry, he had spent two years at the University of Michigan. His interests lay in territorial politics, and he opposed the efforts of Omaha and the North Platte country to dominate territorial affairs. He fought against wildcat banking projects, was nominated four different times for governor of his state, and served from 1858 to 1861 as secretary for the Nebraska Territory. Later he was named Secretary of Agriculture under President Grover Cleveland, a position he filled with such vision and dedication he would have dazzled environmentalists today. Morton saw tree planting as "a communal function with social and educational values," hounded churches, schools and clubs to undertake planting projects, and suggested that Nebraska towns set out young trees to commemorate the visit of a distinguished guest or the dedication of a building. "There is beauty in a well-ordered orchard, which is a joy forever. Orchards are missionaries of culture and refinement. If every farmer in Nebraska will plant out and cultivate an orchard and a flower garden, together with a few forest trees," he said, "this will become mentally and morally the best agricultural state in the Union." In 1872 he published a resolution suggesting a tree-planting day in early April and two years later, his friend Governor Robert W. Furnas, with whom Morton had started a

Above: Arbor Lodge grew from four rooms to a palatial fifty-two-room mansion, complete with pillared porches. (Photo: courtesy Arbor Lodge) *Opposite:* The drawing room walls are covered with patterned sandalwood-brown silk. (All remaining photos: Country Beautiful)

The master bedroom had as its distinguished guests in 1906, Porfirio Díaz, President of Mexico, and his wife. The elaborately carved bed is suitably grand for a chief executive.

large orchard in nearby Brownville, proclaimed April 8 the official Arbor Day. In 1885 the Nebraska legislature legalized the holiday, changing the date to Morton's birthday, April 22, and by 1890 Arbor Day had been adopted by thirty-five other states across the country. Today, eighty years later, Arbor Day lies neglected. The *New York Times* suggests it is too "important to be laid out and embalmed in nineteenth-century costume. . . . In an era of destructive technology, irretrievable waste and the dark stain of poisons in the air and water," Arbor Day, says the *Times,* is "probably the most significant of all holidays."

While he was urging his readers to get busy planting, Sterling Morton practiced his preachings. He and his wife were planting slips and seeds on their property and within a few years their cottage was surrounded with a "jungle of shade trees, shrubbery and vines." Their family grew as they prospered and the cottage they started out with prospered too, with three alterations, ending up T-shaped, three-storied and finished in stucco. The gable roof holds a balustraded widow's walk and on the north, south and east sides there are two-storied porches, each with six Corinthian columns that would do the White House proud. Under each porch on the second floor is a balcony with turned balusters. Morton died in 1902 and his property was inherited by his eldest son Joy, who had settled in Chicago and made a fortune in the salt business. After adding the east portion in 1904 and then enjoying the house for the next twenty summers, in 1922 Morton held a conference with the State Park Board at Arbor Lodge and offered the property as a state park, the mansion as a museum of natural history.

Today, the visitor to Arbor Lodge should be especially aware not only of the original furnishings and wall decorations on the first and second floors, but also of the rich variety of woods throughout the house — Honduras mahogany, apple wood, fumed oak, bird's-eye maple, rosewood, black walnut. Perhaps in no other room is the presence of wood so striking as in the dining room at the west end of a central hall running from the reception room past the double-banistered mahogany main stairway. The exposed ceiling beams and extensive woodwork are fumed oak, while the floor is laid with alternating boards of maple and walnut. Dominating the large room is a massive three-section walnut table which seats twelve and dates from 1877, as do the walnut chairs.

Adjoining the reception room on the left is a high-ceilinged, airy drawing room that succeeds admirably in being at once formal and hospitable: patterned sandalwood-brown silk covers the walls and original candelabra glisten in the large French plate mirror above the fireplace. A fine heavy old

A handsome bird's-eye maple bed and matching dresser dominate Mrs. Morton's bedroom. The wallpaper dates from 1870.

mahogany table sits in the middle of the room opposite a beige upholstered late-Empire-style sofa with straight back and carving on the arm rests. In one corner is a rosewood Chickering grand piano made in 1864, the most elegant piece in the room. By far the most intriguing room, however, is the sun porch directly off the drawing room. Here the visitor is dazzled by the many windows, and especially by the opalescent cathedral skylight with grapevine motif by Louis Comfort Tiffany that stripes the center of the ceiling with light.

The two most historically significant rooms at Arbor Lodge are the master bedroom and the Cleveland Room, largest of the eight bedrooms on the second floor. The master bedroom at the south end of the hall had as its distinguished guests in 1906, Porfirio Díaz, President of Mexico, and his wife. The elaborately carved rare old mahogany bed is suitably grand for a chief executive, as are the two green upholstered armchairs dating from 1850. A large mahogany door opens on to the balcony beneath the south portico, offering a refreshing view of the terraced gardens below.

Occupying the north end of the second-floor hall is the Cleveland Room where former President and Mrs. Grover Cleveland stayed during their visit to Arbor Lodge in 1905. The massive black walnut beds with curved headboards and footboards date from 1830, while an excellent comb-back Windsor rocker by the fireplace and two solid mahogany dressers were first used by Morton's parents about the same time. The fireplace has a wide facing of ceramic tiles with a pink flower motif on cream-colored background that carries out the multicolored floral design of the wallpaper. As in the master bedroom, here there is a door to the balcony, this one with a view of the north drive through the Pine Grove that Morton himself planted — recalling the crusading newspaperman's belief that trees "grow and self-perpetuate themselves and shed yearly blessings on our race."

Tahlequah, Oklahoma
MURRELL MANSION

Remembrance of the Cherokee

It was customary for Indian tribes to adopt an Indian woman's husband, if he was white, and for the white man, in return, to cast his lot with his adopted people and their customs and concerns. This was precisely the pattern followed by George Murrell, a native of Lynchburg, Virginia, who married his boss's daughter, and by doing so, allied himself with a remarkable Indian family. Murrell married Minerva Ross whose father Lewis was a merchant and whose uncle John was to the Cherokee people, "Solomon in counsel and a David in the defense of their rights."

Lewis's and John's grandparents were born in Inverness, Scotland, and their mother was one-quarter Cherokee. Both sons devoted themselves wholly to the Cherokee cause. At the beginning of the nineteenth century the Cherokees were the most powerful and civilized of all the North American Indians and their property extended from the eastern slope of the Blue Ridge Mountains almost to the Mississippi, and from northern Kentucky to central Alabama and Georgia. Their expulsion from Georgia, precipitated by President Andrew Jackson's decree that "the attempt of the Indians to establish an independent government in Georgia and Alabama would not be countenanced," was characterized, according to Thomas Benton, "by a depth and bitterness of feeling such as have never been excelled on the slavery question." Gold deposits in Georgia fanned the white man's desire to be rid of the Indians. Uprooted without recourse, they traveled for over five months, losing four thousand of their people on the route they later called the Trail of Tears. They settled on the site of an old Ute Indian village which they named Tahlequah, in what is now northeastern Oklahoma.

The Ross families, including the Murrells, chose to live in a neighborhood called Park Hill, about five miles south of Tahlequah, already inhabited by a western Cherokee group who had emigrated from Arkansas territory. A church and day mission thrived at Park Hill due to the efforts of Dr. S.A. Worcester. A printing press put out hymns and a primer as well as a Bible in both Cherokee and Choctaw, and the school run by Miss Sarah Worcester and Miss Ellen Whitmire, graduates of Mount Holyoke, specialized in Latin and Greek and taught Watt's *Improvement of the Mind* and Paley's *Natural Theology* and *Intellectual Philosophy*. The newspaper was called the *Cherokee Advocate*. Though the Civil War was fermenting and though the community was plagued by droughts which meant the destruction of crops, the Cherokees were making slow but steady progress, independent of any help except for that of the missionaries.

It was into this hard-working community that George Murrell and his wife moved and received a gift of a log-walled house that Lewis Ross had bought for $2,000. In 1842 Murrell owned the largest of the community's four stores, operated a grist mill and a lumber mill and could afford to have his second wife Amanda (the sister of Minerva who had died of malaria) dress in "flounced silk with the mantle heavily bedecked with spangles which glittered in the sunlight with every movement." He also could afford to build "the largest and finest home in the extensive Indian country," cultivating his land with the help of Negroes, growing grain and raising cotton and an orchard of apple trees. Limestone and sandstone were used for foundations and chimneys, while the neighboring hills and bluffs provided the pine for the framework. The result was a

Above: Murrell Mansion is framed by imposing maple and catalpa trees. (Photo: courtesy Okla. Park Dept.) *Opposite:* An Empire sofa in the parlor combines harmoniously with green brocade curtains. (All remaining photos: Country Beautiful)

stately two-story white frame house with hip roof that today stands like an inviting centerpiece in the middle of a large lawn, framed with imposing maple and catalpa trees. The spacious veranda that encircled the first floor of the house as late as 1956 has been replaced by a simple front porch on the north side. A pedimented second-story balcony above the porch has been retained, although its original massive square columns have been replaced by lighter ones. A fanlight and a narrow window on each side of the large recessed door light the central hallway.

The nine main rooms of the house are each twenty feet square with twelve-foot ceilings. The pine flooring and siding, the windows and oak doors, as well as the furniture and hardware, were imported from France and shipped from New Orleans by boat up the Mississippi and Arkansas rivers to Fort Gibson where they were loaded onto ox carts and driven overland to Park Hill. Though the furniture was scattered far and wide, interested descendants of the Ross family have located several pieces and donated them to the house.

The two principal rooms on the first floor are the parlor to the right of the hall and the dining room across from it. The parlor is dominated by a large portrait of George M. Murrell above the white wooden mantel, a painting returned to the mansion in 1954 by George Murrell Alexander, a direct descendant. To the right of the fireplace is the room's choicest piece, a rosewood Empire sofa with graceful curving arm rests and feet with deep carving. The sofa's upholstery of gold patterned tapestry blends softly with the dark green brocade curtains. A handsome pier mirror with elaborately carved gilt frame hangs above a mahogany pedestal table.

The dining room is an especially appealing room. The cherry Queen Anne banquet table with cabriole legs and a mahogany breakfront are its two most significant pieces. The breakfront is an original piece which contains plates and a brass teakettle that were actually used by the Murrells. The impact of the smashing red wallpaper with delicate black floral pattern and the equally brilliant red curtains is heightened by the snow white wainscoting. A fine Victorian sofa with acanthus leaf and

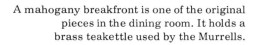

A mahogany breakfront is one of the original pieces in the dining room. It holds a brass teakettle used by the Murrells.

fleur-de-lis carving on the arm rests is an unexpectedly apt addition to this room.

Appropriately enough, grand beds abound in the mansion's five spacious bedrooms on the second floor, one of them being the bed where George and Amanda Murrell's first child was born. Returned in the early 1960's by Mrs. M.G. Murrell of Baton Rouge, it is one of the mansion's French imports whose paneled headboard displays a finely carved cresting of shield-like design. In another bedroom is a massive rosewood four-poster, also original and also imported. Its hexagonal posts and low, simple, curving headboard make it perhaps the mansion's most graceful bed of all. Unequaled in intricacy, however, is an early Victorian bed in the back room and its matching night table and marble-topped dresser with tall mirror. Resting on porcelain casters, the bed is a tour de force of burl-walnut-paneled footboard and headboard crowned with a heart-shaped cresting that nearly rises to the full height of the twelve-foot ceiling.

Tragically, the Civil War changed the course of the Indian community irrevocably. John Ross sided at first with the Confederacy and later restored the Cherokees' allegiance to the Union, abolishing slavery and "involuntary servitude in the Cherokee nation." Murrell had left Park Hill at the very start of the Civil War, in 1862, returning to Lynchburg where he helped to equip a Confederate company at his personal expense and received the rank and title of major. He never returned to Park Hill and his property, according to Cherokee law, reverted to the Cherokee nation. After passing through various hands, his house was bought and secured for posterity in 1948 by the Oklahoma State Planning and Resource Board.

Above: Resting on porcelain casters, this early Victorian bed has burl-walnut panels inlaid in both its footboard and headboard.

Below: Perhaps the mansion's most graceful piece, this massive rosewood four-poster has hexagonal posts and low, curving headboard.

Salt Lake City, Utah
BEEHIVE HOUSE

Greek Revival Mansion of the Mormons' Pioneer Leader

Above: A portrait of Young hangs in the entry hall with its hardwood paneling.

Beehive House was aptly named. From the time the Mormon leader Brigham Young built the elaborate, pillared, Greek Revival mansion in 1854, it swarmed with family and followers who had labored their way west by oxen and mule-drawn covered wagons, by cart and by foot, through ominous Indian country and soaring mountains, to enter the valley of the Great Salt Lake, to colonize and literally to found the forty-fifth state of the Union. If the Mormons, more accurately known as Latter-Day Saints, had had their way, Utah would have been called Deseret which, in their own language, means a honeybee, the Mormon symbol of Industry. Instead, they settled for a beehive-shaped gilded finial crowning the square cupola atop their leader's house as a symbol of their persistent belief that if they wanted to build up the Kingdom of God or establish Zion upon the earth they would have to work — to heed Young's plea to "labor with our hands, plan with our minds and devise ways and means to accomplish that object."

He and his followers believed they had accomplished the impossible and took immense pride in it. "Not a person among all the mountaineers . . . believed that an ear of corn would ripen in these valleys," yet they had achieved the miracle of

The balconies and tall pillars of Beehive
House echo the mansions of Brigham
Young's native Vermont.

fertility. Tough, ruthless, fearless and passionately dedicated, Brigham Young charged his people to allow nothing to "hinder or stay them," that together they would "build our furnaces, open our mines, make our railroads, till the soil, follow our mercantile business uninterrupted; that we may attend to the business of beautifying the earth."

Young, who was born in Vermont to a farmer and Revolutionary soldier from Hopkinton, Massachusetts, was a journeyman house painter and glazier, a handyman and farmer as well. He was living in Mendon, New York, when he was introduced to the teachings of Joseph Smith, the founding father of the Church of Jesus Christ of Latter-Day Saints. In 1830 Smith published the *Book of Mormon;* a few weeks later it was in Young's hands and after two years of study, Young left the Methodist Church irrevocably. At Smith's violent death, Young assumed leadership of the Mormons whose faith evoked bitter criticism from outsiders who did not share their view of right to plural marriage or polygamy as a religious

Molded extension table on pedestal base and Victorian sideboard with spool-turned legs furnish mansion's dining room.

principle. The Mormons, therefore, were made unwelcome in state after state — expelled from Ohio, from Missouri, from Illinois — and finally they made their way west to settle on what was then Mexican soil, beyond American jurisdiction. They were free now to follow the principles of Mormonism so ardently espoused by Young himself who had nineteen wives and fifty-six children in all. The Territory of Utah was organized in September of 1850 and Young appointed governor by President Millard Fillmore and reappointed by President Franklin Pierce. Congress in President Lincoln's administration passed a law in 1862 against plural marriages and it was only when the Mormons would forsake polygamy entirely that the Territory of Utah was admitted into the Union, in January of 1896.

The history of the Church of the Latter-Day Saints during Young's thirty years of leadership is largely the history and settlement of the inter-mountain west during the same period. Young and the Mormons founded schools (the University of Utah was known originally as the University of Deseret), built theaters, a newspaper, and created Zion's Co-operative Mercantile Institution which grew into the largest institution of its kind in the West. Though Young had no more than two months of formal schooling he valued education "to enable us to understand the laws and principles of life, and how to be useful while we live." His florid sermons spanned an amazing variety of topics — from dishwashing to empire building. Though he hated gambling or card playing he recognized that "recreation and diversion are as necessary to our well-being as the more serious pursuits of life."

It was probably Young's personal wealth, as well as his breadth of interests and his practicality, that enabled him "to give polygamy a grace it had nowhere else." It was just seven years after Young reached the Great Basin that he was able to build a handsome three-story house with the help of Truman O. Angell — its deep porches and balconies, its tall pillars echoing, in many ways, the mansions of Young's native Vermont with their high ceilings and expansive rooms. The Beehive House served as his office, as well as a dwelling for one family or another; the adjacent Lion House coped with overflow for the last twenty-three years of Young's life.

After his death in 1877, the Beehive House underwent two major alterations. When Young's son purchased the house in 1888 he rebuilt the rear section into a three-story wing and added an upstairs sitting room and a parlor, now called the Victorian Room. In 1893 the house was purchased by the church to be the residence of its presidents, but only two of them lived in it. The house stood empty after the death of President Joseph F. Smith until a number of years later when it was remodeled again to make it into a residence for young women. Most of this second remodeling was torn away after the church decided in 1959 to restore the structure. Using old

Detail of honeybee motif, elsewhere carved in wood relief, embellishes doorknob escutcheon. (Photo: Country Beautiful)

manuscripts describing the house in Young's time and old photographs, the Beehive House has been made to look as it did while Young lived in it, except for the 1888 additions.

Once more the stuccoed adobe brick is accented with forest green shutters and immaculate white trim. Additions, false ceilings, have been ripped away and the furniture, including many pompous Victorian pieces, gathered from old houses in Utah including some of the original Young pieces.

The eleven tall, white pillars supporting a continuous second-floor balcony extending all the way across the entrance, or south, façade, and part way around the east side, give the exterior an impressive and architecturally harmonious appearance. Inside, the principal rooms are spacious with high ceilings and there are many satisfying details, such as the honeybee motif on the doorknob escutcheons.

There are two basic sections to the house. The entrance hall with its finely wrought pine paneling extends the width of the south portion of the house that includes the downstairs room on the right and Young's office and bedroom to the left. The north section, which is larger, contains two dining rooms, kitchen and the octagonal reception room. Above are a children's schoolroom, the Victorian Room, a sitting room, a sewing room and the elaborately furnished Gardo Room, an octagonal room like the reception room directly below it.

Adjoining the entrance hall is Young's bedroom, historically perhaps the most interesting one in the house, although modest in appearance. A few of his personal possessions are here, including his cherry-wood bookcase-secretary with carved cresting over the cornice and turned finials. The massive mahogany bed repeats the bee motif in the center panel of its headboard. The sitting room across the hall has muted green walls with white woodwork and typical Victorian pieces such as the tall glass-enclosed walnut bookcase with heavy, carved cresting and the Paisley-shawl-covered table.

The two most elegant rooms — the octagonal Gardo Room, done in the rococo manner with much gilded ornamentation, and the great parlor or Long Hall — are on the second floor. It was in the Long Hall with its coved ceiling that Young, as territorial governor and church president, entertained many distinguished visitors through the years, including President Grant and Mark Twain. The original piano which made music for these gatherings is here, and the thirty-two-foot length of the room is dominated by the five pairs of red damask draperies and the square-patterned carpet with panels of flowers on a black background. The furnishings are Victorian, including two Belter sofas, one triple-arched and upholstered in red satin. It is the remainder of the house, however, with its many sturdy pieces of pioneer workmanship, that probably comes closest to the true spirit of Brigham Young. It exudes a kind of homely affluence which the Mormon leader and his many wives and children enjoyed.

Photo: courtesy Church of Jesus Christ of Latter-Day Saints

Young's brown felt hat and well-used cane lie on top of
his bed. Cherry-wood secretary is crested with carving
and mahogany bed's center panel carries bee motif.

Washoe County, Nevada
BOWERS MANSION

Palace of the Tragic Queen of Washoe

No queen was more ambitious, more extravagant, or more pathetic than Allison Orrum Hunter Cowan Bowers, Queen of Washoe, the pleasant Nevada valley with precious deposits of gold and silver known as the Comstock lode.

Allison Bowers, called Eilley, was born in Scotland and married in America, first to a bishop of the Church of Jesus Christ of Latter-Day Saints, a practicing polygamist, then to another Mormon. Divorced from both, she stayed on in Carson City to seek her fortune and to marry, in 1858, one of her boarders who claimed footage adjacent to her own stake in the Comstock lode. Eilley and her new husband, Sandy Bowers, a mule-skinner from Missouri, fourteen years her junior, consolidated their land and shortly were faced not with finding a fortune, but spending one. At that point the mine provided them with $100,000 a month. As they prospered, their stature grew and Sandy, whose original name was Lemuel Sanford, was appointed a delegate to the convention in Carson City on territorial expansion, and, besides mining enterprises, apparently he owned a brickyard, a lumber yard, teams and wagons, and eventually a mansion fit for a mining queen.

An architect was called in from San Francisco to design the Bowers Mansion. A canyon a few miles away yielded the granite. Scotland sent on the stonecutters. Plate glass and etched glass (for panels and transoms) were imported from Belgium. And the Bowerses' own mines yielded the silver for the hinges and door knobs. Furniture was another matter and one of the main reasons for the Bowerses' eighteen-month-long excursion abroad. Welcomed as "Yankee royalty," they bought suites of furniture, marble fountains and mantels, mirrors, Turkish carpets and morocco-bound books gilded with their name. Eilley sent home for the bullion to be made into flatware with a grape design. Silks and brocades were her favorite materials for her Paris-made wardrobe, and the dress she planned to wear for her presentation to Queen Victoria was purple silk with roses embroidered in gold thread. Whether it was because Charles Francis Adams, Minister to Great Britain, did not recognize her appeal to the Queen, if she made one, or whether the Queen could not see her because she was in mourning or *would* not see her because of Eilley's two divorces seems to be one of the uncatalogued aspects of this trip. The fact that Eilley did obtain a few cuttings of ivy from Westminster Abbey or Windsor Castle (depending on the sourcebook) was widely mentioned. In the end, the Bowerses' trip yielded a surprise more meaningful than any possessions Eilley might have cherished. A few days out on their return voyage to America aboard the *Persia*, it is believed that the mother of a day-old infant aboard was buried at sea. Eilley adopted the child and named her, for her mother and the ship, Margaret Persia.

The winter of 1867 and 1868 was crucial for the Bowerses. Heavy rains followed the snow, cutting a channel nine feet deep through the ravine. The Bowerses' newly repaired mill at the mine was wrecked by debris. And the mine itself was no longer producing bounteously. The market was fluctuating and speculators were absorbing the best gold resources. At thirty-eight, Sandy Bowers was dead and his wife was in debt. The house had cost over $400,000 and the entire

Above: Three balustrades and a pair of arched windows emphasize the Mediterranean air of Bowers Mansion. *Opposite:* The choicest piece in the parlor is a tufted satin Louis XVI sofa with Eastlake details. (All photos: Country Beautiful)

estate was appraised for almost $89,000 and Sandy had mortgaged more than he had invested. He had also sold stock in the mine he and Eilley owned and had lost control of it. In 1871 Eilley could no longer afford the mansion for which she had shopped with such frenzied extravagance years earlier. A committee thought it might be suitable for Nevada's much-needed insane asylum but Eilley dreamed instead of making it into a resort hotel. In the end she lost her mansion and went to live in a small cottage on its grounds. The sudden death of her daughter Persia crowned her misfortunes and shattered her stability. When she was thought to have set fire to the outside stairway of the mansion and to the kitchen floor of her cottage, she lost her last claims to the mansion or any of its property. A large, clumsy, halting figure in middle age, Eilley rented a basement room on O'Farrell Street in San Francisco in 1887 until she could no longer work and then went to live in a place not inappropriately named King's Daughters Home of California, in Oakland.

Bowers Mansion changed owners many times before it and fifty-six acres of forested hills surrounding it were rescued from further exploitation in 1946 by the Reno Women's Civic Club who interested the Washoe County Board of Commissioners in its purchase. Maintained now by the Washoe County Parks and Recreation Department, the mansion, with the help of five hundred contributors, has been since 1968 a sincere credit to Eilley Bowers's ambitions and Nevada's fantastic mining episodes.

The U-shaped mansion has had its Victorian-trimmed façade lifted to reveal an Italianate villa of fine proportions and genuine elegance. Two raised stories of gray granite complete with quoins and a bracketed overhang are surmounted by an octagonal cupola in the center of the flat room, while a wide square-columned porch with a wooden balustrade runs around three sides of the house and is painted beige. Two other balustrades, one atop the porch and the

Above left: Mrs. Bowers's bedroom and adjacent sitting room are papered in a delicate maroon floral pattern.

Above: A massive 1879 Steinway square grand piano adds taste and opulence to the east end of the parlor.

Below: Part of a valuable collection, this bronze statue of a Scottish hunter with his horse and dog stands on a night table.

other along the roof, a pair of arched windows in the middle of the second story and a thirty-foot-wide patio between the wings accentuate the mansion's Mediterranean air. The arched windows and the main doorway below them on the first story are each flanked by a pair of large two-pane windows. A wide six-stepped stairway leads up to the porch and main door in the east façade.

The spacious interior is the cream of the Victorian era, filled with gilded mantel mirrors, ornate chandeliers, flowered paper and flowered carpets that are fittingly contrasted with primly tufted satins and velvets. The furniture throughout is of Renaissance-baroque-style of the period 1830 to 1870. Elaborate Corinthian frieze molding with egg-and-dart under it runs through the central hall and the south parlor to the left. A splendid period crystal chandelier graces the parlor ceiling, illuminating stark white walls and trim and a white Carrara marble fireplace with two scrolled brackets beneath the mantel and a deeply carved keystone showing a head of Queen Anne. Contrasting with the pervading whiteness are red velvet draperies and valance framing four large windows and a tufted red satin Louis XVI sofa with Eastlake details and a back formed by three shaped panels separated by exposed framing. Also in this room are two highly prized beige-green satin armchairs in the Renaissance-revival style, their trumpet-shaped legs supporting a broad, deeply padded seat, while comfortable padded armrests appear above caryatids with Egyptian heads. The projection in the center of the front seat rail is an appendage often found on Renaissance-revival furniture. Other signs of opulence in this room are a multicolored Kirman rug and an 1879 Steinway square grand piano at the east end.

The library and dining room, as well as a reception room, all on the first floor, are equally lavish, but do not rival the two principal bedrooms upstairs, Sandy's in the northeast corner and Eilley's across the hall. A century ago, Sandy himself bought and slept in the walnut and burl-walnut double bed with elaborately carved headboard that still sits in his room. Covering the bed is a crocheted bedspread with popcorn stitch and folded at one end is a quilted silk comforter dating from 1845. On the marble-topped night stand, which is original, is a bronze statue of a Scottish hunter with his horse and dog, part of a valuable group collection.

Mrs. Bowers's elaborate bedroom and adjacent sitting room are papered in a delicate maroon floral design and carpeted with a finely patterned rug with leaf motif. The walnut bed with carved headboard flanked by carved swags is covered with fine handmade lace pillow shams and an intriguing satin and velvet quilt depicting in bright colors the state flowers of the thirty-six states that comprised the Union in 1864. A walnut marble-topped dressing table and pier mirror are both hand-carved and outlined in gold. Altogether, the colors and the furniture here, and indeed throughout the house, are as exuberant as Eilley Bowers was in her young and most hopeful days when her trusty crystal ball (which she read in times of stress) promised her great fortune — for a while anyway.

San Juan Bautista, California
CASTRO ADOBE

Where Two Cultures Meet

If you stop to think of where the Castro Adobe is built, why it was built, how it was built, who built it *and* who bought it, you have a clue to the exotic composition of California's culture and people. The slender, plain, white, two-storied house with its sloping tile roof that shades second-floor balconies in front and back was built by Don José María Castro of adobe bricks and was constructed by Castro's father, Tiburcio, with the help of the Indians of the Mission San Juan Bautista. Castro's adobe is one of the early examples of what is known as Monterey architecture, a style that blends Spanish, Mexican, Indian and American tastes, and that has influenced the look of southern California and American territories everywhere.

Castro built this adobe in 1838 on a grant of 1,500 Spanish varas from the Mexican government. Don José was interim governor of Alta California from 1835 to 1836 and interim *comandante general* from 1845 to 1846 and this adobe was to house the secretary of the prefecture. California during the Mexican regime was divided into two districts and San Juan became the *cabecera*, or head town, of the first district and was known as San Juan de Castro, its *comandante* an uncompromising opponent of American aggression. So strongly did Castro feel about American occupation that he and one other man were the only Mexican subjects to decline American citizenship when it was offered them.

Identity was a matter of crisis not only to Castro, however, but to this entire region and had been since about 1540 when the Spanish began their flirtation with California. It was a full two centuries later, spurred by fear of the Russian explorations in Alaska and the need for a refitting point on the California coast for their galleons from Manila, that the Spanish occupied San Diego in 1769, when San Francisco Bay was discovered, and Monterey in 1770. At this time, the Jesuit property on the peninsula was turned over to the Franciscan monks and then, in 1772, to the Dominicans who took over the twenty-one missions built from 1769 to 1823, and helped for the next fifty years to feed, clothe and instruct the inhabitants. When the revolution broke out in Mexico in 1810, the Californians remained loyal to Spain, but by 1822 they had sided with Mexico and under the Mexican federal constitution of 1824, first Upper California, and then Lower California, received representation in the Mexican congress. In 1834, secularization of the missions started, a process which was not completed until 1840. By 1848 Mexico had ceded California to the United States and one year later, Castro Adobe had changed owners and nationality and had entered into a totally new chapter in its existence.

On February 7, 1849, Don José María Castro deeded the Castro Adobe to Patrick Breen, who with his wife had emigrated from Ireland in 1819 by way of Toronto and Iowa. With their children they had joined the Donner Party, named for people who led the tragic venture, and with a group of eighty-seven people in all, tried in the winter of 1846 to reach the summit of the Sierra Nevadas. They were trapped by snow in

Opposite above: Built in 1838, the Castro Adobe is an early example of Monterey architecture. *Opposite below:* A Japanese silk fire screen in the parlor was used to reflect heat into the corners of the room. (All photos: Country Beautiful)

the passes, and only half survived to reach California. The same year the Breens settled at the Castro Adobe with their eight children, the eldest son John went off to the mines to dig gold, first at Mormon's Bar and later at Placerville, and returned most successfully eleven months later with $12,000 worth of gold. He used the money to buy the Castro Adobe and four hundred acres of rich land in the San Juan Valley.

The story, then, of the Castro and the Breen family on the Monterey peninsula encompasses the story of the Americanization of California and explains the region's ties to the Spanish language and people, the food and the architecture, all most evident today, and certainly strongly felt by any visitor to the Castro-Breen Adobe in what one writer describes as the "sleepiest, sunniest, dreamiest place in the world."

The adobe remained in the Breen family's possession for eighty-four years, until 1933, when it was sold to the State of California to become a monument to the early pioneers. The state Department of Parks has restored the house and refurnished it with period pieces and mementos of the Mexican and Early American periods. It sits among other Spanish-style buildings as part of the restored village of San Juan Bautista. The first floor contains three major rooms — the parlor, the kitchen and Castro's office, all with white walls — the latter is entered directly from the outside. Furnished most austerely, as is the rest of the house, the Mexican-style office has a wooden desk, a cowhide rug and a framed painting of Our Lady of Guadalupe, patronness of Mexico, on the wall — all relics of an older culture. A choice piece is the fluted diamond point glass pitcher on the desk, made in Albany, circa 1810, and said to have been used by Castro. The green-painted woodwork adds a pleasing dash of color.

The unadorned principal entrance leads into a small hall that on the left opens into the parlor, the largest room on the first floor, and on the right takes the visitor past the kitchen and turns toward the elegant cherry staircase in the rear. A Japanese silk fire screen with a black-on-white pattern in the parlor, used to reflect heat into the far corners of the room, stands near the fireplace. On the plain wooden mantel are an Amorita clock made in Connecticut and a pair of candle holders from the Breen cache, goods the exhausted travelers left behind buried in the snow and not recovered until five years after the Donner Party was rescued. By far the most

Above: A handmade shell cross in the window of the Mexican Bedroom speaks at once of religious bonds and nearby Monterey beaches.
Below: The austerity of Castro's office is evident in the plain desk, the cowhide rug and the simple unadorned chairs.

impressive piece is a massive square grand piano with seventy-eight keys. Made in 1845 by Dubois and Seabury of New York, it was once owned by Patrick Breen, Jr.

The rustic kitchen contains a "Jewell Triumph" wood stove and such curious utensils as a Sutherland Liverpool griddle and monk's pan for making Danish pancakes. The table appears to be waiting for the Breens at mealtime: It holds complete settings for six, including unmatched bone-handled tinware and silver napkin rings on a bright red tablecloth with white floral design.

The three bedrooms on the upper floor of the house represent both the American and Mexican cultures. The Mexican Bedroom holds a cut-down four-poster bed that was used in the Castro house during the Breen ownership. Beside the bed is an adjustable wrought-iron candle stand and in the window is a handmade shell cross that speaks at once of religious bonds and nearby Monterey beaches.

The spacious master bedroom was used by Patrick and Margaret Breen and still contains a massive Victorian-style bed they ordered from Australia, a luxurious piece of furniture by nineteenth-century California standards. The space-saving Rancho-style wardrobe was a great convenience in the days before built-in closets.

The Breens' only daughter, Isabella, who died in San Francisco in 1935, occupied the remaining bedroom. At the foot of the Spanish-style bed with its intricate leaf-and-stem carving is her wooden camphor chest, and against the wall is a dresser with mirror and plied leaf-design drawer handles that was shipped to California via Cape Horn.

The austere Castro Adobe must have looked palatial to the Breen family when they came down out of the merciless snows of the Sierra Nevadas into the warmth and beauty of this radiant part of the world — especially so to the haggard survivors of the doomed Donner party.

The table in the rustic kitchen holds complete settings for six, including unmatched bone-handled tinware and silver napkin rings.

289

Monterey, California
LARKIN HOUSE

Archetype of the Monterey Style

Above: Larkin House displays the long horizontal lines characteristic of the Monterey style. *Opposite:* Most sophisticated room in the house today, the living room was once used for commercial purposes. (All photos: Country Beautiful)

Thomas Oliver Larkin did just what a classic Horace Greeley hero ought to do. Born in Charlestown, Massachusetts, of *Mayflower* ancestry, and orphaned at sixteen, he worked in North and South Carolina before he went west to "grow up with the country." On September 5, 1831, at the age of twenty-nine, Larkin sailed for California and seven months later docked at Monterey. He clerked for his half-brother until he saved $500, the foundation of a fortune that would make him one of the pioneer practitioners of the theory of diversification so dear to the present economy.

Larkin built the first double-geared flour mill in the region, along with a lumber mill, and traded in both, as well as in beaver and sea-otter skins, potatoes, soaps and horses, with Mexico and with the Sandwich Islands. He acquired vast amounts of real estate both in northern and southern California and founded, with Dr. Robert Semple, the town of Benicia, across the bay in San Francisco which never grew into the great seaport its developers had envisioned. He owned trading vessels, operated a wholesale and retail store which branched out to Santa Cruz, a construction company and a mining company; his reports on the discovery of gold in 1848 were among the first to reach Washington. Larkin is also considered to be among the first bankers, possibly because his office was said to be the only one around that had a safe.

Thus far, we have the portrait of a visionary entrepreneur.

What makes Larkin of more impressive historical interest is the role, however secret, he played in the United States acquisition of California from Mexico. He seems to have held two official positions in this regard, one as the United States Consul, the first and only one to Mexico, from 1844 to 1848, and another as confidential agent in California, an appointment awarded by a secret dispatch dated October 17, 1845, signed by Secretary of State James Buchanan. James Polk was President then, and territorial expansion one of his aims. Larkin was instructed to work for the "secession of California from Mexico, without overt aid from the United States, but with their good will and sympathy." At the same time United States naval officers were instructed to occupy the ports in case of war with Mexico, but first and last to work for the good will of the natives.

Buchanan's dispatch advised Larkin to warn the Californians against designs of the English or French and to "arouse in their bosoms that love of liberty and independence is natural to the American continent." In view of later embattled episodes, principally the outbreak of the Mexican War over the acquisition of Texas, a war that Ulysses S. Grant regarded as

Above: The antique Chinese teakwood bed in Mrs. Toulmin's bedroom is typical of the furniture favored by wealthy Mandarin families.

Below: Over the nineteenth-century American sleigh bed in Mr. Toulmin's room is a wall case with glass pieces from Cyprus and Syria.

"one of the most unjust ever waged by a stronger against a weaker nation," other parts of the Buchanan dispatch are pertinent. "Whilst the President will make no effort and use no influence to induce California to become one of the free and independent states of this Union, yet if the people should desire to unite their destiny with ours, they would be received as brethren, whenever this can be done, without affording Mexico just cause of complaint." Though it was through military rather than diplomatic means that California finally entered the Union, Larkin was credited with obtaining the Mexicans' "good will and sympathy."

There is still another phase of Larkin's accomplishments that is of interest — his unique house that set a precedent for what is known as "Monterey architecture," a remarkably pleasant blend of totally disparate influences, East and West, New England and California, Georgian and Spanish. Larkin had married a New Englander he met on his original voyage West, and had begun building his home just two years after arriving in Monterey. Between the years 1834 and 1838 he paid $38 for a piece of land on which he constructed a sturdy adobe of sun-hardened mud bricks with a hip roof, embellishing this essentially Spanish-style dwelling with mantels, windows and doorway moldings brought from New England to Monterey via Cape Horn. Another feature from the East is the use of a central stairway rather than the traditional Spanish patio. The result, known as the Monterey House, was later widely copied along the West Coast.

Rooms were added to the original structure to house Larkin's nine children, all of whom were educated first in Hawaii and then in New England, because Monterey did not have English-speaking schools at the time. Larkin also added a small office next to his house that served as headquarters for Lieutenant William Tecumseh Sherman, who later became famous during the Civil War, during his time in Monterey. Larkin returned briefly to the East around 1850 and then moved to San Francisco, where he died of typhoid fever five years later, on October 27, 1858. His house was repurchased by his granddaughter, Mrs. Harry W. Toulmin, who donated the six-bedroom house to the State of California in 1957. It is restored and intriguingly furnished.

The exterior readily displays characteristic features of the Monterey style: two stories, hip roof and the long horizontal lines of the veranda and a covered second-story balcony that surround the house. Nearly blinding in the sun, the plastered, whitewashed façade contains three twelve-over-twelve-light windows on the first floor and four smaller ones on the second. A short flight of steps leads up to the porch.

The living room, once used for commercial purposes, is nevertheless the most sophisticated room in the house today. Over a fine English Sheraton mahogany writing desk hangs an unusual carved gilt-wood and gesso Federal mirror with double columns. The woodwork, mantel and redwood flooring are original as is the pair of wing chairs, circa 1780, on each side of the fireplace. Serpentine-arched with closed frame, they are covered with mauve velvet, a gift to the family from a Revolutionary War general.

Across the hall is the dining room which was originally used by Larkin as the trading post. The only principal room without cornice molding and with a rafter ceiling, it is the most primitive room in the house. Today it is nicely furnished with several late Sheraton and Hepplewhite-style pieces and two large circular portraits of Larkin and his wife. The upstairs room the Larkins used as a dining room has one original Larkin item, a caned chair beside the fireplace, but the most valuable things are two French fruitwood pieces — an armoire and a *poudreuse* with molded brass drawers and lined with a mirror. This room served Mrs. Toulmin as a guest room and is delightfully furnished with an American sleigh bed and an American Sheraton chest of drawers.

The upstairs front room now furnished as a bedroom is the mansion's most historic room. Originally the Larkin family parlor, in 1847, before California was granted statehood, it was briefly used as the headquarters of General Stephen W. Kearny when he was in charge of the American Military Government. Thus, Larkin House was, in effect, the capitol of California. After Kearny left, his young adjutant, Lieutenant Sherman, moved into the room. Much later it became Mrs. Toulmin's bedroom and it reflects her taste for Oriental treasures. The antique Chinese teakwood bed was bought from the Chinese Mission in China, in 1910, and is typical of the furniture favored by wealthy Mandarin families. To the side of the bed, on an elaborately carved and inlaid Annamite teakwood altar table, rests a Persian jewel box brightly painted with court scenes both inside and out. The bronze bowl in the window is a Han Dynasty verde antique dated from 400 B.C. and filled today with fragrant potpourri.

The front upstairs bedroom, now called Mr. Toulmin's Bedroom, again reminds us of the mansion's commercial origins, for it was originally used as a storage room for merchandise. The trap door in the floor allowed goods to be passed directly through to the trading post below. The function of the room changed drastically when Mr. Toulmin made it his bedroom because in it he kept his splendid collection of *objets d'art*, still housed there today. Over the nineteenth-century American sleigh bed is a wall case with his glass pieces from Cyprus, Syria and Rome, Egyptian figurines and Chinese tomb figures from the Sung and Ming dynasties. Other unusual treasures are in the exceptional Irish corner wall cupboard of Adam design. Painted white with modillioned and arched interior facing and fluted pilasters, it holds Byzantine cloisonné enamel and bronze fragments, Roman alabaster tomb utensils and pre-Columbian terra-cotta heads. Beneath the cupboard is an uncommon mahogany "bachelor's chest" in the Chippendale style with a fold-down top. Between two of the windows is a French serpentined-back mahogany sofa, covered in green velvet, called a "governess sofa."

The Toulmins' bedrooms reveal them both as people of diverse and wide-ranging interests, as was Thomas O. Larkin. Apart from this house in Monterey, there is another memorial to Larkin, a street named for him in San Francisco. It is appropriately situated high over the city looking out toward an endless horizon.

This office next to the house served as headquarters for Lieutenant William T. Sherman, who later became famous in the Civil War.

Sacramento, California
LELAND STANFORD HOUSE

A Keepsake of the Extravagant Past

Gold was not the only source of fortune-making in California in the middle of the nineteenth century: Railroad construction was definitely another way up the financial ladder. When Theodore Judah, a Connecticut-born civil engineer, conjured up the idea of a transcontinental railroad that would straddle the formidable Sierra Mountains, he was encouraged and backed by four bearded and unique pioneers who braved ridicule and risked funds on behalf of his dream. The Big Four, who influenced the politics, economy and scope of California, as well as of the entire country, included Collis P. Huntington and Mark Hopkins, hardware dealers, Charles Crocker, a dry goods store proprietor, and Leland Stanford, "dealer in groceries and provisions." Stanford, an Easterner and a lawyer who was far from the run-of-the-mill pioneer, arrived in California on the steamer *Independence* in 1852, just two years after the state's admission to the Union. During his lifetime, Stanford served as governor of his state and as senator, and left an enduring monument in the form of the superb educational institution, Stanford University, named after his son who died of typhoid fever at the age of fifteen.

On January 8, 1863, ground was broken for America's first railroad, and Governor Stanford promised the work would go on with "no delay, no uncertainty in the continued progress." He also envisioned the day "when the Pacific will be bound to the Atlantic by iron bands that shall consolidate and strengthen the ties of nationality and advance with giant strides the prosperity of our country." By 1876, with the help of twelve thousand Chinese laborers, the special "Lightning Express" was completed. A passenger was able to make the run from Jersey City to Oakland, including the ferry ride to San Francisco, in eighty-four hours and seventeen minutes, or about the time it takes, a century later, to reach the moon.

It was inevitable that a man with Leland Stanford's vision would have the desire and the need for a splendid setting for his increasingly affluent life and social responsibilities. Stanford bought the house on 8th and N streets in Sacramento in 1861, the year the Big Four banded together. It had been built for Shelton C. Fogus, a Virginian and veteran of the Mexican War who had gone off to fortune hunt in Nevada and to help found Reno. Stanford's new home was the work of Seth Babson, an emigré from Maine, who had been commissioned to design a "fine house of brick and plaster." It turned out to be that and much more, a marvelous Victorian concoction of French and Italian inclinations, "finished in a costly manner."

Stanford was elected Governor of California the year after his purchase and he is supposed to have rowed home from his inaugural ceremony due to a flood that submerged his house in water up to its parlor windows. About three hundred wagon loads of silt and debris later, and the planting of seven or eight hundred trees, plants and vines afterwards, Stanford's house was once more in order and ready for some extraordinary expansion: The first floor was raised one story, and a stairway and porch were added to maintain the same entrance.

Most likely it was an architect named Nathaniel D. Goodell who was called in to make the final embellishments on the Stanfords' Sacramento house. A mansard roof with gracefully sloping lines, a new set of harmonizing windows, enclosed porches, a billiard room and a ground-story ballroom helped to make this house the talk of San Francisco in 1872. The *Chronicle,* reporting on the forty-four-room house where seven

Opposite and above: A gracefully arching double staircase of white-painted wood rises to a porch with Corinthian columns. The porch protects tall carved mahogany doors with their superb etched and cut glass. (All photos: B.B.M. Associates)

The top of this finely crafted Italian inlaid table depicts an elaborate design of a mandolin, stems, leaves and berries.

hundred guests might easily be received, commented that, "Good taste and cultured imagination have been exhausted in furnishing the establishment." Frescoes, "exquisite in artistic perfection," ornamented the walls and ceilings, bouquets of real and artificial flowers brightened the tables, lace curtains draped the windows where two hundred guests were dining. On one occasion a seven-piece orchestra was "practically lost" in the banquet hall that measured thirty by eighty-six feet, while another played in the equally large lower hall, adding up, according to the *Chronicle's* "hurried mathematics," to "six thousand feet of space covered with the tireless dancers. . . ."

The Stanfords left Sacramento for San Francisco in 1874 and seven years after her husband's death in 1893, Mrs. Jane Lathrop Stanford deeded the Sacramento home to the Catholic Diocese of Sacramento. The adolescent girls who live there now are enveloped in the pageantry of the nineteenth-century interior, its furniture a keepsake of the extravagant past.

The lofty four-story mansion still has its mansard roof and mansard windows with scrolled side panels, as well as its cornice, which was enlarged to suit the massive roof. The ten ornamented and sunken panels across the front separate the eleven brackets that support the cornice overhang. The second-story main entrance on the west side is reached by a gracefully arching double staircase of white-painted wood, lighted by two carriage lamps. A porch with Corinthian columns guards the tall carved mahogany doors with their superb etched and cut glass.

The spacious central hall is half filled by a long stairway with a walnut banister that winds upward to the second floor and is embellished with an elaborately carved, tapered newel post, seven feet tall, designed in a squat, ribbed column with small panels and pendant finials. Despite its imposing size, however, it is not the stairway that dominates the hall, but rather an ingenious wooden hat and umbrella stand in the Eastlake style with a marble-topped seat and a drawer where people placed their wet boots. Monumental in size, it rests against the wall at the foot of the stairs, complete with two delicate, carved, fluted columns flanking a short mirror and a broken pediment with elaborately carved cresting.

At the right, the former reception room has been converted into a chapel, while to the left, the parlor and music room retain both a number of the original furnishings and a strong sense of bygone grandeur. Lace curtains surmounted by a gilt valance and deep swags with floral design grace the wide windows. In the parlor, an original pier glass, ten feet tall, and an elaborately crafted Italian inlaid table are two of the most prized possessions. The artful design, against a subtle black and pale brown background, shows swirling sprigs of wheat and stems, leaves and scrolls. The top is centered with a romantic composition of a mandolin embellished with stems, leaves and berries. The massive blue velvet tufted sofa with padded arm rests adds solidity to the room. Salvaged from the flood that ravaged Sacramento and Governor Stanford's mansion is the Chickering square grand piano in the adjoining music room which is still used occasionally. Over the piano are portraits of Stanford and his wife, facing, on the opposite wall, a portrait of Leland, Jr., painted some three years before his early death. A posh white Italian marble fireplace and a round marble-topped pedestal table are interesting accents in this room with several colorful and heavy Victorian sofas and upholstered side chairs.

Beyond the parlor is the former banquet hall, now used as a dining room. Gigantic in its proportions, the room has tall, narrow niches in the corners and a massive crowned gilt pier glass at the south end above a white marble fireplace. Facing each other across the large functional table are two immense Eastlake Renaissance-style sideboards, heavily carved and both with broken pediments and elaborate cresting. In a sense, nothing in Stanford's house epitomizes the governor's sense of opulence or histrionics better than the silver tea set here, including the "Leland, Jr., platter." According to legend, Stanford sat his baby son upon the platter as he took him around to introduce him to his dinner guests, one by one.

Above: Dominating the entrance hall is a massive Eastlake-style hat and umbrella stand complete with fluted columns.

Below: The gigantic dining hall, formerly a banquet hall, has an immense crowned gilt pier glass above a marble fireplace.

Drawn by J.Brown.

Engraved & Printed by
Fenner Sears & C°

THE PRESIDENT'S HOUSE, WASHINGTON.